smart investing
@ your library®

A partnership between American Library Association
and FINRA Investor Education Foundation

ALA American Library Association

FINRA Investor Education FOUNDATION

FINRA is proud to support the American Library Association

Investing for a Lifetime

The Wiley Finance series contains books written specifically for finance and investment professionals as well as sophisticated individual investors and their financial advisors. Book topics range from portfolio management to e-commerce, risk management, financial engineering, valuation and financial instrument analysis, as well as much more. For a list of available titles, visit our Web site at www.WileyFinance.com.

Founded in 1807, John Wiley & Sons is the oldest independent publishing company in the United States. With offices in North America, Europe, Australia and Asia, Wiley is globally committed to developing and marketing print and electronic products and services for our customers' professional and personal knowledge and understanding.

Investing for a Lifetime

Managing Wealth for the "New Normal"

RICHARD C. MARSTON

WILEY

Published by John Wiley & Sons, Inc., Hoboken, New Jersey.
Published simultaneously in Canada.

For general information on our other products and services or for technical support, please contact our Customer Care Department within the United States at (800) 762-2974, outside the United States at (317) 572-3993 or fax (317) 572-4002.

Wiley publishes in a variety of print and electronic formats and by print-on-demand. Some material included with standard print versions of this book may not be included in e-books or in print-on-demand. If this book refers to media such as a CD or DVD that is not included in the version you purchased, you may download this material at http://booksupport.wiley.com. For more information about Wiley products, visit www.wiley.com.

Library of Congress Cataloging-in-Publication Data:

ISBN 978-1-118-90094-9 (Hardcover)
ISBN 978-1-118-91869-2 (ePDF)
ISBN 978-1-118-91868-5 (ePub)

Printed in the United States of America

10 9 8 7 6 5 4 3 2 1

To Jerrilyn Greene Marston

Contents

I believe that investing is relatively easy: Investors simply need to choose a portfolio of stocks and bonds appropriate to their age. When they are young, they can be more aggressive in terms of stock allocation than when they grow older. Regardless of age, they need to diversify their portfolios with different types of stocks and bonds. The hardest task facing investors is to stick with their strategy when times are very good or very bad. When times are good, it is tempting to chase after "opportunities" in NASDAQ stocks, or Las Vegas real estate, or gold. When times are bad, investors are tempted to abandon stocks and hunker down until "markets look better." Still, in normal times, investing is the easiest task facing investors.

It is much harder to save than to invest. Too many baby boomers are approaching retirement without sufficient resources. Many do not even know what their savings goals should be, that is to say, how much wealth they need to sustain them in retirement.

In the past, those approaching retirement could count on company pensions that were guaranteed to last a lifetime. Starting in the 1980s, however, many companies decided to get out of the pension business by shifting employees from traditional defined benefit plans to defined contribution plans that leave it to the employee to save enough for retirement. It's true that in many cases employers contribute to these savings plans. But if employees decide not to save enough, or invest unwisely, then their savings will fall short, thereby jeopardizing their retirement.

When I was 40 years old, I never thought in terms of how much I needed to save in order to have a comfortable retirement. What do I mean by comfortable? I assume that when investors retire that they would like to *spend as much as when they were working*. In order to do that, they must save enough to fund their retirement. Recently a mutual fund company announced that investors needed to save eight times their income to keep spending intact once they retire. We might call this the *savings goal* for retirement. Despite the fact that it is very difficult to save eight times income, the goal the company proposed seemed too low to me. So I set out to determine what the savings goal *should* be for investors with different levels of income.

Retirement savings goals depend crucially on how much investors can spend per year out of their accumulated wealth once they retire. Conventional wisdom says that investors can spend 4 percent per year. When investors are told of this spending rule, they often express disbelief. How can it be *so low*? In what follows, I try to convince investors why the spending rule must be this low by citing actual experiences in the past. For example, investors retiring in the 1960s actually ran out of money within 25 years if they followed this 4 percent rule. It's true that investors retiring later ended up with much more money than they needed in retirement. But how can retirees take a chance that their money will run out just when they need it the most?

Although many investors believe that a 4 percent rule is too low, there are many investment experts who believe that this spending rule is *too high*. With growth slowing in the industrial world, they believe that we are unlikely to earn the high returns that we have experienced in the past. In May of 2009, a few months after the onset of the worst financial crisis since the 1930s, Bill Gross of PIMCO coined the term the *New Normal* to describe a future where investors must rely on their "301(k)s" rather than their 401(k)s of past years. He envisions a future with stock returns much lower than in the past. If the New Normal accurately describes the future facing investors, then investors will have to save more in their working years and spend less in retirement.

Once investors have decided on their retirement savings goal, how much do they actually have to save per year? The *savings rate* depends on how long they intend to save. It's important for investors to learn that starting to save early really helps. But the savings rate also depends on whether the investor has other goals for savings. The chapters that follow consider two important goals. One common choice that parents make is to fund their child's education. They should do so with their eyes open, realizing that funds spent on education are no longer available for retirement. Remember that the sum spent on a child's education would have compounded into an even greater sum by the time of retirement. Consider another common choice. If investors decide to buy a larger home or a second home, these funds are also removed from retirement savings. I will try to convince readers that homes are "consumption," not investment. Indeed, in the past, homes have proven to be a poor investment (even if investors sold at the peak in 2006!).

I also show that, for most investors, retirement plans depend crucially on Social Security. For investors who fail to save enough for retirement, Social Security is the one guaranteed source of income that they have. Even if investors follow good advice and save enough, Social Security still provides a good portion of their retirement income. It's only if the investor is quite wealthy that Social Security fades into the background of retirement planning.

As an investor approaches retirement, further challenges arise. First, the investor has to decide whether to retire at 62 or at the full retirement age of 66. The financial consequences of that decision are greater than most investors realize. Then the investor has to settle on a spending rule during retirement. And, to implement that spending rule, the investor must choose a portfolio that will support a potentially long retirement. The investor must formulate these plans while facing the enormous uncertainty about how long savings must last. It shouldn't be surprising why I regard investing, rather than saving, as the easier task facing investors.

Yet investors do need to understand the basics of investing. I believe it is possible to discuss investments in a nontechnical way. First, there is the basic distinction between stocks and bonds. Investors need to understand how these two assets have performed in the past and how well they are likely to perform in the future. Second, investors need to understand the benefits of diversifying into different types of stocks and bonds. Should investors choose corporate bonds or municipal bonds? Are there arguments for owning foreign stocks or emerging market stocks or real estate stocks? Third, what should the overall portfolio look like? Need it be complicated? Fourth, how should the investor keep track of how the portfolio is performing?

I have trained enough financial advisors to know that they prefer informed clients. It is much easier to explain how their portfolios are being managed if clients understand the basics of investment. An informed investor knows that there will be times when markets do badly. For example, stocks fall when an economy enters a recession. But they also know that stocks recover as the economy recovers. Bond prices fall when interest rates rise. An informed investor also knows that we are currently living in a time of exceptionally low interest rates. That won't last forever. Such an investor knows that the only way to accumulate enough wealth for retirement is to save consistently and to keep investment strategies steady as they can be.

I have spoken to enough clients directly to know the types of concerns that they have. Not only have I given many seminars to the clients of securities firms, but I have also been an advisor to very wealthy families. The latter have portfolios much more complex that the ones that I will recommend for ordinary investors. But many of the same concerns are raised by very wealthy families. Is the portfolio doing badly because there is something wrong with the investment strategy or is it because markets periodically behave badly? How do we know whether investment managers are performing as well as they should? How do we measure the performance of these managers?

Investing wisely is vitally important in this new world where most investors have to provide for their own retirement. This book is designed to help ordinary investors understand better how to invest. But the book is also about the challenges of saving enough to retire and ensuring that these savings last a lifetime.

Richard Marston
Philadelphia, March 2014

Acknowledgments

Three years ago I published a book on asset allocation, *Portfolio Design: A Modern Approach to Asset Allocation* (John Wiley & Sons, 2011), based on my 20 years of teaching in the Certified Investment Management Analyst (CIMA) Program at Wharton. That book was aimed at financial advisors rather than the clients of those advisors. And it was focused on asset allocation decisions rather than more broadly on saving and investment issues. I felt that the book was too technical for the average investor, so I set out to write a book that would help ordinary investors to think about how they might save for retirement, invest those savings, and then stretch their resources through retirement.

I would like to thank the many financial advisors that I have met through the years both in the CIMA program and in other programs at Wharton and throughout the country. Their insights have helped to shape many of my ideas about investing. A thoughtful advisor can make so much difference to the financial well-being of a family. I have also learned a lot from listening to investors who have attended my seminars. These investors have asked me many challenging questions, which have helped to guide me in writing this book.

I would also like to thank Charlotte Beyer, the founder of the Institute for Private Investors, for her many insights about investing for private clients. Charlotte and I founded the Private Wealth Management Program at Wharton in 1999, a program where ultra-high net worth investors can learn about investment management. Very wealthy families have more complex portfolios than those that I describe in this book, but they also share with ordinary investors many of the challenges in managing wealth.

I owe special thanks to Bill Falloon of Wiley for encouraging me to write this book and to develop the website that accompanies it. I also want to thank my agent, John Wright, whose wise counsel is much appreciated.

Finally, I would like to thank my spouse, Jerrilyn Greene Marston, for her lifelong support. There is nothing like having a brilliant wife to inspire you in all of your work, so I am dedicating this book to her.

PART
One

Saving and Investing

CHAPTER 1

Introduction: Investing for a Lifetime

Investing for a lifetime is really hard. First, investors have to figure out a way to force themselves to save. It's not easy because they have so many other things to do with their income. Savings often becomes just the residual after they have finished their spending. Yet savings are so essential if they are to enjoy a long retirement. This book won't teach anyone how to save. But it will show them how essential it is to save throughout the working years.

What amount of savings is necessary? That depends primarily on how much an individual hopes to spend later on in retirement. Ideally, investors may want to maintain their current standard of living once they retire. It's true that in retirement it may be possible to spend less than in their working years, but it's best not to count on spending much less. Individuals vary widely in their savings level because their incomes differ so much. But savings rates, expressed as a percent of income, should not vary nearly as much. In practice they do. That's because many Americans don't save enough.

Second, investors have to figure out how to invest. That's more complicated than it appears because there are so many pitfalls to successful investing. The most important pitfall is that investors can't control themselves. They shift in and out of investments, and mostly at the wrong time. They chase after "hot" investments even though most investment fads end up poorly.

I believe that investing can be very simple. Investors should be able to pick a portfolio of stocks and bonds and stick with it. I will argue later that the portfolio should be well diversified with different types of stocks and bonds. But that doesn't mean the investments have to be complex or difficult to understand.

Third, investors need a plan for retirement. That means assessing how much savings is needed for retirement. Then they have to figure out how to stretch their resources through retirement. That means having a spending plan that is reasonable given the wealth that investors have accumulated during their working years.

THE NEW RETIREMENT REALITY—WE ARE ON OUR OWN

This book is about investments. But it is also about saving for retirement and stretching resources during retirement. The primary reason people invest is that they need to fund their retirements. Of course, many people have other motives to invest. They may save for a down payment to buy a house. They may save to buy a car rather than to finance it. And they may also save to help pay for the education of their children. But the retirement goal is the primary savings goal for most people.

Some Americans are fortunate enough to have guaranteed pensions that provide them with a steady income throughout their retirements. These are the old-style *defined benefit pensions* that were once quite common in corporate America (and are still provided by most state and local governments). The pensions provide a guaranteed income to the employee and often to the employee's spouse in the event of the death of the employee. Sometimes the income is indexed to inflation, rising with the cost of living during retirement. Today, the balance has shifted away from defined benefit pension plans to *defined contribution* pension plans, like the 401(k) plan, where workers contribute part of their salaries to the plan with firms often matching or supplementing the employee contributions. Figure 1.1 shows the share of private sector employees in each type of plan over the past 25 years.[1] There is a dramatic downward trend in defined benefit plans and a corresponding upward trend in defined contribution plans. Employees with the latter type of pension plan are, in a sense, responsible for their own retirement. If they save enough during their careers and invest wisely, they can enjoy a comfortable retirement.

How much is "enough"? That depends on how much they hope to spend in retirement and how much income they can derive from their portfolios. Later chapters will explore both investing and spending in retirement. Decisions that Americans make about investing and spending can make a big difference in determining how financially secure they are in retirement.

Most baby boomers will find the new retirement system quite challenging. It's true that since the 1930s Americans have had a Social Security retirement system to help fund their retirements. But benefits are limited. Retirees typically receive much less in Social Security benefits than they earned in their working years. So savings are necessary if retirees are to come close to matching their preretirement income.

LONGEVITY

Many Americans don't really understand how long their retirement may be. Life expectancy has increased steadily over the past 50 years at the same

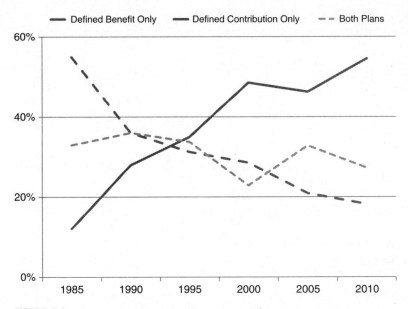

FIGURE 1.1 Retirement Plans in Private Sector by Type
Source: Employee Benefit Research Institute, 2012.

time that the age of retirement has fallen. According to the Labor Department, the median age of retirement for both men and women is less than 62 years of age.[2] That's down from an average age between 66 and 67 in the 1950s. Americans at 62 can often look forward to 20 or even 30 more years of life in retirement. Yet few Americans have a coherent plan to make sure their resources will last that long. Savings are often inadequate and spending is often too high to be sustainable. Investment decisions, moreover, are often inconsistent with spending rates.

In formulating a savings plan for retirement, it will be helpful to know just how long our savings must last. Figure 1.2 presents some estimates of how long current 65 year-olds are likely to live.[3] For a 65-year-old man today, the median age of death is estimated to be 83 years, with 25 percent of his cohort likely to live to be 89. For a 65-year-old woman, the median age is 86 and 25 percent are likely to reach 92. For a married couple at 62 years old, the relevant statistic is the life expectancy of the *surviving* spouse. The median age of death for the surviving spouse is over 90 years of age! So the nest egg accumulated for retirement must last a long time.

With lifetimes this long, investment horizons must be just as long. In fact, they need to be longer because individuals may live longer than the average person their age. Yet Americans entering retirement often choose

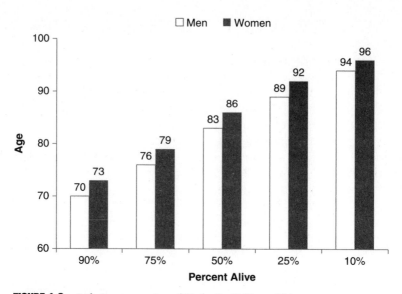

FIGURE 1.2 Life Expectancies of Today's 65-Year-Olds
Source: National Vital Statistics Reports, 2011.

portfolios appropriate for retirees of their grandparents' generation who typically lived only a few years after they retired. Retirees of that generation used to invest in bonds during retirement. Investing in bonds surely seems the safe thing to do. It helps you sleep at night if you avoid stocks and other volatile investments. That's all well and good for emotional well-being, but does the average investor realize how little can be spent if a portfolio is weighted heavily toward bonds?

An even bigger question is whether investors understand how much money needs to be saved before retiring. Chapter 17 explains why retirees should keep their spending in retirement at 4 percent or less of their wealth. Do the arithmetic. If investors save enough to be millionaires, guess how much they can spend if they follow this rule? Four percent of a million is only $40,000 per year. And do you know how hard it is to accumulate that much wealth? The task of saving is truly daunting.

THE SQUIRREL MODEL OF SAVING AND SPENDING

Saving and retirement planning is often viewed as so complex that many Americans just tune out. Unfortunately, we cannot afford to do that. We need to understand how imperative it is to save. If that lesson is learned, then investing is relatively easy. Fortunately, we have squirrels to guide us in saving.[4]

Let's imagine a squirrel is only concerned about the next 12 months and that it lives in a very cold place where winter lasts for six months. Then a good plan would be to "squirrel away" some nuts. The squirrel would like to eat one nut per day. To store up enough nuts for the winter, the squirrel has to find two nuts per day and save 50 percent of them. At the end of six months, the squirrel will have 180 nuts saved (i.e., half of the 360 days in a squirrel year)—just enough to last the winter. A 50 percent savings rate is very high, but the squirrel does not want to run short of nuts late in the winter. Figure 1.3 illustrates the saving and spending plan of this squirrel. For the first six months, the squirrel steadily builds up its store of nuts. Then when winter sets in, the squirrel can sit back and consume them. By planning wisely, the squirrel can eat one nut per day for the whole year.

What if the squirrel lives in Pennsylvania where there are only four winter months? Then the squirrel can cut its savings rate to 33 percent since it can save nuts for 8 out of the 12 months. By working for two more months, the squirrel can eat more nuts (1⅓ nuts per day!) and save less. That savings and spending plan is illustrated by the dotted line in Figure 1.3. Total nuts stored peaks after eight months. Then the squirrel sits back and eats

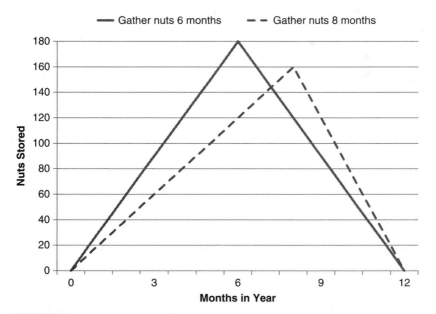

FIGURE 1.3 Squirrel Model of Saving

his store of nuts during the remaining four months. In Pennsylvania, the squirrel has to work two months longer. But he will enjoy so many more nuts than his cousins in the cold north.

Now let's imagine how this works for a person saving for retirement. To make things simple, assume that the person starts saving at 30 years of age, retires at 60, and dies at 90. Let's assume that this person earns zero return on savings and, like the squirrel, does not pay taxes. Then to have enough wealth to retire at 60, this person has to save *half of all income* to maintain the same spending level in retirement as in the working years. Saving at a 50 percent rate is quite onerous. But that's because retirement lasts so long.

How might we find a way to lower the savings rate to a more manageable level? Let's examine four possibilities.

1. **Postpone retirement.** The individual could decide to work longer. Let's assume that the retirement age is postponed until the person is 70 years old. Since the individual works for 40 years rather than 30 years, savings can be less during the working years. In fact, savings can drop from 50 percent of income to 33 percent. That is, you save one third of your income for 40 years, then live off your savings for 20 years. And you can spend more all of your life.

2. **Spend less in retirement.** In the squirrel example, spending needs are as high in retirement as during working years. If spending in retirement were to be reduced to only two thirds of spending during the working years, the required level of savings drops from 50 percent to 40 percent. In the meantime, spending during the working years can rise as well. Of course, anyone already in retirement will quickly object that such a drop in spending is unrealistic. This topic is discussed in Chapters 16 through 19.

3. **Earn a rate of return on your savings.** The example assumes that the individual earns no return on savings. In Chapter 2 we discuss long-run returns on retirement portfolios. Then in Chapter 5, we discuss how positive investment returns can reduce the amount of savings necessary for retirement. Investment returns are crucially important to the success of the retirement strategy. No wonder so much of this book is devoted to investing.

4. **We have Social Security benefits.** Unlike the squirrel, Americans have Social Security benefits for the retirement years. For an individual retiring at full retirement age in 2012, those benefits might be as high as $30,000 per year depending on lifetime earnings. We will have to take those benefits into account when we consider savings strategies in Chapters 4 through 6 and retirement spending in Chapters 16 through 19.

Despite these important qualifications, the squirrel's strategy has a lesson for us all. Retirement savings are really important if we hope to have a decent retirement. And investing those retirement savings in a wise way is also enormously important. That's what this book is about.

OUTLINE OF THE BOOK

Investing for a lifetime requires savings. But how much does an investor have to save to provide a secure retirement? The squirrel's tale gives some indication, but in the first part of the book I will be much more specific. The investor's savings rate will depend on how long that investor plans to save. And it will depend on the extent to which the investor is burdened by taxes and other expenses.

Before we can discuss savings, though, it's important to learn how much can be earned on these savings. If the squirrel could have earned a decent return on his hoard of nuts, he wouldn't have had to work so hard. So the next two chapters discuss how much can be earned on the two basic assets in the portfolio, stocks and bonds. Chapter 2 shows how much we have earned historically on these two assets. Chapter 3 considers whether future returns might be lower in a "New Normal." Then Chapters 4 through 6 discuss savings.

Part Two of the book studies investment options that are available for the average investor (in Chapters 7 through 13). These range from different types of U.S. stocks to foreign stocks and real estate as well as bonds. I will also discuss investment in a home.

Part Three of the book discusses wealth management. Topics include what portfolio is appropriate for the investor (Chapter 14), how can investments in that portfolio be tracked, and what are best practices for investing (Chapter 15). Those topics are for investors of any age. But retirees need special attention. Many retirees are desperately looking for investments that yield income for retirement. Chapter 16 will view the major sources of income available. Then Chapters 17 through 19 will discuss investing and spending in retirement more generally, including a future where a "New Normal" of lower returns prevails.

My aim is to provide some practical guidelines for investing over a lifetime. I hope this book makes the process of saving, investing, and spending much easier to comprehend.

NOTES

1. Figure 1.1 shows participation in defined benefit and defined contribution plans in medium-size and large private establishments. Those

employees who have neither type of pension plan are excluded from the calculations. In 2010, 34 percent of the employees in these same establishments had no retirement plan at all.

2. According to the U.S. Bureau of Labor Statistics, the median age of retirement for the years 2000–2005 was 61.6 for men and 60.5 for women (see Gendell 2008).

3. The estimates are reported by Arias (2011) in a report for the National Vital Statistics System.

4. The squirrel analogy was developed by Keith Sharp of the University of Toronto (sharp@ustat.utoronto.ca).

REFERENCES

Arias, Elizabeth. 2011. "United States Life Tables, 2007." *National Vital Statistical Reports* (September 28).

Employee Benefit Research Institute. 2012. *EBRI Databook on Employee Benefits*. Washington, DC: Employee Benefit Research Institute.

Gendell, Murray. 2008. "Older Workers: Increasing Their Labor Force Participation and Hours of Work." *Monthly Labor Review* (January).

CHAPTER 2

The Building Blocks of a Portfolio: Bonds and Stocks

Investors can invest in a variety of assets from bank deposits to real estate. But it's best to begin a discussion of investment returns by studying two basic assets: stocks and bonds. These are the two fundamental assets in any economy. Bonds promise a steady stream of coupons (at least in nominal terms). Stocks offer dividends, but provide investors with upside potential from capital gains. We will discuss a wider array of assets later in the book, but many of them are highly correlated with U.S. stocks and bonds.

In this chapter, only one type of bond will be considered: the U.S. Treasury bond. By studying Treasury bonds, we can ignore the default risks associated with private sector bonds such as corporate bonds or mortgage-backed bonds. Treasury bonds are not without risk, but these risks stem from the volatility of bond prices and the eroding effects of inflation. We will discuss these risks later. A series for the 20-year U.S. Treasury bond extends all the way back to 1926, so this bond will be analyzed in detail.

Similarly, only one series for stocks will be considered, the S&P 500 stock index. This is a series for large capitalization stocks also extending back to 1926. Investors are often interested in a wider variety of stocks. Indeed, we will have chapters ahead to discuss other types of U.S. stocks as well as foreign stocks. But the S&P is often used to represent the overall U.S. stock market. The S&P 500 consists of only 500 of the 7,000-plus stocks in the U.S. market, but those 500 stocks represent over 90 percent of the total capitalization of the U.S. stock market.[1]

Bonds and stocks are both risky, therefore it is useful to compare their returns with a risk-free asset. Of course, there is no such thing as a perfectly safe asset. But the one-month U.S. Treasury bill comes very close. The Treasury bill (like the Treasury bond) has virtually no default risk. And, unlike the Treasury bond, it has virtually no inflation risk. If inflation were to rise unexpectedly, the next month's Treasury bill would offer a higher interest rate to compensate for that higher inflation (because Treasury bill investors would insist on it). So the Treasury bill is the closest we can come to a risk-free asset.

Although the bond and stock data begin in 1926, we will focus on the postwar period beginning in 1951. That gives us more than 60 years of data while avoiding years of depression and world war (which hopefully we will not see again). But why start so early? Isn't it better to look at recent market performance? The answer is that we will examine more recent periods, but it's important to look at a variety of periods with high growth and low growth, high inflation as well as low inflation. This book is about investing for a lifetime. And that means considering what may happen over 30- or 40- or 50-year periods in the future. Surely, it will help for us to look at a variety of periods in the past.

BONDS AND STOCKS SINCE 1951

How much do we earn on bonds and stocks in the long run? Throughout this book, we will quote returns expressed in annual terms, or *returns per annum*. That's the way that banks are required to quote returns on bank deposits and the way that investment firms quote returns on mutual funds. As shown in Figure 2.1, the average return on the 20-year Treasury bond is 6.4 percent per annum since 1951. A 6.4 percent return may seem like a lot, but we have not yet adjusted for inflation, which averaged 3.7 percent over the same period.

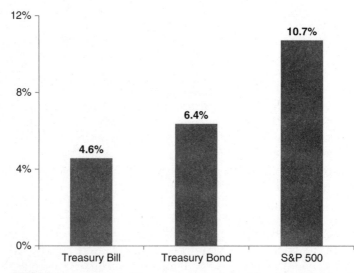

FIGURE 2.1   Compound Returns on Bonds and Stocks, 1951–2012
Source: © Morningstar.

And notice that the 20-year bond does not earn that much more than the one-month Treasury bill, 6.4 percent versus 4.6 percent. If we invest in a one-month Treasury bill and roll over that investment every month, we earn a return that is virtually risk-free. Remember that the 20-year bond exposes us to sudden increases in interest rates. If the interest rate on new Treasury bonds rises, then existing bonds fall in price. In contrast, if the interest rate on new Treasury bills rises, then the next bill that we buy will offer this higher rate.

Figure 2.1 shows the average return over a 62-year period. Over shorter periods, of course, 20-year bonds can earn much higher returns than the Treasury bill. Consider returns during the year 2010. During that year, the 20-year return was 10.1 percent while the Treasury bill earned 0.1 percent. The reason why the Treasury bill return was so miserably low is that short-term interest rates were kept very low by Federal Reserve policy. Long-term interest rates were also low relative to historical experience in 2010, but long-term interest rates fell over the course of that year. So the total return on the 20-year bond was higher than the interest rate itself. In some other years, the return on the 20-year bond falls below that of the Treasury bill. Indeed, Treasury bond returns can actually turn negative as they did in 1973, for example. But over the 62-year period reported in Figure 2.1, the return on the Treasury bond exceeds that of the Treasury bill by 1.8 percent.

Figure 2.1 also shows the average return on the S&P 500 as being 10.7 percent since 1951. That's impressive, particularly compared with a 6.4 percent return on Treasury bonds. The excess return on equity is 4.3 percent over this 62-year period. Experts in finance have given this excess return a special name, the *equity premium*. It's the reward that investors receive from taking on the extra risk of equities. Of course, the equity premium is not steady over time. In some years, equities earn lower returns than bonds. In the recession year of 2008, for example, the S&P 500 earned −37.0 percent, while bond returns soared to 25.9 percent. Figure 2.1 shows long-run averages, not short-run returns.

Looking at returns without adjusting for inflation is a little misleading. For example, if a portfolio earns 5 percent but the cost of living rises by 5 percent, then in some real sense wealth has not increased. In the 1970s, there were high bond and stock returns, but, as we will see, investors did very poorly because inflation was even higher.

THE IMPORTANCE OF ADJUSTING FOR INFLATION

The United States has suffered a lot of inflation since 1950. That's difficult for younger Americans to understand because inflation has been so low for the past decade or so. But there was a time in the 1970s when inflation reached double-digit rates. That was a decade when high inflation combined with slow growth to give us what was termed "stagflation."

Even with modest inflation, however, the cumulative effects of increases in the cost of living are substantial. Suppose that the inflation rate is 2.5 percent. (This is the inflation assumption used in many investment firms when projecting future price increases). Over a 10-year period, a 2.5 percent inflation rate raises the cost of living by 28 percent. That's because inflation compounds over time. Over a 20-year period, the cost of living rises over 60 percent. Since the United States has had inflation considerably higher than 2.5 percent, we need to track changes in the cost of living carefully.

For decades, the U.S. Bureau of Labor Statistics has maintained a consumer price index series for urban consumers. Table 2.1 uses this index to calculate how much a $1,000 basket of goods in 2010 would have cost in earlier decades. For example, in 2000 that basket of goods would have cost $790. Further back, in 1970, that basket would have cost only $178!

The consumer price index is designed to measure the cost of a variety of goods and services. But there is a lot of variation in inflation rates across goods and services. Some manufactured goods have become much cheaper over time, at least measured relative to overall inflation or wage levels. Consider the example of a color television. When color televisions were first introduced in the 1950s, they were quite expensive. But as they became mass-produced, their costs fell. By 1965, a 21-inch RCA cost only $400. What would be the equivalent price for this TV in 2010 if the price had risen as fast as the consumer price index (CPI)? The answer is that this TV (if it still existed) would cost $2,800! In actual practice, the same size TV

TABLE 2.1   Cost of Living and Wages over Time in the United States

Year	Cost of Today's $1,000 Basket of Goods	Wages in Manufacturing Sector Historical	In 2010 Dollars
1950	$110		
1960	$136		
1970	$178	$6,685	$37,576
1980	$378	$14,760	$39,069
1990	$599	$22,703	$37,884
2000	$790	$30,754	$38,951
2010	$1,000	$39,688	$39,688

Source: Bureau of Labor Statistics and Council of Economic Advisors, *Economic Report of the President* (Washington, DC: U.S. Government Printing Office, 2011).

today, though much more technically advanced, would cost even less than $400. It is technical progress in manufacturing that has driven cost down so radically.

On the other hand, some goods and many services cost a lot more today. Take an example that may irritate many parents—college tuition. When I entered college in the 1960s, the cost of tuition, room, and board at an Ivy League college totaled $3,000 per year. If college costs had increased at the same rate as the Consumer Price Index (CPI), the tab today would be about $21,000. Instead, tuition, room, and board at an Ivy League college is over $50,000 per year. Medical care has seen similar inflation rates over time. These rates of inflation matter to investors. Investors in their thirties and forties often have to save for the college costs of their children. It's painful when tuition costs rise faster than overall inflation and faster than wages. Similarly, older investors have to contend with rapidly rising medical costs. Those costs are an important factor affecting retirement planning. But we will focus on overall inflation rates, not those in specific sectors of the economy.

Wages are a lot higher today than they were 30 or more years ago. Or are they? Table 2.1 tracks the average annual wage in manufacturing back to 1970. A worker in manufacturing today earns an average wage of $39,688 (including overtime). Back in 1970, that same worker would have earned a wage of only $6,685. But don't feel sorry for that worker. The cost of living was so much lower in 1970 that this wage was equivalent to $37,576 in today's dollars. So the next time that an older person brags about how little he or she made as a young worker, be skeptical. It's real wages, not nominal wages, that matter. Real wages do increase over time, at least in the long run. But the rate of increase is small for the average worker. In fact, between 1980 and 1990 wages actually fell in real terms in the United States, at least in manufacturing. That was not true once benefits are taken into account.

It's important to take into account inflation in all historical comparisons. That surely is true when it comes to investments. If an investment has doubled in value since 1985, is that good news? Actually, it's terrible news because the cost of living has also doubled since then, so the investor has earned nothing in real terms. Having seen how important inflation can be, let's revisit the returns on bonds and stocks and adjust those returns for inflation.

BONDS AND STOCKS ADJUSTED FOR INFLATION

Since 1951, the inflation rate has averaged 3.7 percent per annum. Adjusting for this inflation rate gives us a set of *real returns* as shown in Figure 2.2.[2] The real return on Treasury bonds is only 2.6 percent. The real return on stocks is a more respectable 6.8 percent. That's still very low.

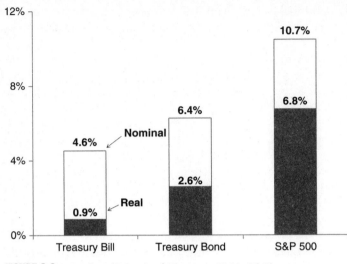

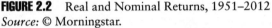

FIGURE 2.2   Real and Nominal Returns, 1951–2012
Source: © Morningstar.

Let's remind ourselves why we are so concerned about real returns as opposed to nominal returns. The reason is that only real returns provide for future spending. A portfolio must keep pace with a higher cost of living just to stand still. In order to grow over time, a portfolio must earn positive real returns.

The difference between earning 2.6 percent on bonds and 6.8 percent on stocks is enormous. Consider a simple experiment where an investor decides between devoting the entire portfolio to either bonds or stocks. Let's consider how much $100,000 in initial wealth accumulates over a 20-year period. And, to keep the example as simple as possible, let's assume the portfolio is tax-free.

The results are shown in Figure 2.3. A portfolio devoted to bonds increases to $167,100 over the 20-year period. Remember that wealth is being measured in constant dollars over the 20-year period. Real wealth increases by $67,100 for a 67.1 percent cumulative return. That's not much for 20 years of patience! Contrast the bond investment with investment in stocks. Over a 20-year period, the $100,000 grows to $372,800 for a 272.8 percent cumulative return. The equity premium makes quite a difference to long-run accumulation! That extra accumulation might come in handy in retirement. In the next chapter, though, we will have to consider periods when the equity premium fails to materialize for the investor.

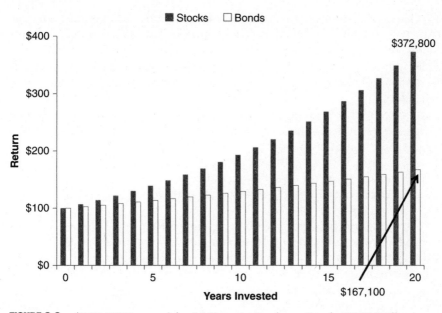

FIGURE 2.3 $100,000 Invested for 20 Years in Stocks or Bonds (2012 Dollars)

How sensitive are these results to the time period? Perhaps the postwar period in the United States has been unusually kind to equities. Earlier in the chapter, we reported that the Treasury bond and S&P series extend back to 1926. For the period from 1926 to 1950, the 20-year Treasury bond earned 2.3 percent, almost matching the return for the post-1950 period. And the S&P return was 6.3 percent rather than 6.8 percent. So for the 25-year period ending in 1950 as well as the 62 years since then, the equity premium was alive and well. It is not merely a fluke of the postwar period.

ASSET ALLOCATION DECISIONS FOR YOUNG INVESTORS: THE CASE OF TIAA-CREF

Because stock and bond returns are so different, it really matters what allocation between stocks and bonds is chosen by the investor. Often investors are asked early in their careers to choose allocations for their 401(k) or other defined contribution programs. And often these allocations remain unchanged for extended periods of time. So it's important to think carefully about what allocation is appropriate early in your working life.

There was an interesting study of investor choice done a few years ago (Ameriks and Zeldes 2004) using data from TIAA-CREF accounts. Until the 1990s, these accounts were open mainly to university professors as well as other university employees. In 1989, there were only two options available to these "professors": TIAA was a fixed-income investment that turns into a fixed annuity at retirement and CREF is a broad-based stock fund. The study showed that professors on the whole are not very sophisticated about their investment decisions. Faced with a choice between two investments, a large proportion of professors clustered on two portfolios:

1. 25 percent chose an all-bond portfolio.
2. 40 percent chose a 50/50 bond/stock portfolio.

Few investment experts would recommend either of these portfolios for young investors early in their accumulation years. Instead, most experts would recommend a higher weighting of stocks than bonds. For example, the "target date" retirement portfolios recommended by firms such as Vanguard and Fidelity call for investors 25 years or more from retirement to devote from 80 to 90 percent of portfolios to stocks. The high allocation to stocks presumes that the equity premium will prevail in the long run, thereby lifting returns over time.

When I was 29 years old, I was faced with the decision about how to invest in TIAA-CREF. I chose an allocation of 75 percent in CREF and 25 percent in TIAA. Looking back now, I would do it all over again. But most highly educated professors seem to have no clue how to proceed with this all-important decision. And they do not have the good sense to seek advice.

Let's consider how much difference this decision can make. Imagine that professors decide to contribute a fixed amount per year for each year of their career. Often this contribution is matched (at least partially) by a contribution from the employer. Let's assume that the total contribution is $10,000 per year in constant dollars. This is admittedly unrealistic in that salaries increase in real terms over time, particularly as the professor is promoted from junior to senior faculty positions, so pension contributions also increase. But let's keep the example simple.

As the professors save, they are assumed to earn returns on their stocks and bonds at the average real returns given in Figure 2.2. That is, bonds earn 2.6 percent in real terms and stocks earn 6.8 percent in real terms. The professors are assumed to choose a bond/stock allocation at the beginning of their work years and leave it unchanged thereafter. Later we will consider "target date" mutual funds that change the bond/stock allocation as the investor gets closer to retirement, but here we assume that the professors are too preoccupied with their research to bother with mundane financial matters. So they leave the allocation unchanged throughout their careers.

Table 2.2 shows the total accumulation at the end of each decade depending on the bond/stock allocation chosen. All figures are measured in constant dollars. Professors are assumed to adopt four alternative strategies ranging from all bonds to all stocks. Professors who invest only in bonds accumulate $446,100 after 30 years. That may seem like a lot, but they have saved a total of $300,000 ($10,000 for 30 years). In contrast, professors who invest 75 percent in stocks and only 25 percent in bonds accumulate $756,600. And those who plunge their whole portfolio into stocks are rewarded with $911,300.

Crucial financial decisions are often made casually even by smart, well-educated people. What segment of the population is better educated than college professors? Professors or other investors who elect all-bond portfolios may make this choice because they believe bonds are less risky than stocks. But what risk are they preoccupied with? If it's short-term volatility, then is that appropriate for a decision about long-run accumulation? Should a 30-year-old be worried about the possibility of market crashes when they are 39 or 47? Or should they focus on how much wealth they will have when they retire at 66?

I remember the market crash of 1987. Stocks fell 25 percent in the space of two days. Since I was far from retirement in that year, I didn't think twice about my retirement allocation. As a finance professor, I was fascinated with the crash. But it didn't matter to me personally. I was confident that the market would rebound. I didn't know when the rebound would occur, but I surely knew it would be before I retired. If I had been about to retire

TABLE 2.2 Accumulation in Retirement Account Based on Bond/Stock Allocation

Allocation				
Bonds	100%	50%	25%	0%
Stocks	0%	50%	75%	100%
Accumulation				
10 years	$112,500	$124,000	$130,300	$136,900
20 years	$258,000	$320,400	$358,100	$401,100
30 years	$446,100	$631,200	$756,600	$911,300

Assumptions: Real bond return = 2.6%, real stock return = 6.8%. $10,000 saved per year (in 2013 dollars).

or even a few years from retirement, this nonchalance would have quickly disappeared.

WHAT ARE THESE LONG-RUN AVERAGES MISSING?

This analysis based on 60 years of data does ignore an unpleasant fact. Stock and bond returns do vary a lot over relatively long periods. Investors who experienced the decade of stagflation during the 1970s know this is true. So Chapter 3 will examine the postwar period in greater detail. It matters to investors when they do their accumulation. Before turning to that chapter, let's ask a simple question about the postwar period. Did it matter when you retired? Were those handsome returns reported in Table 2.2 earned by investors retiring in 1980 or in later decades?

Let's keep the analysis simple by assuming that the investor kept everything in stocks. Like the TIAA-CREF investor, this investor saved $10,000 per year for 30 years. If the investor had hidden the savings under a mattress, the total saved would have been $300,000 in nominal terms. But because of inflation, the total accumulation in constant dollars would have been much less depending on the period. Suppose that an investor saved for 30 years and retired in 1980. How much would he or she have accumulated? And what if the investor started saving 10 years later and retired in 1990? Here are the accumulations in a stock account after 30 years for those investors retiring in 1980 or 1990 or 2000 or 2010, all measured in constant dollars:[3]

- Retire in 1980: $529,000
- Retire in 1990: $689,900
- Retire in 2000: $1,832,800—quite amazing!
- Retire in 2010: $847,800

Look at those lucky retirees who finished accumulating in 2000. They had just experienced two decades of bull markets in both stocks and bonds. No wonder they had accumulated more than three times more than those who retired in 1980. Retirement is not the end of the investing process, of course, and those who retired in 2000 were facing a "lost decade" on returns thereafter.

What's the moral of this story? The moral is that it's not enough to marvel at the long-run equity premium. Stocks outperform bonds in the long run, but we must worry about the huge variation in returns in the postwar period. And we must worry about whether future returns will be lower than in the past. Bill Gross of PIMCO talks about a "New Normal" of low returns. Is this what investors are facing in the years ahead?

NOTES

1. Prior to 1973, the Ibbotson Associates (2012) large-cap stock series based on the Standard & Poor's Composite Index is used. The Composite Index consists of 500 stocks from 1957 onward, but only 100 large-cap stocks prior to 1957. In this book, the whole series is referred to as the "S&P 500 Index."
2. To adjust nominal returns for inflation, you must divide by one plus the inflation rate. The real return on bonds is 2.6 percent because $(1 + 0.064)/(1 + 0.037) - 1 = 2.6\%$.
3. See Table 3.2 for details on these calculations.

REFERENCES

Ameriks, John, and Stephen P. Zeldes. 2004. "How Do Portfolio Shares Vary with Age?," Working Paper, Columbia Business School.

Ibbotson Associates. 2012. *2012 Ibbotson Stocks, Bonds, Bills, and Inflation (SBBI) Classic Yearbook*. Chicago: Morningstar.

CHAPTER 3

Long Swings in Returns: Are We in a "New Normal?"

n 2009 after the financial crisis was beginning to abate, Bill Gross of PIMCO coined the term "New Normal" to describe the world of investing going forward.[1] This is a world of half-size economic growth in the industrial world, painful deleveraging of the balance sheets of both governments and the private sector, and, as a result, disappointing bond and stock returns. It's a depressing vision for younger investors trying to save for retirement. It's a nightmare for retired investors trying to stretch their savings through retirement. Bill Gross is one of the most astute investors around, so his vision commands attention. Could it be that the long-run returns that we discuss in Chapter 2 are gone forever?

To try to answer that question, we need to understand the long swings in the returns on stocks and bonds that we have already experienced in the postwar period. It has been a very rocky ride for investors. There have been thrilling periods when investors rushed to open their investment statements. That was certainly true of the 1950s when stock markets soared. But it was also true of the two decades of the 1980s and 1990s. In other periods, market movements caused despair. Let's try to make sense of those decades.

LONG SWINGS IN RETURNS

The performance of the U.S. economy has varied substantially over the past 60 years. The postwar boom was followed by the high inflation, low growth decade of the 1970s. Then the economy started a 20-year boom that ended with the recession of 2001. These long swings in economic performance helped to generate swings in bond and stock returns.

We might identify four cycles of stock returns in the postwar period: the postwar expansion, the inflation decade of the 1970s, the boom period of the 1980s and 1990s, and the bust period beginning in 2000 (which many observers call "the lost decade"). The timing of these four cycles is arbitrary, but some basis for the timing can be seen in Figure 3.1 and 3.2 where real returns on the S&P 500 are displayed.

Figure 3.1 suggests that the postwar expansion ended either in late 1968 or late 1972 (when returns were only marginally higher in real terms). During the period that ends in November 1968, the S&P 500 had a cumulative real return of 659.1 percent! That's equivalent to a 12.0 percent return per annum. The subsequent period was a different story. The figure breaks up the period in two phases, Dec 1968 to September 1974 when the cumulative real return was –50.1 percent and October 1974 to July 1982 when the cumulative return was +28.6 percent. Over the whole period from Dec 1968 to July 1982, the cumulative return on the S&P 500 was –35.8 percent (in real terms) or –3.2 percent per annum. No wonder stocks fell out of favor during this period.

Figure 3.2 traces stocks over the subsequent boom period of the 1980s and 1990s. The S&P 500 earned an astounding 1268.6 percent compound real return over the 18 years from August 1982 to March 2000. That's equivalent to a 15.9 percent per annum real return. Since 2000, however,

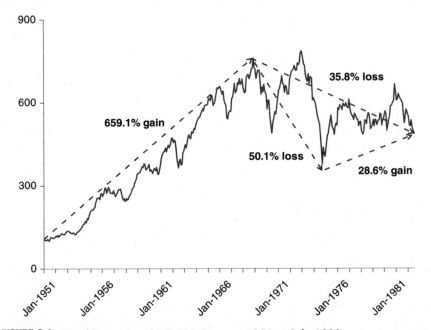

FIGURE 3.1   Real Return on S&P 500, January 1951 to July 1982
Data sources: © Morningstar, S&P Dow Jones Indices, and Bureau of Labor Statistics.

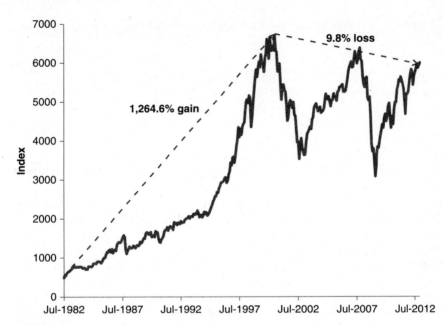

FIGURE 3.2 Real Return on S&P Dow Jones Indices, July 1982 to December 2012
Data sources: S&P Dow Jones Indices and Bureau of Labor Statistics.

stocks on balance have lost almost 10 percent in real terms through 2012. At the bottom of the latest bear market in March 2009, the cumulative loss was almost 50 percent.

Now let's see just how well bonds would have fared over these same periods. Table 3.1 compares the real returns on the S&P 500 with those on the long-term (20-year) Treasury bond. The Treasury bond had negative real returns during the postwar boom period and during both of the inflation-ridden periods of the 1970s. In the postwar boom period ending in 1968 when stocks averaged a 12.0 percent real return, the Treasury bond had a small negative real return. And in the period from December 1968 to July 1982 when stocks were losing ground to inflation, Treasuries earned a cumulative real return of –37.8 percent for an annual return of –3.4 percent! Stocks and bonds, in fact, were equally miserable investments. The S&P 500 had an average annual real return of –3.2 percent. But bonds are supposed to be the safe haven for investors.

Then in the 1980s and 1990s, Treasuries came alive. Bonds had splendid returns in the 1980s and early 1990s for a very simple reason. Inflation and bond returns fell over this period. Soon after Paul Volcker was first named to lead the Federal Reserve in 1979, the inflation rate started to

TABLE 3.1   Real Returns in Four Market Phases, 1951–2012

Dates	S&P 500®		Long-Term Treasury Bonds	
	Cumulative	Per Annum	Cumulative	Per Annum
Jan. 1951–Nov. 1968	659.1%	12.0%	–11.6%	–0.7%
Dec. 1968–July 1982	–35.8%	–3.2%	–37.8%	–3.4%
Aug. 1982–Mar. 2000	1264.6%	15.9%	328.7%	8.6%
Apr. 2000–Dec. 2012	–9.8%	–0.8%	111.2%	6.0%
Whole Period				
Jan. 1951–Dec. 2012	5898.9%	6.8%	397.7%	2.6%

Note: The S&P 500 and long-term Treasury bond returns are deflated by the consumer price index.
Data sources: © Morningstar, S&P Dow Jones Indices, and Bureau of Labor Statistics.

recede from historic highs. That's because Volcker and the Fed instituted a tough monetary regime aimed at sharply lowering the double-digit inflation that we were experiencing. Figure 3.3 shows how the inflation rate turned down sharply soon after Volcker's policies began to take effect.

After Volcker succeeded in driving inflation to low single digits, bond yields stayed stubbornly high for a time. But eventually the bond market adjusted. The yields on newly issued bonds fell to reflect lower inflation, so the prices of existing bonds were bid up. As a result, bond returns soared. Investors in this market benefited whether they bought and held onto bonds with higher yields or sold out their bond positions after registering large capital gains. There was a *once-in-a-lifetime* capital gain on Treasuries (as well as most other bonds).

Paul Volcker ushered in a terrific period for bond investors. As Table 3.1 shows, the long-term Treasury earned an 8.6 percent annual return over the period from August 1982 through March 2000. Even so, Treasury returns paled in comparison with stock returns during this period. Stocks earned an average real return of 15.9 percent/year. Then when the stock market fell astray, Treasuries really started to shine. In contrast with a –9.8 percent return on the S&P 500, Treasuries have earned over 100 percent in cumulative return since 2000.

Some investors are hoping for high bond returns to continue indefinitely. But the driving force for these record real returns was the reversal of the same inflation that had undermined the bond market in the late 1960s and 1970s.

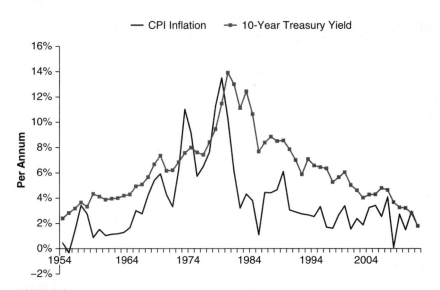

FIGURE 3.3   Inflation and Bond Yields, 1954–2012
Data sources: IMF, International Financial Statistics, and Bureau of Labor Statistics.

WERE YOU LUCKY ENOUGH TO INVEST DURING THE 1980S AND 1990S?

To maximize wealth at retirement, it is essential to be accumulating in decades when returns are high. That much is self-evident. Being lucky enough to invest in the 1980s and 1990s is surely a recipe for investment success. But it is also important to have saved enough by the time that high returns arrive. For example, investors who have $100,000 already in their accounts in 1981 will fare much better than those who start out saving in that year.

Let's extend the experiment considered earlier where an investor saves $10,000 per year. This time we will examine how much the investor has accumulated after 30 years in both the bond market and stock market. So we imagine that the investor is retiring after 30 years of work and saving. We will consider different types of investors. At one extreme, an investor elects an all-bond portfolio throughout the accumulation years. At the other extreme, an investor elects an all-stock portfolio.

Before considering the specific results, we can guess how well the investor choosing an all-bond portfolio will fare in different periods. If the investor retires in 1980 after three decades of negative bond returns, he or she is not going to accumulate very much. Remember that a portfolio earning zero real return will deliver $300,000 after 30 years, since the investor is saving $10,000 per year. Because real bond returns were negative for the previous 30 years, a bond investor retiring in 1980 would have to retire with *less than he or she saved*—at least in real terms after adjusting for the cost of living. But what if the bond investor retired in 2010? An investor retiring in 2010 would have enjoyed the huge positive returns of the past three decades. Naturally, that investor would retire with a nest egg considerably larger than the $300,000 invested over time.

Stock investors also experience widely different fates depending on when they do their accumulation. If the investor retires in 2000, the investment pool has grown huge because of the outsized returns of the previous two decades. But pity the investor who retires in 2010. A decade of negative real returns is the recipe for a diminished retirement.

Table 3.2 gives the detailed results for these different investors. The table shows how much the all-bond investor and all-stock investor accumulates over 30 years depending on the date of retirement. For stock investors, the best results are found for the cohort who retires in 2000. Having saved $300,000 over time, these investors sit on nest-eggs worth over $1.8 million. Investors retiring one decade later in 2010, in contrast, accumulate only $847,800 by the time they retire. There are two reasons why they fare much worse. First, these investors only started saving in 1981, so they had fewer assets to benefit from the 9.0 percent return of the 1980s and 14.4 percent return of the 1990s. Second, the investors accumulating through the 2000s had to contend with negative real returns on stocks in that decade.

For bond investors, the glory days are found in recent decades. An investor retiring in either 2000 or 2010 would have accumulated almost

TABLE 3.2   How Much Does a Retiree Accumulate over 30 Years? Cumulative Wealth in Real Terms (Constant Dollars)

	Accumulation over 30 Years ($ thousands)	
Retire in Year	**All-Bond Portfolio**	**All-Stock Portfolio**
1980	$190.2	$529.0
1990	$451.5	$689.9
2000	$776.0	$1,832.8
2010	$779.0	$847.8

Assumptions: Investor earns actual real return on Treasury bonds or S&P 500 in every year of accumulation period. Each year the investor contributes $10,000 to account (measured in constant dollars).
Data sources: © Morningstar, S&P Dow Jones Indices, and Bureau of Labor Statistics.

$800,000 in wealth. That is far above what the poor bond investor saw in the three decades ending in 1980. The bond investor retiring in 1980 would have accumulated about $190,000 in real terms because rising inflation resulted in negative real returns. The $300,000 nominal savings was eroded by over one third!

What lies ahead for the bond investor? Is there a "New Normal" for that investor? And is there a "New Normal" for the stock investor? Let's consider each type of investor in turn.

THE NEW NORMAL FOR THE BOND INVESTOR

The New Normal described by Bill Gross focused on stock returns, not bond returns. Low growth in the future would limit returns on stocks and other risky assets. As a result, investors would have to switch to a more conservative asset allocation mix with more bonds and stable blue chip stocks. An investment expert as successful as Gross demands respect for his views. But perhaps Gross should have also warned us about a *New Normal for bonds*. In my opinion, lower bond returns are more likely than lower stock returns.

Interest rates are difficult to forecast. Wall Street strategists and bond fund managers are paid big bucks to forecast the future. Yet even they do not know what interest rates will be in a year's time or over the next few years. It's undoubtedly easier to think further into the future to predict interest rates, and therefore bond returns.

Let me begin by describing two extreme scenarios for the bond market: (1) yields stay low and (2) rising rates.

Yields Stay Low

In early 2013, interest rates are near all-time lows. Perhaps they will stay low for a prolonged period of time. After all, the U.S. economy has been growing quite slowly since the beginning of the recovery in June 2009. In the meantime, the Federal Reserve has pumped an enormous amount of liquidity into the financial system to keep interest rates low. In this scenario, investors will have to be content with miserably low bond returns. If interest rates stay low, the return on a bond will be equal to the yield itself. Consider the return on a 20-year Treasury bond. In early 2013, the yield on this bond was a little below 3 percent. With inflation almost as high as the bond yield, investors are barely treading water in real terms. Those saving for retirement in a bond-only portfolio have stagnant portfolios. Those living off bonds in retirement are draining their reserves. This scenario is a cruel one for investors.

We cannot rule out a scenario where interest rates stay low because we have witnessed such a scenario in another industrial economy, Japan. For most of the past 20 years, Japanese interest rates have remained severely depressed despite efforts by the Japanese government and Bank of Japan to stimulate the economy following the collapse of its stock market and real estate market.[2] The Japanese government has run up record fiscal deficits resulting in a debt/GDP ratio over 200 percent (the highest in history). The Bank of Japan has supported this policy by keeping short-term interest rates low. Despite these efforts, Japanese growth has remained sluggish, and Japanese long-term interest rates have remained painfully low. Perhaps U.S. interest rates will follow Japanese patterns.

Rising Rates

There is a worse possibility facing U.S. investors. Interest rates could rise toward normal levels. What is a normal level for U.S. interest rates? Figure 3.3 shows that there is no "normal" level for nominal bond yields. They rise and fall with inflation rates. Real yields also vary over time, though not as much as nominal yields. But in the long run, average real yields are quite stable. Since 1951, the 20-year bond yield has averaged about 2.5 percent after adjusting for inflation. That's also true of the period extending back to 1926. What if real interest rates were to rise back to normal? The *nominal* yield depends on the inflation rate, which itself is difficult to forecast. But let's imagine that in the long run inflation settles at 2.5 percent. (This may be more a wish than a forecast given how much monetary stimulus the Fed has produced since the financial crisis began). Then the nominal yield on a 20-year Treasury bond should eventually rise to 5 percent or so. That is not a pretty picture. It means that bond yields will have to rise by 2 percent or more in the future. During the period when bond yields rise, *bond returns may at times be negative, at least in real terms.*

So there is a plausible case for a "New Normal" for bonds. At least investors should expect the end to the wonderful bond returns of the past 30 years. The bond party has lasted for that long. It may go on for a while longer, but we are running out of champagne and the partygoers are thinking about when to depart. In Chapter 16 we will discuss what this means to current retirees. That chapter discusses various ways for retirees to find income in today's investment market. Retirees will have to be very careful about the maturity of their bond investments. The longer the maturity of a bond, the more vulnerable it is to increases in interest rates. On the other hand, the yields on shorter-term bonds are pitifully low. So the retiree has to choose between income and safety. Long-term Treasury bonds as well as private sector bonds will suffer if bond yields rise. The "New Normal" presents a bleak future for bond investors.

THE NEW NORMAL FOR THE STOCK INVESTOR

Since 2000, the U.S. stock market has delivered zero returns or less to investors. This has truly been a "lost decade." Writing in March 2013, the S&P 500 is barely above its level in March 2000. In delivering near-zero nominal returns (and negative real returns), the market has forced investors on a rollercoaster ride of two deep dips followed by two exhilarating rallies. The thrill has been lost on investors as they earned nothing for all the volatility. Perhaps we have already begun the "New Normal" for stocks.

Bill Gross chose to announce the "New Normal" at an inopportune time. Indeed, his timing was awful. He announced the new normal just two months after the market reached its bottom. Since March 2009, the U.S. stock market as represented by the S&P 500 has rallied over 100 percent. This is not as surprising as it seems because the stock market always rallies during a business cycle upturn. And by March of 2009, the "worst financial crisis since the 1930s" had turned into an ordinary recession (though admittedly a bad one). That's because of the quick action by the Treasury and Federal Reserve in the fall of 2008 after Lehman Brothers failed. This book is not the place to recount the events of that stressful period. But by the spring of 2009 it was clear that the worse had passed. The S&P 500 reached its bottom on March 9, 2009. We would learn later that the recession ended in June 2009.[3]

When the U.S. economy falls into recession, it eventually recovers. Once it recovers, the rally in the stock market is usually quite substantial. Table 3.3 examines the rise in the S&P following each of the nine recessions since 1951. In each case, the stock market rallied strongly as the economy recovered. In all but one case, the rally began *before the recession had actually ended.* For example, the last recession ended in June 2009, yet the market reached bottom on March 9, 2009, three months before the recession ended. Market participants evidently anticipated the end of the recession and the sharp gain in corporate profits that would occur as the economy rebounded. So in some sense, the stock market has been behaving recently as it normally does.

Yet investors are interested in the future, not the past. Even though the stock market has enjoyed a classic cyclical rally, this does not deny the possibility that returns in the future may disappoint investors. Ultimately, stock returns depend on profitability of firms within an economy. If the U.S. economy grows in the future, stock returns will follow. This is not to say that growth and stock returns follow closely one another. Surely stock returns in the 1990s exceeded growth or any prospects for growth in the

TABLE 3.3   S&P 500 Rallies after Recessions, 1951–2012

Recession Months (NBER dating)	Market Bottom	Gain in First 12 months
July 53–May 54	Sept. 53	46.0%
Aug. 57–Apr. 58	Dec. 57	43.4%
Apr. 60–Feb. 61	Oct. 60	32.6%
Dec. 69–Nov. 70	June 70	41.9%
Nov. 73–Mar. 75	Dec. 74	37.3%
July 81–Nov. 82	July 82	59.3%
July 90–Mar. 91	Oct. 90	33.5%
Mar. 01–Nov. 01	Feb. 03	38.5%
Dec. 07–June 09	Mar. 09	49.8%

Note: The market trough is determined by the lowest monthly average of daily prices for the S&P 500 price index.
Data sources: The S&P price data is from Robert Shiller's website, www.econ.yale .edu/~shiller/data.htm. The S&P 500 gain is based on the total return on the S&P (including dividends) from SBBI Ibbotson 2013 (© Morningstar).

U.S. economy. Price-earnings ratios rose sharply in that decade. Conversely, the negative stock returns of the decade ending in 2010 occurred despite substantial growth in corporate earnings per share. Earnings per share in the last decade (2001 to 2010) were 55 percent higher than earnings in the 1990s. Yet stocks stagnated.

One view of this *lost decade* is that we are giving back the returns of the 1980s and 1990s. At the end of 1999, the average real return on stocks measured from 1951 to 1999 was a surprisingly high 8.9 percent. The long-run average had been driven upward by two decades of incredible stock returns. The average measured through 1999 was way above the average real return of 6.4 percent measured from 1951 to 1980. And it was way above the average real return from 1926 to 1950 of 6.3 percent. The lost decade has brought the long-run averages almost back to where they were in 1980. By 2012, the average return measured from 1951 was back to 6.8 percent. So we have spent 12 years reverting to the mean! If this is the case, then there is little reason for pessimism about stocks. According to this interpretation, we are near the end of a decade-long period of adjustment. So going forward, stock returns will behave more normally than in the last decade or so.

An alternative view is based on current valuations of the stock market. We could look at current price-earnings (or P/E) ratios, either based on recent earnings or projected future earnings. Since projected earnings are subject to many revisions, let's consider price-earnings ratios based on the previous year's reported earnings. Since 1951, this P/E measure has averaged 17.9. At the end of 2012, the P/E was 16.2. So by this measure of valuation, the stock market appears to be reasonably valued.[4]

An alternative price-earnings measure has been developed by Robert Shiller (2000). Shiller makes two changes to conventional P/E measures. First, he measures the past 10 years' earnings in order to iron out sharp cyclical changes in earnings. Second, he adjusts both prices and earnings by inflation (necessary because 10 years of earnings are being measured).

The result is shown in Figure 3.4. Notice how overvalued the market looks in the late 1990s. Two sharp corrections in 2000–2002 and 2007–2009 have brought the P/E ratio down to about 22 in early 2013. Comparing current ratios to the average since 1951 (18.8), the market appears to be at least 10 percent overvalued. If this analysis is right, then stock market investors face additional pain as valuations adjust back toward their long-run averages. And there is no guarantee that P/E ratios will not overshoot in the downward direction.

But Bill Gross may be foreseeing even bleaker times for the stock market. If U.S. growth remains depressed in the future, earnings will not grow as

FIGURE 3.4 Price/Earnings Ratios for S&P 500, 1951–2012
Data source: www.econ.yale.edu/~shiller, described in Shiller 2000.

rapidly as in the previous 60 years. Stock returns may disappoint investors because U.S. growth is no longer as rapid as it used to be.

WHAT CAN INVESTORS DO?

The New Normal for bond investors is almost a sure thing. The only uncertainty is about which bad scenario we will face. In the most optimistic scenario, bond yields remain low and inflation is high enough to reduce real returns to zero or less. So savers cannot look to capital appreciation as they try to accumulate wealth for retirement. And retirees will be barely treading water. A more pessimistic scenario involves bond yields rising so bond returns may turn negative. In that case both savers and retirees suffer even more.

A New Normal for stock investors is harder to predict. The conventional measure of price-earnings suggests that the "lost decade" may be over. The evidence based on Shiller's P/E analysis instead indicates that the near-term outlook for stocks is unpromising. That's especially true because we have already been through the rebound in stocks that normally follows a recession. The New Normal suggests that lower stock returns will be experienced even after any further valuation adjustments occur.

Investors cannot control what happens to bond and stock returns. If investors believe in a New Normal, it means they have to work even harder to make sure that they are saving enough for retirement. And they have to make sure that the investing they do is as sure-footed as possible. The bleaker is the future outlook for investing, the more they have to pay attention to the investment plan. Unlike the investors of the 1980s and 1990s, investors of today cannot afford the luxury of mistakes in saving and investing. In Chapters 4 and 5, we will consider how the New Normal may affect required rates of saving. And in Chapters 16 through 19, we will consider how the New Normal may lower how much a retiree can safely spend in retirement.

NOTES

1. Gross introduced the "new normal" at the 2009 Morningstar Investment Conference held in May of 2009.
2. The Japanese Nikkei average reached a peak of 38,900 in December 1989. In early 2013, that index remained at about a quarter of its peak value. A similar collapse of real estate values followed a few years later.
3. The NBER Business Cycle Committee, the unofficial arbiter of recessions in the United States, later declared that the recession ended in June of 2009.

4. It should be noted that this price-earnings measure has been very unstable. For example, during the worst of the financial crisis in 2008, the price-earnings ratio soared over 60 because earnings collapsed so badly that year. Price-earnings based on operating earnings rather than reported earnings were much more stable during this period.

REFERENCES

Shiller, Robert J. 2000. *Irrational Exuberance*. Princeton, NJ: Princeton University Press.

CHAPTER 4

A Savings Goal for Retirement

In the "old days," 20 or 30 years ago, many companies where Americans worked offered pensions to their employees for their retirement years. As explained in Chapter 1, these so-called "defined benefit" pensions were usually guaranteed for life. Some were even indexed to inflation, so that pension income rose along with the cost of living. The companies themselves had to bear all of the risks of maintaining these pensions. If markets were booming, a company could lighten up on its payments to its pension fund. But if markets performed poorly as in the last decade, the company was forced to increase payments to the fund. As a result, many companies chose to get out of this pension fund business. The traditional defined benefit pensions have been replaced for many workers with "defined contribution" pensions that require workers to save for their own retirement.

It should be noted that even in the heyday of defined benefit pensions, only a fraction of Americans were covered by these conventional plans. So the "old days" may be somewhat mythical for many Americans who have always had to save for their own retirement. That has certainly been true for most small business owners, including farmers. Nonetheless, traditional pensions are far less important today that they were 20 or 30 years ago. Americans are increasingly on their own in saving for their retirement.

Employers sponsoring defined contribution plans such as the 401(k) do often "match" some of the pension contributions of their employees. A typical matching plan might have the employer matching the first 3 percent of employee contributions to 401(k) plans. But the bulk of the contributions to these new pensions are provided by the employees themselves. If they contribute enough to their 401(k) plans, they might have a comfortable retirement. If they fail to contribute, they may have to base their retirement on Social Security alone.

This chapter will ask about how much has to be saved for retirement. Is there a rule of thumb that will help guide younger and older workers in their savings? Such a rule of thumb in the form of a specific *savings goal* would be very useful in deciding whether a worker can retire early or must delay retirement. And when workers are still in their 40s or 50s, a specific savings goal would alert them to the need to accelerate their savings rates in order to retire on time.

Providing for retirement is not the only goal of savings. Younger workers save in order to pay off debt including college loans. They save for a down payment on a home. If they have children, they begin saving to pay college tuitions. And, of course, they save for that future trip to Bali Hai (a mystical island, for those who have never seen *South Pacific*). But surely retirement is the most important goal, even for young workers.

WHAT IS RETIREMENT SAVINGS TRYING TO ACHIEVE?

Most investors know that saving for retirement is important. But what is the ultimate aim of this saving? More is better, but how much more? I would like to propose the following objective for retirement saving:

> Retirement savings have to be high enough to sustain preretirement spending.

That is, like the squirrel in Chapter 1, investors have to save enough during their working years to keep spending at the same rate in retirement. If an investor is used to spending based on an income of $100,000, then savings should be sufficient to keep that level of spending going in retirement. This objective may not be attainable, but it is a reasonable one to strive for. Since savings usually cease with retirement, this amounts to matching preretirement income *less* savings. If an individual has been earning $100,000 per year and saving 15 percent of it, then the objective of retirement savings is to generate $85,000 in retirement income (or 85 percent of preretirement income).

Having stated this aim for savings let me qualify it immediately:

- First, taxes may fall in retirement, so retirement income does not have to be as high as prior to retirement. Taxes may fall because Social Security benefits are not fully taxed.[1] Withdrawals from savings, moreover, may be taxed at lower rates than ordinary income. That's especially true if savings are in taxable accounts rather than in 401(k) or other retirement accounts.[2] Withdrawals from taxable investment accounts are often subject to the lower tax rates applying to capital gains and dividends.
- Second, expenses may drop in retirement. Retirees may save on commuting expenses and on other work-related expenses like workday lunches and dry cleaning. More important, housing costs may be

reduced. Retirees can downsize their housing and perhaps move to a smaller house or apartment or to a less expensive part of the country.
- Third, spending can be curtailed *if necessary*. This is a point made by Michael Stein (1998) in his excellent book on retirement. Stein emphasized that if retirees don't have enough resources to come close to their past standard of living, they find a way to live within their means.

On the other hand, retirees have so much more time to spend their income than they did when they were working. So don't presume that they can live on a small fraction of their preretirement income.

IS THERE A RULE OF THUMB ABOUT HOW MUCH YOU HAVE TO SAVE?

One mutual fund company has recently formulated a savings goal to guide retirement savings. The savings goal is that investors save *eight times their income* by the time they retire. So if you are used to earning $100,000 per year, you need to save $800,000. That may seem like a lot of savings, but I will try to convince you that it underestimates the amount of savings actually needed by many savers.[3]

Any rule of thumb for savings has to take into account Social Security. Most Americans qualify for Social Security by the time they retire. In fact, Social Security payments provide a good portion of the income needed for retirement, unless the retiree's income is far above average incomes in the United States.

The savings goal that I will discuss assumes that retirement spending comes from two sources:

1. Social Security provides a steady stream of income. In fact, Social Security income is indexed to inflation, so it rises with the cost of living.
2. Wealth accumulated prior to retirement provides a second source of retirement spending.

Some retirees may also be able to rely on traditional pensions, but let's focus on retirees who have only their own savings to fall back on (including savings within 401(k) and other defined contribution plans). Social Security payments are supplemented by drawing on accumulated savings. But how much can you spend out of savings?

It's not possible to establish a savings goal for retirement unless we know how much can be spent per year out of that savings. Any well-planned retirement should set a rate of spending out of savings that is sustainable over time. This rate of spending is called a *spending rule*. The spending rule should be low enough so that it can be sustained throughout retirement. And it makes sense to choose a spending rule that can keep pace with inflation. So if (say) the spending rule is set initially at 4 percent of wealth, the dollar amount of spending then can increase over time to keep pace with inflation. Let's consider what this spending rule should be based on.

WHAT RATE OF SPENDING IS SAFE IN RETIREMENT?

Foundations and endowments establish spending rules that state that spending must be kept at a set percentage of the total value of their portfolios. Many of these institutions keep spending at about 3 percent of the portfolio's value.[4] Such a low spending rule is adopted since these institutions usually want to keep the portfolio intact (in real terms) indefinitely.

Individuals planning retirement can afford to spend more than institutions because the money has to last only until the end of retirement. Most experts advise spending about *4 percent of investable wealth each year*.[5] This spending rate is kept low so that spending can rise in future years as inflation raises the cost of living for the retiree. Investable wealth is defined as the value of all investable assets such as stocks and bonds (and mutual funds containing them), including assets held in defined contribution pension accounts. If an investor has accumulated $1 million by the time of retirement, then a 4 percent rule would allow that investor to spend $40,000 in the first year of retirement. Some of that spending would be generated by the interest earned on bonds and dividends paid on stock. The rest of it would have to come from harvesting capital gains. In other words, spending would be generated by the *total return* on the portfolio, not just the income. Chapter 16 on investment income will show that in today's low interest rate environment, it might be too risky to try to find assets generating income of 4 percent per year.

The rationale for this rule can be explained more easily if we see the principles behind such a rule. The first principle is the most important one.

Principle 1: The spending rule should be based on the expected real rate of return on the portfolio, not the expected nominal return.

This makes a huge difference. A lot of investors base their spending on nominal returns. So if they earn 8 percent per year on their stock portfolios, they think they can spend 8 percent per year. Let's consider an extreme case to see why this won't work.

Example: An investor decides to invest everything in 30-year bonds paying 4.5 percent. With a $1 million portfolio, the investor knows that for the next 30 years, he or she will receive $45,000 per year in interest income. So, naturally enough, the investor decides to spend $45,000 per year out of this portfolio. What is wrong with this strategy? The answer is that even with moderate inflation, spending at a 4.5 percent rate will gradually undermine the standard of living of this investor. Suppose that inflation averages just 2.5 percent per year for the next 30 years. This is an optimistic assumption given our discussion of the "New Normal" in Chapter 3. With 2.5 percent inflation, the cost of living rises by 28 percent in 10 years and by over 60 percent in 20 years. That means that the $45,000 will buy less and less as we go forward. If an investor spends the nominal return on the portfolio, there is no allowance for a *future rise in the cost of living.* So the investor will have to get by with less and less later in retirement. For this reason, the spending rule must be based on the real return, not the nominal return.

Principle 2: The spending rule depends on the portfolio chosen in retirement.

The second rule should be obvious. If investors choose a portfolio of bonds paying 4.5 percent, the real return is only about 2 percent (still assuming that inflation stays at 2.5 percent). So the spending rule would have to be quite low. On the other hand, a stock portfolio might earn 6.5 percent in real terms in the long run. As Chapter 2 showed, this was the average real return on stocks over the past 60 as well as 90 years. In that case, the spending rule might be quite a bit higher. For retirees, a stock-only portfolio is not a reasonable one because there is too much risk in such a portfolio. But a retiree might reasonably compare a 50-50 stock-bond portfolio with an even more conservative one. In that case, it's important to recognize that the higher the proportion of bonds in the portfolio, the lower the spending rule has to be.

Principle 3: The spending rule has to be low enough to minimize the risk of running out of money in retirement.

Long-run averages are just what they appear to be. Unfortunately, investors often don't get to wait until the long-run average is reached. Markets do misbehave. Investors sometimes retire just before the start of a recession. Recently, some Americans were unfortunate enough to retire just as the financial crisis hit. We have to base our spending rules on bad scenarios as well as long-run averages.

How do we minimize the damage of bad markets? The answer is that we choose a spending rule that is low enough to survive most such markets—so the investor *does not run out of money in retirement.* The spending rule must be low enough to ensure that this is an unlikely possibility. A spending rule as low as 4 percent is based on studies that allow stocks and bonds to suffer from the type of bad markets that we have experienced in the past. There are two common ways to conduct these studies. One is to examine past historical episodes and ask how well each level of spending fares. The spending rule is lowered until the portfolio survives almost all bad episodes. The second approach is to use simulation experiments to find out how often a portfolio with the same average returns as in the past survives intact when buffeted by random shocks like those in the past. A 4 percent spending rule is low enough so that the portfolio falls short in less than 10 percent of the simulations. The results that are obtained are quite similar using both methodologies. We will discuss both types of evidence in Chapter 17 on retirement spending,

It is important to point out that the 4 percent spending rule is based on past real rates of return, whether returns in the postwar period or returns extending back to the 1920s. If a "New Normal" of low returns lies ahead, the 4 percent rule may be too ambitious. I raise this possibility for those readers who think that the rule is too conservative. If a lower spending rule is required, the task of saving enough for retirement will be all the more daunting.

Now that the 4 percent spending rule has been explained, we are ready to ask how much savings are necessary to fund a retirement. Remember that the savings goal is designed to keep spending during retirement as high as it was prior to retirement.

WHAT IF THERE WERE NO SOCIAL SECURITY? SOME SIMPLE ARITHMETIC

It's useful to consider a world without Social Security. That's not because I believe that Social Security will ever be taken away from Americans. After all, there is enormous support for the program. And older Americans already on Social Security cast votes out of proportion to their share of the population.[6] But imagining no Social Security keeps the arithmetic of retirement savings very simple. In fact, the arithmetic is quite shocking. So my later calculations that establish a retirement savings goal in a world with Social Security will be less shocking to the reader. By the way, there are many younger Americans who say that they don't trust that Social Security will be around by the time that they retire. My arithmetic may scare them into saving a lot more!

Let's imagine that an investor is used to making $100,000 per year and saving 20 percent of that income.[7] So the investor wants to save enough so that he or she can spend $80,000 per year in retirement. With a spending rule of 4 percent, this investor must save $2 million by the time of retirement. Why? That is because 4 percent of $2 million is $80,000 per year. In a world without Social Security:

Savings goal is 20 times income.

That surely is a shocking result.

Notice that this savings goal of 20 times income also applies to anyone making either more or less than this investor. If another investor is used to earning $400,000 per year, then the savings goal is still 20 times income, or $8 million. With a spending rule of 4 percent, this second investor withdraws $320,000 per year, or 80 percent of preretirement income.

Americans without Social Security are almost as badly off as the squirrels in Chapter 1. Recall that the squirrels had to forgo half of their current "income" to store enough nuts for winter. Can you imagine how high the rate of savings has to be to reach a savings goal of $2 million by the time of retirement? Fortunately, Americans have Social Security to help support their retirement. Let's factor Social Security payments into the retirement savings goal.

SAVINGS GOAL WITH SOCIAL SECURITY

Once Social Security is factored into retirement planning, the savings rule depends on the level of income of an individual. That's because Social Security payments are capped in value for the same reason that Social Security taxes are capped at a certain level of income ($113,700 in 2013). A worker who makes $400,000 per year will receive not much more in Social Security payments than a worker who makes $100,000. For this reason, we will focus most of our discussion on a worker making $100,000 per year. Later in the chapter we will look at those making more or less than that amount.

A worker earning $100,000 today and equivalent amounts (adjusted for inflation) in earlier years would qualify for almost the maximum amount paid by Social Security. If this individual is retiring at the full retirement age of 66, the Social Security payment will be almost $26,000 per year.[8] That amount, moreover, is indexed to inflation. So in future years, the newly retired person will see his or her Social Security income rise in line with the consumer price index.

If this individual is to match 85 percent of preretirement income or $85,000, he or she must save enough to generate $59,000 per year (adjusted by inflation in future years) to supplement Social Security. If the spending rule is 4 percent of wealth, then it easy to calculate how much savings the individual must accumulate to generate $59,000 per year. That's $1.475 million.[9] What a formidable goal!

Savings goal for individual making $100,000 is almost 15 times income.

Our hypothetical investor is assumed to be single. Suppose instead that this investor is married and that the spouse is also 66 but has not worked enough to qualify for Social Security benefits. Then the married couple qualifies for 1.5 times the benefit of a single individual with the same income.[10] So the couple might receive as much as $39,000 in Social Security payments each year. As Table 4.1 shows, the extra spousal benefit reduces the savings required to match preretirement spending. The married couple needs to generate $46,000 per year in withdrawals out of savings. This withdrawal plus the Social Security payment of $39,000 will generate the required $85,000 a year. To fund this large a withdrawal, the couple must save a total of $1.15 million by the time of retirement.

The savings goal for a married couple making $100,000 is 11.5 times income.

These savings goals are probably much larger than most readers imagined. So it's natural to think about ways in which the goals are too ambitious:

- Many readers may argue that the 4 percent spending rule is too stingy. A higher spending rule would require that less wealth be accumulated prior to retirement. But remember that this 4 percent rule is based on the long-run (real) returns on stocks and bonds. And the "New Normal" casts doubt on whether these long-run returns will be achieved in the

TABLE 4.1 Savings Goal Required to Replace Preretirement Spending

	Individual	Couple
Social Security benefits	$26,000	$39,000
Withdrawal from portfolio	$59,000	$46,000
TOTAL	$85,000	$85,000
Percent of income replaced	85%	85%
Required wealth at retirement	$1,475,000	$1,150,000
Savings goal	14.8	11.5

Assumptions: Retiree earned $100,000 prior to retirement. Retirement is at age 66 so the retiree has reached "full retirement age." Savings goal is adjusted to ensure that postretirement spending is equal to 85% of preretirement income. Withdrawals are based on a 4% spending rule.

next 10 or 20 years. So perhaps the 4 percent rule is too high rather than too low.

■ Other readers may not believe that spending has to be as high in retirement as during the working years. Those readers may focus on the opportunities to cut expenditure in retirement. As mentioned above, taxes may be lower in retirement depending on whether the savings are within taxable or tax-sheltered retirement accounts. And overall spending may also be lower in retirement. That's certainly going to be the case *by necessity* if savings goals fall short. Yet don't pretend that lowering spending will be easy for those with the time (and health) to enjoy retirement.

On the other hand, these formidable spending goals may underestimate the actual savings needed by many families. That's because a *majority of Americans retire prior to full retirement age* (which is currently 66). In fact, two-thirds of Americans retire at age 65 or earlier. If an individual retires at 62, Social Security benefits are 25 percent smaller than they would be at full retirement age. The savings goal would have to be increased accordingly to make up for lower Social Security payments. For example, an individual retiring at 62 would have a savings goal of over 16.4 times income to match preretirement spending. In Chapter 18 on retirement, we discuss the issue of retirement age in more detail.

Spending goals outlined in Table 4.1 may be too modest for another reason if investors have made more than $100,000 prior to retirement. That's because Social Security plays less of a role in retirement for those fortunate enough to have higher incomes. The next section will show how the spending goal varies with preretirement income.

RETIREMENT SAVINGS GOAL AT HIGHER OR LOWER LEVELS OF INCOME

Social Security payments naturally depend on the income of participants. It is true that Social Security taxes are proportional to income up to a limit ($113,700 in 2013). But Social Security payments are not proportional to income. In fact, there are two features of the Social Security system that affect the savings goals of investors:

1. Social Security payments are proportionately more generous the lower your income. As an example, recipients who earned $50,000 rather than $100,000 for most of their lives (in real terms) receive Social Security payments that are about 65 percent of those of the higher earning individual. As discussed earlier, an individual earning $100,000 receives almost $26,000 in Social Security at the full retirement age of 66. But an

individual earning $50,000 receives a little less than $17,000 per year or about 65 percent rather than 50 percent of the other individual's benefit.

2. Because there is a cap on income subject to Social Security and a corresponding cap on Social Security benefits, individuals making much more than $100,000 do not get a proportionate bump in benefits. An individual earning $200,000 per year is capped at about $30,600 per year. So that individual earning twice as much as the $100,000 earner receives benefits less than 118 percent of what the $100,000 earner receives. There is nothing unfair about this since Social Security taxes are also capped. But it does mean that higher earners have to be much better savers than lower earners because post retirement spending depends much more on portfolio withdrawals.

Let's begin with lower-earning workers. The median income of American families is a little over $50,000 in 2013. Let's determine the savings rule for someone earning $50,000 prior to retirement who decides to retire at the full retirement age of 66. If the retiree is single, the Social Security payment is a little less than $17,000 per year (as stated above). In order for this individual to spend 85 percent of preretirement income (or $42,500), the retiree must have saved almost $640,000 or 12.8 times income!

Savings goal for the average individual is 12.8 times income.

That's a tall order for the average American.

What if the retiree is married and the couple qualifies for the maximum spousal benefit? Marital bliss will surely help.

Savings goal for average married couple is 8.5 times income.

With Social Security payments that are 50 percent larger, the required savings at retirement falls to "only" $425,000 or 8.5 times income. But remember that this savings goal is based on the assumption that retirement is delayed until the full retirement age of 66. If retirement is at the more normal age of 62, even this high a savings goal will still fall short.

Let's approach the issue of retirement savings another way. Suppose that a couple has saved only $200,000 by the time of retirement. With a spending rule of 4 percent, this will generate a withdrawal of $8,000 per year (4 percent of $200,000). With Social Security of about $25,500 (50 percent higher than the individual's Social Security of $17,000), the couple will be able to replace about 67 percent of preretirement income ($33,500/$50,000). For most families, cutting back spending by that much is feasible. But it is certainly not desirable.

For the more fortunate families making more than $100,000, savings are much more important to retirement. Consider someone who earned

TABLE 4.2   Retirement Savings Goal for Married Couple by Income Level

Preretirement income	$50,000	$100,000	$200,000	$400,000
Wealth at retirement	$425,000	$1,150,000	$3,100,000	$7,350,000
Retirement savings goal (as multiple of income)	8.5	11.5	15.5	18.4

Assumptions: The retirement savings rule is based on Social Security benefits for a married couple at the full retirement age of 66 as well as 4% spending out of accumulated wealth. All amounts are measured in constant dollars.

$200,000 a year prior to retirement with retirement occurring at the full retirement age of 66. If that individual is married and if the spouse is eligible for a 50 percent spousal benefit, then Social Security totals about $45,600 per year. Despite receiving the maximum Social Security benefit, retirement spending must be supported by a large amount of savings. As Table 4.2 indicates, this couple would have had to save 15.5 times earnings or $3.1 million in order to replace preretirement spending. And if the retiree made $400,000 prior to retirement, the savings rule increases to 18.4 times earnings or $7.35 million. Needless to say, for retirees who were in those income brackets, Social Security matters much less than for those with lower incomes. Savings goals are particularly important to higher income earners.

It should be clear from this discussion that there is no single savings goal that will work for every American. That's because Social Security plays a much more important role for married couples than for individuals and for those with modest incomes compared with higher income Americans. At every income level, the savings goals are formidable. How does a family making the median income save $425,000 by the time of retirement?

HOW DO WE REACH THE SAVINGS GOAL?

The next chapter discusses how savings goals might be achieved. It is one thing to establish how much savings is needed to retire. But how much does someone have to save each year to reach this goal?

NOTES

1. According to the Social Security website, "No one pays federal income tax on more than 85 percent of his or her Social Security." www.ssa.gov/planners/taxes.htm.

2. Withdrawals from Roth IRAs, in contrast, are free of Federal tax.
3. The mutual fund company is careful to state that the savings goal will vary from one investor to another.
4. These institutions often tie the spending rule to the average value of the portfolio over the preceding (say) three years so as to smooth out the effects of market fluctuations.
5. See Chapter 21 of Solin (2009) for a discussion of the 4 percent rule and references to previous work supporting it including an influential early study by Bergen (1994).
6. There is a chance that upper income Americans will see their Social Security benefits taxed more heavily or even partially curtailed. And there are proposals to change the indexing formula for calculating Social Security benefits.
7. I choose a savings rate of 20 percent to make the arithmetic easier.
8. These Social Security payments are for an individual retiring in January 2013 who earned $100,000 the previous year. A benefit calculator is available at www.ssa.gov/oact/quckcal.
9. That is, $1.475 million × 4 percent = $59,000.
10. Social Security benefits are maximized when only one spouse earns all of the income. These and other features of the Social Security system are discussed in detail in Chapter 18 on retirement.

REFERENCES

Bergen, William P. 1994. "Determining Withdrawal Rates Using Historical Data." *Journal of Financial Planning* (October).

Solin, Daniel R. 2009. *The Smartest Retirement Book You'll Ever Read.* New York: Penguin.

Stein, Michael K. 1998. *The Prosperous Retirement: Guide to the New Reality.* Boulder, CO: Emstco Press.

CHAPTER 5

What Rate of Savings?

We find so many different ways to spend our income. There are necessities like food and clothing and shelter and health care. Education, as noted earlier, costs a lot. Then there are luxuries like travel and fancier cars. Savings is one item that is easy to neglect.

There is a life cycle to savings. Everything else being equal, investors find that it is easier to save in the years prior to the arrival of children. And it's easier to save after parents have become "empty nesters," at least once college tuitions are paid. But for the moment, we will assume that savings is steady throughout the working years. That's not a bad approximation for savings within retirement plans. When workers first enter 401(k) or other defined contribution plans, they set their rate of contribution at some rate. Then they leave it alone. Before long, they find that they have contributed a lot to their pensions.

Sadly, some workers elect not to contribute at all. That used to be particularly easy. Until reforms instituted during the Clinton Administration, 401(k) plans depended on workers *electing* to contribute. They had to sign up. We know enough about human behavior to know that automatic signups increase participation. Why? The reason is most people are lazy when it comes to making decisions, especially those that have no immediate payoff. People fail to sign up for 401(k) contributions even in cases where the employer matches their contributions. If they have to take positive action to enter a retirement program, they are less likely to do so. Nowadays, many 401(k) plans automatically enroll workers. Individuals can elect not to participate, but to do so they must take a positive (or should we call it a negative) step to elect not to participate. Automatic enrollment is surely a good thing for savers.

The wonderful feature of a 401(k) is that savings often occur without anyone noticing. Employee contributions are made prior to taxes. Unless employees look carefully at their paychecks, the 401(k) contribution remains as unnoticed as Social Security and Medicare taxes. Sure, everyone complains about their taxes. But they pay more attention to their property tax bills, which have to be paid directly, than the taxes withdrawn from their paychecks. Of course, those who are self-employed would beg to differ about taxes being almost invisible. Those quarterly tax "estimated contributions" are as visible (and painful) for self-employed workers as any other expenses. And for those workers, it takes extra effort to make retirement contributions.

HOW MUCH DOES THE RATE OF SAVINGS MATTER?

Let's see how much difference a higher allocation to a 401(k) program can make. In 2013, employees are allowed to contribute up to $17,500 to their 401(k). (Higher contributions are allowed for those 50 years old or older). 401(k) savings also occur when employers "match" the contributions of the employee. With such high limits, workers making $100,000 per year can in many cases contribute over a fifth of their pretax income to retirement. But to be realistic, let's consider contributions of 5 to 15 percent of income (including any match by an employer). Even if it's not feasible for some workers to save 15 percent within 401(k) plans, savings outside of retirement plans might allow a worker to save 15 percent of income.

To make the discussion of savings as simple as possible, let's assume that savings are invested continually in one portfolio. That portfolio is assumed to allocate 75 percent in stocks and 25 percent in bonds. Following the discussion in Chapter 2, we will assume that bonds earn 2.5 percent real returns in the long run and that stocks earn 6.5 percent real returns. That provides a 5.5 percent real return on the portfolio—at least in the long run. What if the portfolio return is significantly lower? That's a relevant question in 2013 after over a decade of underperformance by the stock market. In a later section, I will allow for lower stock and bond returns. If the "New Normal" is the new norm for returns, it will be important to take into account lower returns.

Let's focus on the investor who is saving 15 percent of income. This investor is saving 15 percent of pretax income of $100,000 or $15,000 per year. That's an aggressive savings rate because taxes have to be paid out of that income as well as all living expenses. Table 5.1 indicates how much this investor has accumulated after 10, 20, and 30 years of saving. The table assumes that the retirement account is invested in a portfolio earning a real return of 5.5 percent. All figures are in constant dollars. After 10 years of saving, the investor has contributed $150,000 to the retirement account, but he or she has accumulated $193,100. Compounding of returns begins to really help the longer the investor saves. By the end of 20 years, contributions total $300,000 (i.e., 20 times $15,000), but wealth has risen to $523,000. By the end of 30 years, the retirement account swells to almost $1.1 million.

How much difference does it make if we contribute only 5 percent instead of 15 percent? The answer is found in Table 5.1. An investor who

TABLE 5.1   Rate of Savings Matters a Lot

	Rate of Savings		
Accumulation Period	5%	10%	15%
10 years	$64,400	$128,700	$193,100
20 years	$174,300	$348,700	$523,000
30 years	$362,200	$724,400	$1,086,500

Assumptions: Savings is based on an income of $100,000. The portfolio chosen devotes 75% of savings to stocks and 25% to bonds. The real return on the portfolio = 5.5%. All amounts are measured in constant dollars.

saves 5 percent of income accumulates a little over $360,000 over 30 years (in 2013 dollars), or one-third as much as someone who saves 15 percent of income. Clearly, the rate of savings makes a tremendous difference to the accumulation of wealth for retirement. But is the extra savings attained by someone saving 15 percent of income really necessary?

HOW MUCH IS ENOUGH?

According to Table 5.1, investors who save 15 percent of a $100,000 in-come accumulate a little more than a million dollars in 30 years. A million dollars sure seems like a lot of money. But is it enough? Do the investors achieve their savings goals?

Table 5.2 reports the annual withdrawals that are supported by the wealth accumulated according to Table 5.1. A savings rate of 5 percent sup-ports about $14,500 of withdrawals per year in retirement. The good news is that this withdrawal rate is designed to increase over time as the portfolio grows in nominal terms. That is, as explained in Chapter 4, the spending rate of 4 percent assumes the dollar amount withdrawn increases over time as the portfolio grows. Higher savings rates naturally support higher levels of withdrawal. A savings rate of 15 percent allows the investor to withdraw over $40,000 per year in retirement.

Table 5.2 also takes into account Social Security benefits. If the worker is married, the benefit is likely to be about $39,000 if that worker retires at the full retirement age (66 in 2013) and if the spouse qualifies for 50 percent ben-efits. So the total retirement "income," consisting of the savings withdrawal plus the Social Security benefit, will be available to support postretirement spending. For a couple saving only at a 5 percent rate, the total retirement income is $53,500 or 53.5 percent of preretirement income. But if the couple

TABLE 5.2 How Much Savings Is Enough? Retirement Income for a Married Couple at Full Retirement Age

	Rate of Savings		
	5%	10%	15%
Accumulation after 30 years	$362,200	$724,400	$1,086,500
Withdrawals	$14,500	$29,000	$43,500
Social Security benefits	$39,000	$39,000	$39,000
Total retirement income	$53,500	$68,000	$82,500
Percent of working income	53.5%	68.0%	82.5%

Assumptions: Savings is based on an income of $100,000. The accumulated wealth at retirement is taken from Table 5.1. Spending (withdrawals) in retirement are based on a 4% withdrawal rate. Social Security payments are for a married couple qualifying for full Social Security benefits (at age 66 in 2013) and full spousal benefits. All amounts are measured in constant dollars.

has saved 15 percent, retirement income rises to $82,500 or 82.5 percent of preretirement income. That's much closer to the 85 percent of income that this couple would have to achieve to match preretirement income (less saving).

Let's discuss further the impact of Social Security benefits on the calculations in Table 5.2. That table assumes that there is a married couple qualifying for maximum spousal benefits. As explained in Chapter 4, a married couple qualifies for 1.5 times the benefit of the single worker, at least as long as the working spouse has qualified for Social Security at full retirement age (66 in 2013).[1] If the worker is single, Social Security payments fall to only $26,000 per year. If this individual has saved 15 percent of income, the lack of a spousal benefit lowers postretirement spending to 69.5 percent of preretirement income. So an individual who has saved as much as 15 percent of income falls considerably short of replacing preretirement spending.

A 15 percent savings rate thus looks adequate for a married couple. But it surely falls short for an individual planning retirement. And very few Americans save at that rate.

THREE KEY FACTORS IN SAVING

There are three key factors that determine the success of any savings program: consistency in savings, starting early, and investing wisely. Let's consider each of these factors.

Savings are easy to neglect. If savings are to be *consistent*, they must be a part of the budget for spending. Budgets usually start with the necessities:

TABLE 5.3   Balance Sheet of a 20-Something

Assets	Liabilities
Cash (bank accounts, money market funds)	College loans
Tax-deferred investments (401(k), IRA, etc.)	Credit card debt
Taxable investments	Mortgage on home or condo
Residence	Other debt
	Net worth

rent, food, transportation to work, debt payments, and so forth. Then there are the discretionary spending items such as restaurants and sporting events. Even if true luxuries are avoided, there is little room for savings. But for someone with long-run goals in mind, savings should come before discretionary spending. That's difficult except to the extent that we are automatically enrolled in a 401(k) plan or some other retirement plan.

It makes sense that it is important to *start saving early*. But is that easy to do? Let's consider the typical balance sheet of someone in his or her twenties as shown in Table 5.3. Notice how the liabilities of a 20-something can burden the savings process. College loans and credit card debt can make it quite difficult to begin the savings process. In such cases, the only savings that is likely is within a 401(k) or IRA. We have already seen how this handicaps the accumulation process.

The third requirement for a successful savings program is *wise investing*. This will be the topic of the middle third of this book. I actually think that investing is the easiest part. It's much harder to save than to invest. But many savers undermine their retirements by being too fancy with their investments. Wise investing requires that you choose a portfolio that is sensible, and then leave it alone. Don't respond to short-run stimuli. Turn off CNBC. Ignore the pundits. Wise investing will require a little more than this, but not much more.

But what about the second factor for a successful savings program, starting early? Does it really matter whether you start saving in your twenties or postpone saving until you reach your mid-thirties? Common sense tells us that it does matter. But how much does it matter?

HOW IMPORTANT IS IT TO START SAVING EARLY?

Given the power of compounding, the earlier we save, the more chance our portfolio has to accumulate wealth. When we start saving depends on two factors. We need to be employed to start saving out of our income. Some men and women start working at an early age, either after completing high school or college. Others extend their schooling much longer.

Professors are a good example of the latter. We usually need at least four years to complete a PhD, so earnings begin four years later than for college grads. Medical doctors have an even more prolonged wait. Medical school itself requires four years after college. Then there is a period of internship and residency that can add another three to five years to that. It's true that interns and residents are paid a wage. But like those of most apprentices, the wage is much lower than that of a doctor who has completed residency requirements.

Other people in their twenties have trouble finding that first job, especially one as good as expected. A lot depends on luck. Those graduating in boom times have a much greater chance of finding that desired job than those graduating in recessions like those in 1981–1982 and 2008–2009.

Still other people in their twenties may have trouble starting the savings process even though they are earning decent incomes. Savings may be sacrificed because they are working hard to pay off student loans. Or perhaps they are saving for a specific goal such as buying a car or taking a trip. Or perhaps they are just not interested in starting retirement savings. After all, they are so many decades from retirement. Isn't it true that only older people save?

Let's study the savings of 26-year-olds who do find employment by that age and decide to save. And let's assume that their wage in the first year of employment is $50,000 per year (in today's dollars). That's on the high end for 25-year-olds, even for those with college degrees. But it's not an unreasonable starting salary for someone who will eventually earn $100,000 in today's dollars.

In many industries, wages increase with experience. But the pattern of increase varies a lot by industry. Unionized carpenters or plumbers may reach peak wages within 10 years of starting unless they are promoted to managerial positions. That's also true of teachers. But attorneys may have steadily rising earnings throughout their careers.

To try to capture some of this variation in real earnings over a career, we will assume that a 26-year-old worker will manage to earn $100,000 in 10 years (at the age of 36). Thereafter, we will assume that earnings are constant in real terms. (That is, nominal income will rise only fast enough to keep pace with inflation, so real income stays at $100,000). Throughout the initial 10-year period of work, the portfolio grows. If the worker saves 15 percent of income, then after 10 years the portfolio has grown to $136,000 and after 20 years to $425,000. That's not bad for someone earning only $50,000 a year to start. To achieve this accumulation, the worker has to be continuously employed. And that worker has to be smart enough to keep saving and to invest wisely.

TABLE 5.4   Wealth Accumulation with Early Start

Accumulation at Age	Age Savings Start		
	26	31	36
35	$135,800	$70,700	$0
45	$425,100	$313,900	$193,100
55	$919,200	$729,300	$523,000
65	$1,763,200	$1,439,000	$1,086,500

Assumptions: Savings is based on an income of $50,000 at 26 rising to $100,000 at age 36 (and staying constant in real terms thereafter). The portfolio chosen devotes 75% of savings to stocks and 25% to bonds. The real return on the portfolio = 5.5%. All amounts are measured in constant (2013) dollars.

Now let's ask how much difference it makes that this worker has started saving early. Let's compare that worker with those who save nothing until 31 or 36 years of age. Perhaps those other workers are not saving for retirement because they are paying off college loans or saving for down payments on homes. Or they decide to postpone savings for other reasons. So no funds are contributed to retirement. That can't make a difference, can it? After all, the workers are still in their twenties or early thirties.

Table 5.4 shows how much wealth is accumulated by the age of 65 if the investor starts at 26 years of age rather than when he or she is 31 or 36 years of age. The difference is very dramatic. Workers who start saving at 26 accumulate over $1.7 million by the time they reach 65. Workers who postpone saving for 10 years until they are 36 years of age accumulate a little less than $1.1 million, or 37 percent less at retirement. That is true despite the assumption that the 26-year-old starts with a salary of $50,000 rather than $100,000. The starting point for savings matters a lot.

Table 5.4 also gives a hint about how important it is to keep working until full retirement age (currently 66). The longer the investor saves, the larger the accumulation for retirement. In Chapter 18, we will also factor in the higher Social Security benefits available for those who retire later rather than sooner.

WHAT IF SAVINGS ARE WITHDRAWN FOR COLLEGE?

Tables 5.1 and 5.2 presume that there is only one savings goal—retirement. But surely investors have other major goals in mind as they save. Most families aim to save enough to buy a home. First they have to save for a down payment. Then they have to pay enough in mortgage payments to cover both interest and principal repayments on the mortgage. Second, families with children aim to save enough to help cover the costs of education. These are secondary goals that are quite important to many families.

Let's begin with saving for a home. In Chapter 13, I try to convince readers that the home is a poor investment. And that is true even if they lived in California (where house appreciation has been the fastest) and sold their homes in 2006 before the housing bust! But let's face it. Most Americans want to own the residence where they live. Let's ignore the savings necessary to purchase that residence. Perhaps investors have found a way to save a down payment independent of the savings rates in the previous tables and treat mortgage payments as a pure expense. Or perhaps they have postponed saving for retirement until they have assembled that down payment.

That leaves college educations as a major savings goal. Let's first discuss how tough it is to pay for college. Then we will assess how college costs make it more difficult for parents to save for retirement.

In 2012, the average cost (tuition, room, and board) of an Ivy League college education was over $50,000 per year. Some private colleges cost considerably less, but many of the more competitive ones cost as much as Ivy League colleges. Many prominent state colleges cost at least half as much as the Ivy League even for in-state residents, although there is huge variation in costs from state to state. It should be noted that the cost of state colleges has been increasing faster than the cost of private colleges as state and local governments struggle with the effects of the financial crisis.

If a family elects to send one child to college, it can easily cost $200,000 for a four-year Ivy League education or $100,000 for a four-year state college education. Think of college costs as if you are buying a BMW each year for four years. (That's the way I came to think of it when my daughters attended college). You write a check every summer and dream of that new car. Then at the end of four years, you attend graduation—still driving your Honda Civic.

If a family were planning today for college tuitions 15 or 20 years hence, how much would they have to save? Naturally, they would have to save more than the current cost of college because the cost of living rises over time. But college tuitions have been increasing much faster than the overall cost of living. One set of measures of the inflation rate for college costs is provided by the College Board. Over the 26-year period ending in 2012, college tuition at four-year private colleges rose by 6.0 percent per year at a time when the Consumer Price Index was rising 2.9 percent per year. College tuition at four-year state colleges was rising even faster at 7.4 percent per year. Tuition, room, and board at private colleges rose by 5.6 percent per year over this same period. That's still 2.7 percent faster than the CPI inflation rate. So if your child is attending an Ivy League college in 15 years, the actual real cost of that college (in constant dollars) will be about $73,700 per year rather than $50,000 per year![2] No wonder parents and students are struggling with college payments.

How does the cost of college affect the retirement accumulation process? The answer is that there is an obvious tradeoff between retirement savings and college savings. The more parents help their children, *the less they will have for retirement*. Let's be a little more specific. Suppose that parents pull $100,000 out of their savings to help fund one child's education. I am referring to savings in taxable accounts, not tax-deferred accounts like a 401(k). Withdrawing savings from a 401(k) would incur severe penalties prior to the age of 59. The actual withdrawal is assumed to occur at the end of the 15th year of savings (in a 30-year savings program). What happens to the wealth accumulated for retirement by the end of the 30th year? Withdrawing $100,000 to help pay for one child's education reduces wealth at retirement by $223,000. That is, the investor accumulates $863,000 after 30 years rather than the $1.086 million accumulated if there are no college costs. The reason why accumulated wealth drops so sharply is that the $100,000 spent in year 15 could have compounded over the next 15 years until retirement.

This calculation just emphasizes the truly important tradeoff between generations. Parents can help their children with their educations, but only at the expense of their future retirement. This shows why it is so important to try to save for your children's education *with additional savings*. It's a separate (and very important) goal for savings. To the extent possible, college tuition should not come at the expense of retirement.

WHAT IF THE PORTFOLIO RETURNS FALL SHORT?

The results obtained so far assume that investment returns will be as high as they were on average over the past 60 years or so. Real returns on bonds averaged about 2.5 percent and real returns on stocks averaged about 6.5 percent. A portfolio with 75 percent invested in stocks and 25 percent invested in bonds earns 5.5 percent on average. What if investment returns fall short? What if we are entering the "New Normal" discussed in Chapter 3?

It's important to emphasize that we are talking about returns over 30 years of saving, not over any given five-year period. As explained in Chapter 3, stock returns are subject to wild fluctuations in a recession. They fall sharply prior to the recession and rise sharply as the recession ends. The business cycle exerts a powerful influence on stock returns. Fortunately, the accumulation of wealth for retirement depends on returns over 30 years

TABLE 5.5   Wealth Accumulation If Portfolio Returns Are Lower than Expected

Accumulation by Years of Saving		Real Rate of Return		
	5.5%	4.4% (20% lower)	3.3% (40% lower)	2.2% (60% lower)
10 years	$193,100	$183,500	$174,400	$165,800
20 years	$523,000	$465,700	$415,600	$371,800
30 years	$1,086,500	$899,800	$749,300	$628,000

Assumptions: Savings are based on an income of $100,000 and a savings rate of 15%. The portfolio chosen devotes 75% of savings to stocks and 25% to bonds. The real rate of return on the portfolio ranges from 5.5% down to 2.2%. All amounts are measured in constant dollars.

rather than over a business cycle. Yet as shown in Chapter 3, there can be wide variations in returns even over 30 years. So it is important to consider how wealth accumulation changes if returns are lower than previously assumed.

What would be a reasonable range to consider? Table 5.5 examines wealth accumulation under the assumption that returns are 20, 40, or 60 percent lower than their long-run averages. So instead of assuming a real portfolio return of 5.5 percent, we assume that returns are 4.4 or 3.3 percent or even as low as 2.2 percent. A return of 2.2 percent is below the long-run real return of 2.5 percent on bonds, so surely that is low enough for even the most pessimistic of observers. We assume the investor is saving 15 percent of income.

The results are distressing, but not surprising. If returns in the next 30 years are 60 percent below those of the past 60 years, then wealth accumulation drops by over 40 percent (from $1,086,500 to $628,000). With a constant spending rule, this means that withdrawals from the portfolio in retirement also have to be reduced by over 40 percent. Recall that the investor is saving $450,000 over the 30 years of work (15 percent of $100,000 saved for 30 years). With a return of only 2.2 percent, those savings compound to only $628,000. Even if investment returns are only 20 percent lower than they have been in the past, 4.4 rather than 5.5 percent, retirement savings are 17 percent below what they would be with normal investment returns. So the failure to earn normal rates of returns leads to a large shortfall in retirement savings. That's the reason why the "New Normal" vision of lower returns haunts today's investors.

Yet we have left out other troubling aspects of the accumulation process. What if the low returns occur early in the investor's lifetime? Does that make

much of a difference? Or what if the low returns occur late in the accumulation process—just before retirement? Financial returns are subject to wide
fluctuations. That is true of stocks, but even bond returns can vary widely over
time. So a portfolio diversified between stocks and bonds can also fluctuate
quite widely. If portfolio returns are low at crucial times in the process of building wealth, then our wealth accumulation will fall short and our retirement
plans will have to be modified. How do we account for the variation in returns?

To answer these questions, we need to pull out some heavy artillery. The
guns will remain in the background. But in order to answer these questions,
we must run thousands of random experiments allowing the investors' returns to vary based on their underlying volatility. The method we will use
has an imposing name, Monte Carlo simulation. Despite the name, we will
not be entering any casinos for our answers. Instead, we will use a methodology developed in the 1940s to help solve problems in physics. The method
has since been used in a variety of disciplines in the sciences and social
sciences. In the past 40 years as computing capabilities have improved, investment experts have begun using Monte Carlo simulations to solve problems like the ones with which we are grappling. The simulations allow us to
see how wealth evolves when investment returns are allowed to fluctuate as
randomly as they do in practice. What happens to our wealth accumulation
if investment returns are subject to random fluctuations? Simulations will
help to answer this question.

For these simulations, we will maintain the same return assumptions as
in our base case: an expected real return of 5.5 percent based on a historical real stock return of 6.5 percent and bond return of 2.5 percent. And we
will be assuming that the portfolio is as volatile as it has been over the past
30 years. Let me summarize the results: Recall from Table 5.1 that if there
is no volatility in returns, the investor will accumulate $1.086 million after
saving for 30 years. But with volatility in the returns, worse results can occur.

At the 10th percentile of returns (that is, in 10 percent of the cases studied), wealth accumulation at retirement drops in value from $1 million to
$570,000 (in constant dollars).

Let me clarify this result. There is a 10 percent chance that an investor
saving $15,000 per year for 30 years will accumulate only $570,000 rather
than $1.086 million. Since the investor has saved $450,000 over 30 years
($15,000 times 30), this means that the average real return on the portfolio
is small indeed.[3] Naturally, there is also a significant upside to returns.

At the 90th percentile of returns, the portfolio rises to $1.74 million at
retirement.

But somehow the good scenarios do not make up for the bad scenarios.
Most investors would find it much easier to cope with too much wealth than
too little.

Don't dismiss these simulations as just academic experiments. The simulations are based on the actual volatility of returns in the past. In the "real world," similar results can occur. Let me prove this to you. Suppose an investor was unlucky enough to have started saving in 1955 and ended in 1984. For a few years, that investor earned handsome returns, including a 28.7 percent real return in 1958. But this investor later saw annual returns of –13.0, –18.5, and –27.6 percent. At the end of 30 years of savings in 1984, the investor had accumulated only $640,000. Investors retiring a few years earlier suffered similar fates. So the simulation results do simulate reality. Bad results can occur even over a 30-year period. The best laid plans can go awry if the markets conspire against us. Surely, that's also a lesson of the past decade of disappointing returns.

What can prudent investors do to protect themselves against living (and saving) through bad times? The answer is a disheartening one: Err on the side of caution. Save more than you think is necessary. Then the worst that can happen is that you postpone your spending dreams until you know that you have enough to retire. If the good returns roll in as they did in the 1980s and 1990s, then you can think about saving at a more normal pace.

HOW DO TAXES AFFECT SAVINGS?

This chapter has shown why consistency in savings is important. And so is starting early. It has also shown why it is important to invest wisely. But we have yet to focus on how taxes affect wealth accumulation. We can save at a fast clip, but our efforts might fall short if we ignore the effects of taxes. That's the next topic that is worth examining.

NOTES

1. If both spouses have qualified for benefits (but their combined income is still only $100,000), the total payment depends on how much each of the individuals has earned, but it will fall short of the amount assumed in Table 5.2. See the discussion of this feature of Social Security in Chapter 18.
2. This assumes that college inflation can stay so much higher than general inflation in the future. Hopefully that will not be the case.
3. Even at the 25th percentile of returns, the investor ends up with only $727,000.

CHAPTER **6**

Savings and Taxes

Investors have to save in order to accumulate wealth. And they have to invest wisely to earn high enough returns on those savings. But how much wealth they accumulate depends on three other factors. These three factors, all of which inhibit the accumulation of wealth, are *inflation, taxes,* and *fees.*

In Chapter 2, I emphasized how important it is to take into account inflation. *Real returns*, not nominal returns, are important to wealth accumulation. Investment fees are discussed in Chapter 15 where we explain the importance of benchmarking portfolios. In this chapter we discuss taxes. Taxes drag down returns, so they limit the amount of wealth that is accumulated for retirement. But taxes vary by asset class. Even within an asset class, investments differ in their "tax efficiency." U.S. tax law, moreover, provides methods for deferring taxes for retirement. So it's important to study how taxes affect the accumulation of wealth.

HOW TAXES REDUCE INVESTMENT RETURNS

In Chapter 2, we study returns on stocks and bonds in the long run. But those returns ignore taxes. Only a tax-exempt investor would actually earn those returns. We need to consider the effects of taxes on those returns.

Investment returns are taxed in various ways. Interest earnings on bonds are taxed at the same rates as ordinary wage income, while long-term capital gains on any asset are taxed at capital gains rates. Capital gains for holding periods of a year or less are also taxed at ordinary rates. Until the tax changes instituted in 2003, dividends were taxed at the same tax rates as ordinary income. But the 2003 law reduced taxes on dividends to capital gains rates. The law passed on January 1, 2013, made those changes permanent, although it increased taxes on both dividends and capital gains to 20 percent for taxpayers making more than $400,000 ($450,000 for a married couple). Under the new law, taxpayers in the top tax bracket pay 39.6 percent tax on interest earnings and short-term capital gains, but only

20 percent on dividends and long-term capital gains.[1] Taxpayers making $100,000 in income pay 28 percent ordinary income tax (25 percent if married) and 15 percent tax on dividends and long-term capital gains.

Lower tax rates allow investors to accumulate more wealth. But the deferral of taxes also helps. To see the effects of each, consider three $10,000 investments subject to different tax rates. In each case, the pretax return is assumed to be 5 percent.

The first investment, perhaps in a corporate bond, is subject to ordinary income tax of 28 percent each year.

The second investment, perhaps in a portfolio of stocks, earns both dividends and capital gains subject to a tax of 15 percent each year.

The third investment, perhaps in the stock of a single company that pays no dividends, will remain untaxed until it is sold at the end of year 10. At that point it is subject to capital gains taxes of 15 percent.

If pretax returns are 5 percent, the first two investments have after-tax returns at the end of the first year of 3.60 percent and 4.25 percent, respectively. For example, the investment subject to ordinary income tax receives a return of 5 percent $(1 - 0.28) = 3.60$ percent. The third investment earns the full pretax return of 5 percent the first year because capital gains taxes have been deferred.

Table 6.1 traces the returns on these three investments through the 10th year. The third investment is assumed to be sold after the 10th year, so capital gains taxes are paid at that time. After 10 years, the first investment accumulates to $14,243 or 3.60 percent/year after-tax. The second investment accumulates to $15,162 or 4.25 percent/year after-tax. So the lower tax rate has a major impact on wealth accumulation. The third investment has the additional advantage of being able to defer capital gains taxes, so the total accumulation after-tax is $15,346 or 4.38 percent/year. Tax deferral therefore helps, but *it's the lower tax rate that helps even more.*

TABLE 6.1   Investments Subject to Different Tax Rates: $10,000 Investments Earning a Pretax Return of 5 Percent

End of Year	Ordinary Income Tax (at 28% rate)	Dividend/Capital Gains Tax Paid Yearly (at 15% Rate)	Capital Gains Tax Deferred until Year 10 (at 15% Rate)
Year 1	$10,360	$10,425	$10,500
Year 10	$14,243	$15,162	$15,346
After-tax rate of return	3.60%	4.25%	4.38%

The choice between investing in stocks and bonds has to be influenced by the different tax rates affecting these investments. Even when dividends were subject to ordinary income tax rates, a large part of the returns from owning stocks consisted of capital gains. So investors could have sheltered that part of the return from ordinary income taxes. Over the 60-year period from 1951 to 2010, the average return on large-cap stocks was 12.3 percent, but the income portion of that return averaged only 3.4 percent.[2] So the rest of the return could have been sheltered from all except capital gains taxes. Now that dividends are taxed at the same rate as capital gains, even the income portion of the stock return is subject to lower tax rates than those on bond yields.

How much difference do these taxes make to investment returns? James Poterba studied aftertax returns on stocks, Treasury bonds, and Treasury bills over the period from 1926 to 1996. Poterba assumed that investors had incomes of $75,000 in 1989 and equivalent incomes in real terms in earlier years. He took into account the actual tax rates applying to these investors in each year. (Tax rates have varied widely over this period, so it is important to keep track of them.) The results of his study are shown in Table 6.2.

Large-cap stocks earned an average pretax return of 12.7 percent over this 71-year period. If taxes are taken into account, the return drops to 9.2 percent. So taxes reduce the pretax return by 27.6 percent. Bonds have a much lower average return of 5.5 percent, but a higher percentage of this return is sacrificed to taxes in the case of bonds. After taxes are taken into account, the return on bonds falls to 3.4 percent per year, or 38.2 percent lower than before taxes. Returns on Treasury bills are affected even more.

If we consider that other "tax" on investment returns, inflation, the contrast between stocks and bonds is even starker. Poterba went on to calculate after-tax real returns on stocks and bonds. These are the returns after both inflation and taxes have been taken into account. The *real* after-tax return on stocks is only 5.9 percent. But at least investors are accumulating

TABLE 6.2   How Taxes Affect Investment Returns: Pre-Tax and After-Tax Returns, 1926–1996

Asset Class	Pretax Return	After-Tax Return	% Decline
Large-cap stocks	12.7%	9.2%	–27.6%
Long-term Treasury bonds	5.5%	3.4%	–38.2%
Treasury bills	3.8%	2.2%	–42.1%

Note: The last column reports the percentage decline in the return due to taxes.
Source: Poterba, 2001.

some wealth. The real after-tax return on bonds is only 0.2 percent! That is, with a pretax return on bonds of 5.5 percent, the investor is left with only 0.2 percent once inflation and taxes are taken into account. The real after-tax return on Treasury bills is –1.1 percent.

Recall that the Poterba study is for an investor earning $75,000 in 1989. (That's equivalent to $138,400 in 2013 if inflation is taken into account). If an investor were in the top tax bracket, the results would be even more dramatic. No doubt the investor would earn negative real after-tax returns on Treasury bonds. So it's clearly important to judge investments on an after-tax basis.

What is the most important lesson of the Poterba study?

Taxes make stocks even more attractive relative to bonds.

Chapter 2 showed that the long run real return on stocks was much higher than on bonds. The lower taxes on stocks make them even more attractive.

It is important for investors to pay attention to the taxes they pay on investments. But they also have to realize that tax regimes change quite often. The tax code providing 15 percent taxes on capital gains and dividends expired at the end of 2012. The tax bill passed on January 1, 2013, preserved most of the "temporary" changes (except for those in the top tax bracket). But in the meantime, the Patient Protection and Affordable Care Act ("Obamacare") passed in 2010 raises taxes on investment income by 3.8 percent for individuals earning more than $200,000 ($250,000 for couples) starting in 2013. The one thing investors can count on is that tax rates will change often. So keeping investments "tax efficient" is a continuing struggle.

Consider the variation in tax rates over the past 30 years as shown in Table 6.3. (This is an updated version of a table appearing in Swensen 2005). The top ordinary income tax rate has fallen from 70 percent in 1980 to 39.6 percent in 2013. But dividend taxes have fallen even more dramatically from 70 percent in 1980 to 20 percent in 2013. That has obviously increased the relative attractiveness of stocks over bonds. But there is no guarantee that these rates will stay the same in future years. It would be more plausible to guarantee that they will change.

TAX EFFICIENCY

Within any given asset class, taxes vary. That's because investments differ in their "tax efficiency." Some investments yield lots of income subject to ordinary income tax rates. Other investments are subject only to capital gains taxes. We can measure the vulnerability of investments to taxes using the "tax efficiency ratio." Tax efficiency is the ratio of after-tax returns to pretax returns. For

TABLE 6.3 Historical Federal Tax Rates for Top Bracket Income

Year	Long-Term Capital Gains Rate	Short-Term Gains and Current Income	Dividends
1980	28.0%	70.0%	70.0%
1985	20.0%	50.0%	50.0%
1990	28.0%	31.0%	31.0%
1995	28.0%	39.6%	39.6%
2000	20.0%	39.6%	39.6%
2005	15.0%	35.0%	15.0%
2010	15.0%	35.0%	15.0%
2013	20.0% (23.8%)	39.6% (43.4%)	20.0% (23.8%)

Note: The 2013 tax rates in parentheses include the new 3.8% tax on investment income mandated by the Patient Protection and Affordable Care Act beginning in 2013.

Source: Swensen 2005, Table 1.6, updated using IRS data.

example, if an investment earns 10 percent pretax, but only 7.5 percent after tax, then its tax efficiency ratio is

$$\text{Tax efficiency ratio} = 7.5\%/10.0\% = 75\%$$

A higher tax efficiency ratio means that the investors get to keep more of their returns.

Consider the example of two stock mutual funds, each earning a return of 10 percent pretax. The manager of Fund A understands that most of his or her investors hold the fund in taxable accounts. So that manager tries to keep all capital gains long-term subject to the 15 percent capital gains rate. The manager of Fund B believes that most investors pay attention only to pretax returns. That manager chooses to trade a lot, so the fund's capital gains are subject to the short-term ordinary income tax rates of 25 percent. The results are shown in Table 6.4.

Even though both funds earn the same pretax return, investors in Fund A pay taxes at the dividend and capital gains rate of 15 percent. So taxes reduce returns by only 1.5 percent. The tax efficiency of this fund is 8.5 percent/10 percent = 85 percent. Investors in Fund B, in contrast, must pay ordinary income taxes on the capital gains, so taxes reduce returns by 2.3 percent.[3] The tax efficiency of this fund is only 77 percent.

Is such a difference in tax efficiency plausible? Consider a study of the tax efficiency of mutual funds by Dickson and Shoven (1995). In their sample

TABLE 6.4 Comparison between Two Mutual Funds: Taxes and Tax Efficiency

	Tax Rate	Fund A	Fund B
Dividend	15%	2.0%	2.0%
Short-term capital gain	25%	0.0%	8.0%
Long-term capital gain	15%	8.0%	0.0%
Pretax return		10.0%	10.0%
Taxes		1.5%	2.3%
After-tax return		8.5%	7.7%
Tax efficiency ratio		85%	77%

of 147 mutual fund returns over the 10-year period ending in 1992, Dickson and Shoven show that tax efficiency ratios ranged from 67.4 percent to 78.3 percent with a median value of 72.8 percent. This means that investors in the most tax efficient fund managed to keep much more of their after-tax return than investors in the least tax efficient fund. Which was the most tax-efficient fund? Interestingly enough, it was Fidelity's Magellan Fund run by the legendary Peter Lynch. Not only did Peter Lynch score the second best *pretax return* among the 147 funds, but he also achieved the highest *after-tax return* in part due to the tax efficiency of his fund.

Investors are not interested in tax efficiency per se. They are interested in *after-tax returns*. That's what they can take to the bank. In this sample of 147 mutual funds, the top after-tax return of 15.4 percent per year, was earned by Peter Lynch's Magellan Fund. The lowest after-tax return was 6.9 percent. That's quite a range! So what is the lesson for investors? It's a simple one: Compare performance on an after-tax basis. That's now simple to do because starting in 2001, the *SEC required all mutual funds to publish after-tax returns*. This was an important breakthrough for investors. Take advantage of the new rule.

Tax efficiency is desirable. But Americans have another way to reduce taxes, their defined contribution retirement plans like the 401(k) and IRA plans. For the past few decades, investors have had an opportunity to completely shield their investments from taxes until they retire. So let's study the effects of these tax deferral programs.

HOW IMPORTANT IS TAX DEFERRAL?

So far, we have emphasized one advantage of defined contribution retirement programs. These programs force us to save. That's true at least if we agree to sign up to participate. A second advantage is that employers often contribute to them, "matching" employee contributions in some way. For example, an employer might agree to match employees' contributions dollar for dollar up to 5 percent of their contributions. That's an important feature of these programs because it increases the incentive for employees to participate. If an employee declines participation in a 401(k), then the employer's matching contribution is usually forfeited.

Yet there is a third advantage of retirement plans, *tax deferral*. Contributions can be made with pretax dollars.[4] And these plans are sheltered from all capital gains and dividend taxes. If an investor contributes 10 percent of a $100,000 income or $10,000 to a 401(k) plan, for example, the $10,000 escapes immediate taxation and begins to accrue dividends and capital gains free of tax. Taxes are levied only when the investor withdraws monies from the account. At that point, ordinary income taxes are due on the accumulated account.

Consider an example of a married couple that is in the 25 percent tax bracket for ordinary income. In 2013, this is the tax bracket for married couples earning between about $72,500 and $146,400. The capital gains and dividend tax for that bracket is at a 15 percent rate. If this couple stays in the same bracket all of their lives, then the 401(k) allows them to postpone payment of the 25 percent tax rate on any 401(k) contributions until after they retire (or when they turn 70 and a half). They are able to accumulate returns on every dollar of their savings because these accounts escape all capital gains and dividend taxes. Contrast that with investors who have only taxable accounts. Every dollar of savings is subject to income tax. So if they set aside $10,000 of pretax income for savings, only $7,500 ends up in their portfolio because they have to pay taxes equal to 25 percent. And this taxable account has to pay taxes on dividends every year and taxes on capital gains whenever any assets are sold.

Let's compare the two accounts at the end of one year. Assume that both accounts are invested only in stocks and that stocks earn 9 percent/year.[5] (If the accounts also included bonds, this would make the taxable account look even worse because taxes are higher on bonds than stocks.) To make things simple, let's assume that the portfolio is turned over at the end of that year, so that capital gains are paid on any appreciation of the assets (and taxed at the long-term capital gains rate). That may seem like high turnover for a portfolio, but 37 of the 147 funds in the Dickson-Shoven database turned over that often.

The taxable account will start with only $7,500 because income has already been subject to a 25 percent income tax rate. During the first year, the stocks earn $675 in dividends and capital gains, but are then hit with a 15 percent tax. The net return is $574, so the taxable investor accumulates $8,074 by the end of the first year.

In the tax-deferred account, the pretax sum of $10,000 earns a return of 9 percent or $900. But since we are assuming that the account is closed after one year, it is hit with income tax of 25 percent on the full amount. So net of tax, the $10,900 becomes $8,175. The tax-deferred account thus saves the investor only $101. That's because the advantages of tax-deferral are small when the deferral is for only one year. But notice that the tax advantage is not the deferral itself. Instead, the advantage consists of avoiding the capital gains/dividend tax.

The longer these taxes are avoided, the better the tax-deferred account. Continuing the example, what happens if the tax-deferred account is held for 20 years? The investor is going to invest $10,000 per year (10 percent of pretax income of $100,000) for 20 years. To make this example as simple as possible, let's assume that the whole account is withdrawn in the first year of retirement at which time the investor must pay income tax on the entire portfolio. Does it pay to save within a tax-deferred account? The answer is given in Table 6.5 where taxable and tax deferred accounts are compared.

Before examining the table, let's mention a few caveats. I am assuming that all returns in the taxable account are subject to capital gains and dividend taxes on the entire return *each year*. In practice, taxable accounts invested in stocks can avoid yearly capital gains taxes by being very tax efficient (as explained earlier in this chapter). On the other hand, I am assuming that the accounts are invested entirely in stocks rather than in bonds (which are less tax efficient). I am also ignoring the possibility that tax rates might fall in retirement which would make tax-deferred investing more attractive.

With those caveats in mind, consider the results in Table 6.5. Remember that investors in the taxable and tax-deferred accounts have saved the same amount each year, $10,000. And they have invested in the same portfolio of stocks earning 9 percent per year. Because the tax-deferred investors have avoided capital gains and dividend taxes throughout the

TABLE 6.5   Wealth Accumulation Based on $10,000 Savings Per Year

Year Account Closed	Taxable Account	Tax-Deferred Account	Advantage of Tax Deferral
Year 1	$8,074	$8,175	$101
Year 20	$355,454	$418,234	$62,780

Assumptions: Ordinary income tax = 25%, capital gains and dividend tax = 15%, stock return = 9% (in nominal terms). In the taxable account, taxes on dividends and capital gains are assumed to be paid every year. In the tax deferred account, ordinary income taxes are assumed to be paid in the year the account is closed.

20 years, they end up with an account that is $62,780 larger—*even after paying income tax on the full account at the end of year 20!* That's a sizable advantage. Notice what it's dependent on: If taxes on capital gains and dividends were to go up, then the advantages of tax deferral would increase.

Before leaving the subject of tax deferral, one important fact should be pointed out. When investors are nearing retirement, they often total up their wealth to see if they "have enough" to retire. That subject is a tricky one that is addressed in Chapters 17 through 19. But let's focus on investors who have both taxable and tax-deferred accounts. The tax-deferred account is *smaller than it appears to be.* That's because it has a tax liability attached to it. If an investor has saved $1 million in a tax deferred account and is in the 25 percent tax bracket, the amount available for spending is only $750,000. The taxable account may also have tax liabilities attached to it in the form of embedded capital gains. But the basis itself—the original amount invested plus any dividends and capital gains already taxed—is tax-free. It's only the subsequent capital gains (plus any current dividends and interest) that are subject to tax. So investors have to be careful when calculating their wealth available for retirement.

ASSET LOCATION

Since investors have the option of shielding some of their investments from taxes in their retirement plans, it makes sense to think carefully about "asset location." This is important for any investor who has significant wealth invested both in taxable and tax-deferred accounts. The basic idea of asset location is very simple. Choose relatively tax efficient investments for your taxable account. And choose tax inefficient investments for the tax-deferred account. What a simple but powerful idea.

Investments that are relatively tax inefficient include high yield corporate bonds, Treasury Inflation-Protected Securities (TIPS), and real estate investment trusts (REITs). High yield bonds provide, as their name implies, high yields subject to ordinary income taxes. TIPS provide investors with two types of returns, an interest yield, and an inflation adjustment that raises the par value of the bond. Investors must pay tax on both the interest payment and the inflation adjustment even though the latter is not realized until the bond matures or is sold. REITs pay relatively high dividends that are normally taxed at ordinary income tax rates, not the low rates (currently 15 percent) applicable to most corporate dividends. Hedge funds and commodity futures funds are also very tax inefficient because most of their returns take the form of short-term capital gains subject to ordinary income

TABLE 6.6 Asset Location

Taxable Account	Tax-Deferred Account
Municipal bonds	High-yield bonds
Real estate—directly held	TIPS
Private equity and venture capital	REITs
Foreign stocks	Hedge funds and futures funds
Tax-efficient stock funds	Tax-inefficient stock funds

tax. Table 6.6 illustrates how the portfolio might be allocated between the taxable and tax-deferred accounts.

Investments that are relatively tax efficient include municipal bonds (normally subject to no tax at the federal level), real estate directly held (subject to favorable tax treatment under certain conditions), and private equity and venture capital. The latter investments earn most of their return in the form of long-term capital gains. Foreign stock funds may or may not be tax efficient, but investors get to claim credit for foreign withholding taxes only if these funds are held in taxable accounts. Notice that within any asset category, such as U.S. stock funds, it always makes sense to place the more tax efficient funds in the taxable account and relegate the tax inefficient funds to the tax-deferred account.

Asset location should not be allowed to alter the overall asset allocation. It should only help determine where assets are held. But unlike many efforts to minimize taxes, asset location need not involve any extra cost. It just requires careful planning as investors build their portfolios. If taxes on capital gains and dividends rise further in the future, this will only increase the advantages of asset location.

CONCLUDING COMMENTS

Remember the three drags on investment returns: inflation, taxes, and fees. This chapter has examined the many ways that taxes can affect investment returns. Tax rates naturally matter a lot. Stocks benefit from lower tax rates. The favorable treatment of capital gains and, more recently, dividends produces higher returns after tax than investments subject to ordinary income tax rates. Among investments in the same asset class, tax efficiency matters. Finally, tax deferral also makes a big difference, so investors should maximize the amount of savings in their 401(k)s and other retirement accounts.

NOTES

1. Starting in 2013, investment returns are subject to an additional 3.8 percent tax rate (to fund the Affordable Care Act) if the taxpayer earns more than $200,000 ($250,000 for a married couple).
2. The average returns are simple averages using the breakdown of the large-cap return in Ibbotson SBBI (2011).
3. The investor pays 0.3 percent tax on the dividends (15 percent of 2 percent) and 2 percent tax on the short-term capital gain (25 percent of 8 percent) for a total tax of 2.3 percent.
4. An exception is the Roth IRA account where contributions are made with post-tax dollars, but no taxes are paid at withdrawal.
5. Chapter 2 showed that stocks earn about 6.5 percent in real terms in the long run. If inflation is 2.5 percent per year, the nominal return on stocks is about 9 percent.

REFERENCES

Dickson, Joel M., and John B. Shoven. 1995. "Taxation and Mutual Funds: An Investor Perspective." *Tax Policy and the Economy 9.*

Ibbotson®. 2011. *SBBI® 2011 Classic Yearbook.* Chicago: Morningstar.

Poterba, James M. 2001. "Taxation, Risk-Taking, and Household Portfolio Behavior." NBER Working Paper No. 8340. Cambridge, MA: National Bureau of Economic Research.

Swensen, David F. 2005. *Unconventional Success: A Fundamental Approach to Personal Investment.* New York: Free Press.

PART

Two

Investment Choices

CHAPTER 7

Investing in U.S. Stocks

In Chapter 1, I state that investing is easier than saving. That doesn't mean that it is easy. Too many investors make investing hard by trying to be too smart for their own good. They choose the latest fad for their investments. Recently it has been popular to invest in gold, but no one wanted gold 12 years ago. In the late 1990s, it was high-tech stocks. Then six years later it was condos in Vegas or Miami.

Many investors don't understand how important it is to diversify. This part of the book emphasizes diversification. But I promise that readers will also know a lot about each potential type of investment. None of these will be "*the* investment" to focus on. But all will be useful additions to an investor's portfolio. We will begin with U.S. stocks.

In the "old days" wealthy investors might choose a handful of U.S. "blue-chip" stocks for their portfolios. That was all they needed because they were confident in the long-run viability of these blue-chip companies. In the 1960s, the list might have included AT&T, General Electric, and Procter & Gamble. But the list might have also included other companies in the Dow Jones Industrial Average like Eastman Kodak and Bethlehem Steel. In the 1990s, the list surely would have included Citigroup and General Electric, two companies run by star executives. What investor would not want to place a big bet on companies run by Sandy Weill and Jack Welch? In both periods, General Motors was also viewed as a blue chip. In fact, it was one of the most widely held stocks. With the benefit of hindsight, we can see how these investors would have fared depending on which handful of stocks they selected. Those who held General Electric, for example, earned 1.5 percent per annum over the past 15 years.[1] Procter & Gamble investors fared much better with a 5.5 percent per annum return. But investors in General Motors, Eastman Kodak, and Bethlehem Steel were wiped out. Investors in Citigroup and Alcoa earned negative returns. By contrast, the S&P 500 index gained 4.5 percent during the same 15-year period. Concentrated stock portfolios are risky even if they are made up of "blue-chip" stocks.

MUTUAL FUNDS AND ETFS

Some individual investors still believe in this type of stock investing. But they are in the minority. Most investors invest in the U.S. stock market (as well as in the U.S. bond market) via mutual funds. In 2012, there was a total of $13.0 trillion invested in all types of U.S. mutual funds, and $5.9 trillion invested in U.S. stock mutual funds (ICI 2013). 53.8 million U.S. households owned these mutual funds. So most investors refrain from "do-it-yourself" investing in the sense of picking their own companies to invest in. Instead, they leave it to professional managers to pick stocks, while the investors themselves (in many cases, guided by financial advisors) decide how much to invest in stocks, bonds, and other assets.

Stock mutual funds come in many shapes and sizes. Many mutual funds focus on large company stocks, while others specialize in small companies. Some mutual funds favor so-called "value" stocks while others favor "growth" stocks. In this chapter, we will investigate all of these types of stocks. Most mutual fund managers choose a subset of stocks that they consider superior rather than invest in all of the companies in their segment of the stock market. Such "actively managed" mutual funds are to be contrasted with "index" mutual funds that closely track the universe of stocks in that segment of the market. For example, a mutual fund manager who invests in large-cap stocks might choose to invest in only 30 companies even though there are 500 companies in the large-cap S&P 500 index. An S&P 500 index mutual fund, in contrast, tries to track movements in that index as closely as possible.

In the past 20 years, investors have been offered another method for investing in stocks (as well as bonds): the exchange-traded fund or ETF. Mutual funds are valued at the close of the market each day. So if an investor wishes to sell a mutual fund at 10 A.M. EST, the trade is not executed until the end of the trading day. ETFs, in contrast, are continuously traded throughout the day. So an investor can execute the sale of an ETF at any time during that day.[2] The ETFs themselves can be aimed at a particular segment of the market just like a mutual fund. Most ETFs are indexed, so they provide investors with an alternative to an ordinary indexed mutual fund. Thus, for example, there are ETFs indexed to the S&P 500. So investors can choose between an S&P 500 index mutual fund and an ETF tied to the same index. In some cases, both products are offered by the same firm. In 2012, there was a total of $1.3 trillion invested in ETFs in the United States compared with $13.0 trillion in mutual funds (ICI 2013).

Mutual funds and ETFs offer simple ways to invest in stocks and bonds. But some of these also have hidden perils. Some mutual funds and ETFs are so narrowly focused that investors end up with too much risk. Examples are tech mutual funds in the late 1990s when the NASDAQ was reaching its peak or mortgage-backed bond funds in 2006 on the eve of the financial crisis or gold ETFs today. Concentrated positions are risky even when mutual funds or ETFs are involved.

WAYS TO SLICE UP THE U.S. STOCK MARKET

In earlier chapters we talked only about the S&P 500 large-cap index. The reason was simple. Over 80 percent of the value of all U.S. stocks is in this index. It is a much more representative index than the Dow Jones Industrial Average. The latter has only 30 stocks included, and those stocks are chosen arbitrarily. Until 1999, for example, all 30 Dow Jones companies were listed on the New York Stock Exchange. Only in that year were two firms listed on the NASDAQ—Microsoft and Intel—included in the Dow Jones index. In contrast, the S&P 500 has, as its name implies, 500 stocks, and most of them are among the 500 largest in the United States.[3] Just as important, the index is value-weighted, whereas the Dow Jones is price-weighted. (If an index is price-weighted, the weight of each stock is arbitrarily related to its price. It makes much more sense to have the value of the company be the basis for its weight in the index.)

Because the S&P 500 is so widely recognized as the best large-cap index, it is often used to benchmark large-cap managers. That is, a manager's performance is compared with that of the S&P 500. Chapter 15 will discuss benchmarking in detail. The S&P 500 index, however, is not the best benchmark for the U.S. stock market as a whole because it contains only large U.S. firms. Investors may also choose to invest in small-cap stocks. After all, researchers have discovered a "small-cap premium," by which they mean an excess return on smaller companies' stocks.

The *SBBI 2013 Yearbook* displays a graph showing the cumulative returns of different kinds of stocks and bonds since 1926. A dollar invested in the SBBI small-cap index in 1926 grows to $18,365 by the end of 2012. Even after adjusting for inflation, the index grows to $1,434 over the same period. In contrast, a dollar invested in the large-cap index grows to $3,553 and a dollar invested in long-term Treasury bonds grows to $123. Adjusted for inflation, these assets grow to $277 and $10, respectively. That's quite a cumulative premium for small-cap stocks.

Besides the small-cap premium, there is another premium that many investors believe in. Ever since Graham and Dodd published their classic study of security analysis in the 1930s, investors have believed in the wisdom of "value" investing. Value stocks are usually defined as those whose price is low relative to their book values. Stock indexes have been developed to distinguish value stocks from "growth" stocks. The most prominent of these indexes are the Russell value and growth indexes. We will investigate whether there is a "value premium" found in the Russell series.

WHAT DO WE MEAN BY SMALL-CAP STOCKS?

Perhaps the best-known small-cap index is the Russell 2000. That's a good place to start in defining small-cap stocks. The Russell 2000 index consists of the smallest 2,000 of the stocks in the Russell 3000. The Russell 3000, in turn, represents the top 3,000 U.S. stocks in terms of capitalization.[4] The left size of Figure 7.1 shows the breakdown of the Russell 3000 into its two components: the Russell 2000 small-cap index and the Russell 1000 large-cap index.

The largest firm in the Russell 2000 has a capitalization of $3.3 billion, while the smallest firm is worth only $130 million (as of May 2013). In contrast, the Russell 1000 large-cap index has firms ranging from $3.3 billion to $422 billion. Because firms are relatively small in the Russell 2000, the whole index represents only 10 percent of the value of the overall Russell 3000 index (as shown on the right side of Figure 7.1).

What types of firms do we find in the Russell 2000 small-cap index? Table 7.1 presents a breakdown of the industries represented in this index (as of June 2013). Financial services, a category that ranges from banks to insurance companies to real estate investment trusts, represent 23.7 percent of the index, while the next four industries represent over 10 percent each.

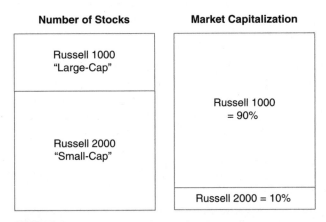

FIGURE 7.1   Breakdown of Russell 3000
Data source: Russell.com

TABLE 7.1   Russell 2000 Small-Cap Index

Industries	Market Cap	Top Firms	Market Cap
Financial services	23.7%	Pharmacyclics Inc.	0.36%
Consumer discretionary	15.8%	Ocwen Financial	0.33%
Producer durables	14.0%	Starwood Property Trust	0.31%
Technology	13.2%	Two Harbors Investment	0.29%
Health care	12.6%	3D Systems	0.28%
Materials	7.4%	Alaska Air	0.28%
Energy	5.9%	Genesee & Wyoming	0.28%
Utilities	4.1%	Alkermes PLC	0.28%
Consumer staples	3.2%	Dril-Quip	0.26%
Other	0.1%	Omega Healthcare	0.26%

Source: July 2013 capitalizations from ishares.com.

The top 10 firms in this small-cap index, listed in the same table, are hardly household names. But each of these has capitalizations of over $1 billion. The manager of a small-cap fund has to be knowledgeable about a host of smaller companies. On the other hand, with so little analyst coverage of these firms, active managers may be able to exploit market inefficiencies that are difficult to find in the large-cap space.

Figure 7.1 shows that the lion's share of valuation in the Russell 3000 is taken up by the Russell 1000 large-cap index. The Russell 1000 has 90 percent of the value in the all-cap index. It's a little confusing that we refer to the Russell 1000 as being a large-cap index. After all, this index has twice the number of stocks as the other well-known large-cap index, the S&P 500 index. The reason is the Russell 1000 also includes stocks that are best described as "mid-cap" because they are generally so much smaller than stocks in the S&P 500. In fact, Russell also defines an index popularly known as the "SMID" index for small and mid-cap stocks, the Russell 2500. This consists of all stocks in the Russell 3000 index except the top 500. This index represents 19 percent of the capitalization of the Russell 3000. Firms in this index range in size from $130 million to $8.1 billion. So the largest firms in the mid-cap space are more than two times as large as the largest firms in the small-cap space ($3.3 billion).

If large-cap stocks constitute such a large percentage of the overall market, why should investors bother to include small-caps in their portfolios? This is a sensible question. The belief that small-cap stocks offer investors a "small-cap premium" may justify the extra effort. We will search for such a premium by examining returns on the Russell Indexes since they began in 1979. Then we will extend the study to stocks prior to 1979 using a different data set.

RELATIVE PERFORMANCE OF LARGE-CAP AND SMALL-CAP STOCKS

Over the 30-plus years since the Russell indexes began, small- and large-cap stocks have fluctuated widely relative to one another. In some years, small-caps outperform large-caps by 10 percent or more. In other years, large-caps shine. In 1998, large-caps outperformed small-caps by almost 30 percent. Overall, however, there seems no clear winner. Table 7.2 summarizes the performance since 1979. The Russell 2000 small-cap index has a return that is about the same as its large-cap counterpart, the Russell 1000 Index. So there is no small-cap premium in the Russell data set. The only index with a decided advantage is the Russell 2500 "SMID" index. Apparently, the addition of mid-caps to the small-cap index makes a big difference.

Where did this notion of a small-cap premium come from? The answer is that it came from some very prominent academic studies published in the early 1980s.[5] These studies showed that there had been a sizable small-cap premium in the past. And, mysteriously enough, most of this premium performance occurred in January. The so-called "January effect" where small-caps outperformed large-caps mainly in January drew a lot of attention to small-cap stocks. Unfortunately, the academic studies seemed to have jinxed small-cap stocks. In the period since these studies appeared, small-caps haven't outperformed large-caps. But perhaps we should look at a longer period than that made available by the Russell series.

The longest small-cap series available is the small-cap index developed by Ibbotson Associates. This is the series shown in the SBBI Yearbooks that

TABLE 7.2   Returns on Large-Cap, Small-Cap, and Small/Mid-Cap Stocks

Russell Indexes	Average Return 1979–2012	SBBI Indexes	Average Return 1951–2012
Russell 1000	11.5%	S&P 500	10.7%
Russell 2000	11.4%	SBBI Small-Caps	13.1%
Russell 2500	12.7%		

Data sources: Russell and Morningstar.

extends back to 1926. The series includes many of the small-cap stocks found in the Russell 2000 as well as even smaller stocks that we might term "micro-caps." According to the SBBI 2013 Yearbook, the series contains approximately 1,900 stocks with a median capitalization of $225 million. So the capitalization of the average stock in this index is much smaller than the average in the Russell 2000.

The SSBI small-cap series begins in 1926, but as in the previous chapters we will begin the analysis in 1951. The right side of Table 7.2 reports the returns on the SBBI small-cap series and the S&P 500 large-cap series for 1951 to 2012. The results are quite different than those reported for the Russell series. The SBBI small-cap index has a return that is 2.4 percent above that of the large-cap index. Evidently, small-caps must have done well in the period prior to the beginning of the Russell series.

Figure 7.2 shows excess returns for small-caps over large-caps using the SBBI series. The returns are measured as one-year moving averages. (If small-caps have outperformed large-cap stocks over the preceding year, the

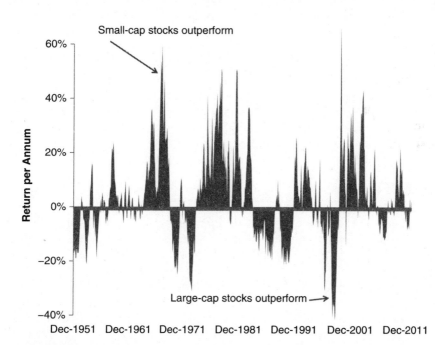

FIGURE 7.2 Excess Returns on Small-Cap Stocks: Rolling One-Year Average Returns, 1951–2012
Data source: Morningstar.

moving average rises above the horizontal line). It is evident from this figure that small-caps did particularly well in the late 1960s and in the period from 1975 to 1983. In 1969, for example, small-caps had an excess return of almost 60 percent. Over the period from 1975 to 1983, moreover, small-cap returns exceeded large-cap returns by over 19 percent per year on average. It's this extended period of small-cap dominance that explains the higher average returns found over the period beginning in 1951. It's interesting that studies of the small-cap premium emerged near the end of this period of small-cap dominance.

Is there a small-cap premium? The answer must be an ambiguous one. Yes, there is a premium if you examine stocks over the past 60-plus years using the SBBI data set. That's because small-caps did so well in the late 1960s and in the 1970s. But the answer is no if you look at only the past 34 years using the Russell indexes.

Where does this leave the investor? Many investment firms choose to overweight small-caps in their recommended portfolios. The overweight is found in the "model portfolios" used by these investment firms to guide decisions by their investment advisors and clients. What do I mean by an "overweight?" If small-caps are 10 percent of the Russell 3000 all-cap index, then any allocation to small-caps greater than 10 percent is an overweight. So if the portfolio has a 40 percent weight for U.S. stocks, any allocation to small-caps over 4 percent (10 percent of 40 percent) is an overweight. I don't necessarily recommend that investors overweight small-caps. But there is surely a good reason to include small-caps in a well-diversified U.S. stock portfolio. And, judging from the high returns on the Russell 2500 small-mid-cap index as reported in Table 7.2, there is any even better reason to include mid-caps in a portfolio.

THE VALUE PREMIUM

Investors in U.S. stocks also must decide whether there is a "value premium," an excess return on value stocks relative to growth stocks. This value premium attaches to stocks that have a low market price relative to the book value of their assets. Think about the types of companies that attract Warren Buffett's attention. These are firms like Geico or Dairy Queen, businesses that produce a steady stream of profits. Many investors are attracted to the more exciting growth companies such as those in the tech sector. Perhaps that's one reason why the prices of growth stocks are so high relative to their book values.

The notion of a value premium in the U.S. stock market is a long-standing belief. After all, the Graham and Dodd text written in the 1930s

(Graham and Dodd, 2008), which inspired Warren Buffett's career, provided a strong case for value investing. But it was the influential papers by Eugene Fama and Kenneth French in the early 1990s that provided the best evidence of this premium.[6] We will look for this premium in the Russell 1000 large-cap and Russell 2000 small-cap indexes.

Russell defines its value and growth indexes using two criteria that assign firms to each index: (1) price-to-book ratio and (2) estimates of the long-run growth of earnings provided by the Institutional Brokers Estimate System (IBES). At the end of every June, the indexes are reconstituted using current market capitalization weights. The firms are arrayed in order according to the two criteria (using an algorithm that is proprietary). Seventy percent of the firms at the two ends of the array are assigned to the value or growth indexes, respectively, depending on the two criteria. The remaining 30 percent of firms in the middle of the array are then divided proportionally into value and growth depending upon the same two criteria. So these firms are included in both indexes, but with different weights. IBM, for example, is assigned weights in both indexes, but with a greater weight in the growth index.

Table 7.3 gives the breakdown of the Russell 1000 Growth Index by industry in July 2013. The largest sector is consumer discretionary stocks with over 22.9 percent of the market weight. The technology sector is not far behind with a 21.5 percent share. Prior to the collapse of the NASDAQ in 2000, however, technology dominated this index. As of October 2000, technology was 50.5 percent of the index as compared with a weight of only

TABLE 7.3 Russell 1000 Growth

Industries	Market Cap	Top Firms	Market Cap
Consumer discretionary	22.9%	Apple	3.6%
Technology	21.5%	Microsoft	3.4%
Producer durables	12.4%	Google	2.9%
Health care	11.6%	IBM	2.4%
Consumer staples	11.2%	Coca-Cola	1.9%
Financial services	8.2%	Phillip Morris	1.7%
Materials	5.3%	Verizon	1.7%
Energy	4.6%	Pepsico	1.5%
Utilities	2.1%	Home Depot	1.4%
Other	0.2%	Oracle	1.3%

Source: July 2013 capitalizations from ishares.com.

TABLE 7.4   Russell 1000 Value

Industries	Market Cap	Top Firms	Market Cap
Financial services	29.6%	Exxon Mobil	4.9%
Energy	15.1%	General Electric	2.9%
Health care	12.7%	Chevron	2.8%
Producer durables	9.5%	Procter & Gamble	2.6%
Utilities	9.2%	Johnson & Johnson	2.5%
Technology	8.4%	Berkshire Hathaway	2.4%
Consumer discretionary	6.8%	JP Morgan	2.4%
Consumer staples	5.5%	Wells Fargo	2.4%
Materials	2.8%	AT&T	2.3%
Other	0.6%	Pfizer	2.2%

Source: July 2013 capitalizations from ishares.com.

16.2 percent for health care. So the nature of the growth index has changed significantly since the height of the tech market. Table 7.3 lists the top 10 firms in the index listed by market capitalization. Technology firms such as Apple, Microsoft, and Google are included on the list, but there are also other nontech firms (like Phillip Morris and PepsiCo) in the index.

Table 7.4 gives the industry breakdown for the Russell 1000 Value Index. The stocks of financial services firms dominate this index with energy and health care stocks far behind. But the financial crisis in 2007–2008 has reduced the share of financial services from over 35 percent to less than 30 percent. There are now only two banks, JP Morgan and Wells Fargo, among the top 10 value stocks.

Is it plausible that the value firms in Table 7.4 can have higher returns than the exciting growth firms in Table 7.3? The answer is that there are some growth firms such as Google that have larger returns. But the 400-plus firms in the Russell 1000 Growth index as a whole have lower returns than those in the Value index.

RELATIVE RETURNS ON VALUE AND GROWTH STOCKS

Table 7.5 reports the average returns on the Russell indexes since 1979 when the series begin. Let's focus on the large-cap series. Over this 34-year period, value stocks deliver an average excess return of 1.4 percent per annum.

TABLE 7.5   Returns on Russell Growth and Value Indexes, 1979–2012

Index	Russell 1000 Large-Caps	Russell 2000 Small-Caps
Growth Index	10.6%	9.2%
Value Index	12.0%	13.2%

Source: Russell.com.

That's quite a differential. The cumulative return on value stocks exceeds that of growth stocks by 1,640 percent (i.e., 4,614 versus 2,974 percent).

The outperformance of value is even greater in the small-cap space. The Russell 2000 Value index has an average return of 13.2 percent whereas the average return on the Russell 2000 Growth index is a miserable 9.2 percent. That's an astonishing gap. Perhaps investors are too busy searching for the next Google among small-cap growth stocks to pay attention to returns! Some investment experts will counter that active small-cap growth managers provide so much excess return by stock selection that the low index return doesn't matter. That may be true of some managers, but surely small-cap growth managers as a whole can't overcome that much of a deficit.

Just because one index has a higher return does not mean that it always pays to invest in that type of stock. Figure 7.3 shows how much variation there is in value and growth performance. This figure shows a one-year moving average of returns on large-cap growth stocks relative to value stocks. So if returns are above the horizontal axis, growth stocks have outperformed value stocks over the previous year. The opposite is true if returns are below this axis. Notice that the swings in relative returns are often huge. In early 2000, for example, growth returns rose above value returns by 35 percent measured as a moving average over the previous year. But then markets reversed. Within a year later, value stocks outperformed growth stocks by 48 percent. Imagine how investors would feel if they had all of their U.S. investments in one sector or another. In times when that sector soared, they would feel triumphant. But then there would be times when the sector tanked. That's a good reason for diversification.

Is the value premium found in earlier periods? Stock market data collected by the University of Chicago's CRSP data set are available back through 1926. These market data form the basis for the Ibbotson dataset of large- and small-cap stock returns. To develop value and growth indexes, however, it's necessary to obtain the book value of common equity from the balance sheets of the firms being studied. In the early 1990s, Fama and French developed indexes for value and growth extending all the way back to 1926. The results are quite definitive. There is a large excess return of

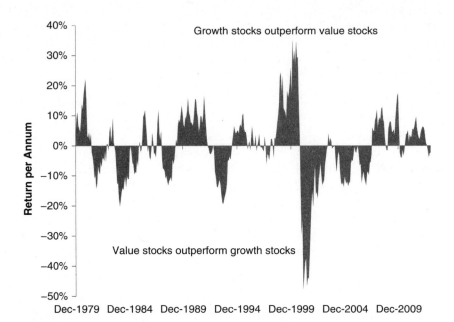

FIGURE 7.3   Excess Returns on Large-Cap Growth Stocks: Rolling One-Year Average Returns, 1980–2012
Data source: Russell.

value over growth for both large-cap and small-cap stocks in this earlier period as well. This is true whether returns are measured beginning in 1926 or 1951. (The results are reported in Chapter 4 of Marston 2011.) So the "value premium" is not a fluke of the Russell data set.

The long-run performance of value stocks is quite impressive. In all of the data sets reported, value stocks give higher average returns than growth stocks. There is no doubt that there is a value premium in the U.S. stock market.

IMPLICATIONS FOR PORTFOLIOS

What does all of this mean for a portfolio? (1) The evidence for a value premium is so overwhelming that I would recommend overweighting value stocks in the portfolio. Or at the very least, make sure that investments in value stocks are at least as large as investments in growth stocks. That would be ensured if the investor chose a "core" large cap fund that is benchmarked to the S&P 500. (2) The evidence in favor of a small-cap premium is mixed for the reasons given earlier. But even if the investor does not believe in a small-cap premium, it still makes sense to allocate at least 10 percent of the investment in U.S. stocks to a small-cap stock fund.

Why not focus entirely on value stocks? As Figure 7.3 shows all too clearly, there are periods when growth stocks shine. Investors don't want to miss out on those returns. That's particularly true if an investor is easily swayed by recent performance. A string of good years for growth stocks might cause the investor to abandon a well-chosen asset allocation so as not to miss out on a tech boom. After all, investors are continually enticed by the siren call of "this time it is different." Focusing on either growth or value to the exclusion of the other would not be sensible.

The important point about portfolio choice is that investors want to avoid concentration in one particular style (growth or value) and want to avoid excessive investment in small-caps. Diversification is the key since we are investing for the long run.

NOTES

1. The 15-year returns are reported in June 2013 on Morningstar.com, http://performance.morningstar.com/stock/performance-return.
2. This feature doesn't matter to me because I make only a few changes to my portfolio in any given year.
3. The S&P 500 index also includes the American Depository Receipts (ADRs) of some large foreign companies. Chapter 8 discusses the ADR market. Siegel (2013) describes the Dow Jones and S&P 500 indexes in more detail.
4. The Wilshire 5000 index includes almost all stocks in the U.S. market, but the stocks left out of the Russell 3000 represent only about 2 percent of the total capitalization of the U.S. market.
5. Two classic studies are Banz (1981) and Keim (1983).
6. Fama and French (1992, 1993) show that the small-cap premium and value premium are both influential factors in stock market returns.

REFERENCES

Banz, Rolf W. 1981. "The Relation between Return and Market Value of Common Stocks." *Journal of Financial Economics* (March): 3–18.
Fama, Eugene F., and Kenneth R. French. 1992. "The Cross-Section of Expected Stock Returns." *Journal of Finance* (June): 427–465.

Fama, Eugene F., and Kenneth R. French. 1993. "Common Risk Factors in the Returns on Stocks and Bonds." *Journal of Financial Economics* (February): 3–56.

Graham, Benjamin, and David Dodd. 2008. *Security Analysis*, 6th ed. New York: McGraw-Hill Professional.

SBBI 2013 Classic Yearbook. Chicago: Morningstar.

Investment Company Institute. 2013. *2013 Investment Company Fact Book, 53rd Edition*. www.icifactbook.org.

Keim, Donald B. 1983. "Size Related Anomalies and Stock Return Seasonality," *Journal of Financial Economics* (June): 13–22.

Marston, Richard. 2011. *Portfolio Design: A Modern Approach to Asset Allocation*. Hoboken, NJ: John Wiley & Sons.

Siegel, Jeremy J. 2013. *Stocks for the Long Run: The Definitive Guide to Financial Market Returns and Long-Term Investment Strategies*, 5th ed. New York: McGraw-Hill.

CHAPTER 8

Foreign Stock Markets: Industrial Countries of Europe and the Pacific

Back in the early 1990s, investors considered themselves adventurous if they invested overseas. Foreign stock returns had exceeded U.S. returns for 20 years. But somehow Americans were more comfortable investing in the likes of General Electric and AT&T than in European companies like Phillips or Nestle or Japanese companies like Toyota. Americans might buy European or Japanese products, so their tastes were not exactly parochial, but their portfolios were U.S.-centric. Many investment advisory firms were recommending international diversification. But the 10 percent allocation to foreign stocks that they typically recommended seems quite timid by today's standards. And hardly anyone was recommending emerging market stocks. It's true that pioneers such as John Templeton were introducing some American investors to emerging markets, but most investors kept clear of those markets.

Contrast the situation today with that of the early 1990s. There is a wide array of foreign stock funds available to ordinary investors. Some funds offer broad diversification into markets across the globe. Others specialize in Europe or the Pacific or elsewhere. Today one leading investment bank urges that its private banking clients devote 40 percent of their stock allocation to foreign stocks. It's ironic that the recommendation is so much higher today since the advantages of diversifying into foreign stocks are not as great as they used to be. We show evidence about that below. This chapter will consider the case for diversification into the stocks of the industrial countries. The next chapter considers the so-called "emerging markets," those with relatively low per capita incomes.

The world stock market had a capitalization of $46.8 trillion in 2011. Of that total, the U.S. stock market represented 33.4 percent of this total. Another 41.1 percent consisted of stocks from the other industrial countries, with the remaining 25.5 percent being stocks of the emerging markets.

FIGURE 8.1   World Stock Market Capitalization
Source: S&P *Global Stock Markets Factbook*, 2012.

The capitalization of the world stock markets is shown in Figure 8.1. There is quite a wide world out there. Even if investors focused on industrial countries alone, they could diversify across European countries, including those that have adopted the euro, and across the Pacific in markets such as Japan, Australia, and New Zealand, and Singapore and Hong Kong.

Why would an American investor bother to invest overseas? The traditional argument for diversifying overseas was that the foreign markets were not highly correlated with U.S. markets. That's no longer the case as we will show later. But it still remains the case that foreign markets provide a way to diversify the portfolio across industries more effectively than a portfolio devoted to U.S. stocks alone. Moreover, while monthly correlations are quite high, that doesn't mean that investors always earn the same returns on U.S. stocks and foreign stocks. As shown later, in recent years the emerging markets have beaten developed markets, while in the 1970s and 1980s European and Japanese markets outperformed the U.S. market.

RETURNS ON FOREIGN STOCKS

Just as in the American market, investors use stock price indexes to track returns in foreign stock markets. The most widely used foreign stock index is the MSCI EAFE index, an index developed in the 1970s to measure returns in the industrial countries outside the United States. The EAFE index is a capitalization weighted index (like the S&P 500) of large-cap stocks in the industrial countries of Europe and the Pacific. EAFE stands for Europe, Australasia, and the Far East. The countries in the index are shown in Table 8.1. Europe makes up over 60 percent of the index, while the Pacific makes up the rest. The Canadian market was left out of the EAFE index, presumably because of its high correlation with the U.S. market.

Table 8.2 compares the average return on the EAFE index with that of the S&P 500 over the period 1970–2012. It's evident that after 43 years the two indexes have ended up very close to one another. EAFE's returns exceeded those of the United States throughout most of the 1970s and 1980s. The S&P 500 surged ahead in the 1990s with the huge boom in U.S. stocks. Then more recently EAFE has almost caught up. That it's a close horse race should not be surprising. After all, most industrial countries are at the same level of development. Individual countries may excel in one industry

TABLE 8.1 Country Composition of MSCI EAFE Index

Europe Index	63.0%	Pacific Index	37.0%
Austria	0.5%	Australia	7.4%
Belgium	1.4%	Hong Kong	5.5%
Denmark	1.1%	Japan	21.8%
Finland	0.9%	New Zealand	0.4%
France	9.7%	Singapore	1.9%
Germany	7.3%		
Greece	0.2%		
Ireland	0.2%		
Israel	0.9%		
Italy	2.7%		
Netherlands	3.7%		
Norway	1.3%		
Portugal	0.4%		
Spain	6.3%		
Sweden	2.9%		
Switzerland	5.7%		
United Kingdom	17.9%		

Source for market capitalization: S&P *Global Stock Markets Factbook*, 2012.

TABLE 8.2   Returns on U.S. and Foreign Stocks in Dollars and Local Currency, 1970–2012

Market	Returns in Dollars	Returns in Local Currency
S&P 500	9.9%	9.9%
MSCI EAFE	9.7%	7.9%
MSCI Europe	10.3%	9.7%
MSCI Pacific	9.5%	6.3%

Data sources: MSCI and S&P Dow Jones Indices.

or another. But overall no country or region has a clear advantage in firm profitability and stock market performance.

The second column of Table 8.2 reports returns measured in dollars, while the third column reports the returns in local currency. Since the dollar returns are substantially higher than the local currency returns, this means that the American investor has benefited from a significant appreciation of foreign currencies. When a foreign currency rises relative to the dollar, the dollar value of foreign assets rises.

Notice that all of the returns measured in dollars are clustered near one another. The return for the U.S. market is 0.4 percent above that of the Pacific market, but 0.4 percent below that of the European market. Returns for EAFE are only 0.2 percent below those of the U.S. So for the 43-year period as a whole, the returns on foreign and U.S. stock markets as seen by American investors are remarkably similar.

MARKETS HAVE BECOME MORE CORRELATED

If U.S. and foreign stock returns are so close to one another, why does it pay to invest in foreign stocks? It used to be the case that foreign and domestic markets were relatively low in correlation with one another. That is no longer the case. Sometime in the late 1990s, U.S. and foreign stocks started to move much more closely together. (When stocks move together, we say that the "correlation" between the stocks is high). Experts on international markets had a ready explanation for this increased correlation: "The world has become more integrated." That surely is a plausible explanation. But does it explain why the correlations increased so abruptly in the late 1990s?

What does it mean that the world is more integrated? Over the last 20 or 30 years, international trade and international capital flows have both increased substantially. Barriers to international trade have fallen sharply since the high-tariff period of the 1930s and 1940s. There are regional free-trade agreements such as the North American Trade Agreement as well as worldwide free-trade agreements. Barriers to international capital flows have also fallen. Today's world of free-flowing capital is in sharp contrast to the capital control world of the early postwar period. (When I was a student at Oxford in the late 1960s, British residents were allowed to take only £50 out of the country. Needless to say, you did not see many Englishmen sipping cappuccino in Florence.) There has also been a marked improvement in information flows. Information has long been transmitted almost instantly between countries, at least since the establishment of the worldwide telegraph system in the 1860s. But now there is so much more information readily available about markets and companies than there was as recently as the 1970s. Databases of corporate performances, for example, are available for many foreign companies. And the web has provided instant access to annual reports and other corporate records.

Nonetheless, it's hard to explain why this trend in integration should lead to an abrupt increase in correlations in the late 1990s. There is no evidence of an abrupt increase in international trade or capital flows around that time. Nor did instant communications become even more instantly available in the late 1990s. The internet became important in the late 1990s, but just a little bit earlier, 1866 to be exact, a telegraph cable across the Atlantic linked New York markets with those in London and Paris. However, without an alternative explanation of this phenomenon, all we can do is observe the change in correlations and admit that low correlations are no longer a major reason to invest overseas. Markets worldwide often rise and fall in response to the same events.

WHY DOES IT PAY TO DIVERSIFY INTO FOREIGN STOCKS?

If markets in the United States and other industrial countries are now highly correlated, is there any reason to invest overseas? I believe that two reasons are most important. First, even though returns on the S&P 500 and EAFE indexes since 1970 are almost identical, these returns differ widely over shorter periods, even periods as long as a decade in length. Second, investors who confine themselves to U.S. stocks alone don't properly diversify across industries, depriving themselves of some great firms and industries overseas.

Let's first look at returns over periods shorter than 40 years. Here is an interesting experiment. Compare returns by decade across four markets: the U.S. market, the European portion of the EAFE index, the Pacific portion of that same index, and emerging markets. Emerging market data only begin

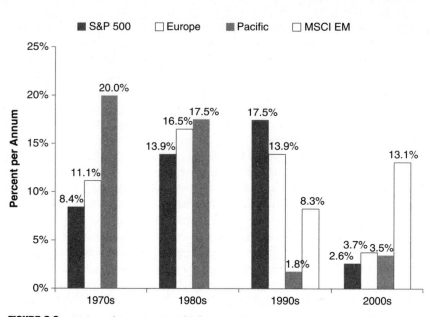

FIGURE 8.2   U.S. and Foreign Stocks by Decade, 1971–2012
Data sources: MSCI and S&P Dow Jones Indices.

at the end of the 1980s, so only three markets will be compared in the first two decades. The results are shown in Figure 8.2.[1]

In the 1970s, 20 percent returns per annum from the Pacific stock markets led the other markets, with the United States trailing Europe by 2.7 percent per year on average. In the 1980s, markets in the Pacific and Europe again outperformed the U.S. market with the gap between Europe and the United States averaging 2.6 percent. No wonder that some American investors became enthusiastic about foreign stocks as these first two decades evolved. In the 1990s, the tables were turned as the U.S. market outshone all the others. Since 2001, returns in the emerging markets have beaten those in the United States by over 10 percent per year after having lagged far behind the United States and Europe in the 1990s.

An investor examining this record of returns must focus on the following question. Which markets will outperform in coming decades? The sensible response is that investors do not know the answer to this question. That is the most compelling argument for diversifying abroad. Ignore correlations for the moment and focus on Figure 8.2. Should investors be concentrated in U.S. stocks if we could plausibly face decades more similar to the 1970s and 1980s and 2000s than the 1990s? The answer is an obvious one. So why are U.S. investors so U.S.-centric?

To see to what extent markets can vary relative to one another, consider the sad experience of Japanese investors over the past 20 years or so. In the late 1980s, the Japanese stock market was the largest in the world as Japanese stock market values soared. The Nikkei stock market index (the Dow Jones of Japan) reached its peak of 38,900 in December 1989. Shortly thereafter, the Japanese market collapsed. In early 2013, it is still below 12,000. Over the 23 years since the peak of the market, the Japanese investor has earned −3.7 percent per year on average. In dollar terms, the return has been −1.5 percent per year. What a disaster for Japanese investors. Over this same period, the S&P earned 8.6 percent per year (in dollar terms). And the EAFE index, pulled down by negative Japanese returns, earned 4.4 percent per year.[2] How much better off would Japanese investors have been if they had chosen a global rather than a national portfolio?

The second reason to invest in other industrial countries is to diversify the types of firms in an investor's portfolio. American firms are great in some industries, but foreign firms are better in others. American firms excel in pharmaceuticals, medical equipment, entertainment, and software. But the Japanese are better at making most consumer electronics and autos and heavy machinery. German industry is supreme in machine tools and specialty chemicals. The French excel in design, high-speed trains, and nuclear engineering. Why should American investors confine their portfolios to U.S. firms alone?

In early 2013, the top five firms in the EAFE index were Nestle (Swiss), HSBC (U.K.), Novartis (Swiss), Roche (Swiss), and British Petroleum (U.K.). Why would American investors want to exclude such companies from their portfolios? Is Nestle inferior to all U.S. food companies? Similarly, are U.S. banks so superior to HSBC that we should exclude it from our portfolios? The answers to these questions are quite obvious, yet why are Americans so willing to remain American-centric in their investment decisions?

One reason may be that the stocks of foreign companies are denominated in foreign currency. And currency movements cause foreign stock returns to vary more than U.S. stock returns. I don't regard the currency issue as a deal breaker because there are so many other benefits of investing in foreign stocks. But it's important for investors to know how currency movements affect stock returns.

ROLE OF CURRENCIES IN RETURNS EARNED BY U.S. INVESTORS

The returns shown in Table 8.2 are measured both in dollars and in local currencies. The returns measured in dollars reflect not only the underlying returns in the local market, but also the capital gains on foreign currencies relative to the dollar. A Japanese resident measures stock returns in Japanese yen, while a U.S. resident measures stock returns in dollars. In 2003, for example, the Japanese stock return in yen was 23.0 percent. But because the yen appreciated quite sharply that year, the American investor received a return of 36.2 percent.

Over the shorter run, currency movements can lead to large changes in the returns on foreign stocks seen by Americans. Currencies sometimes swing a lot. A good example is found in the euro, introduced in most of Western Europe in 1999. The euro began trading at about $1.18/€ in January 1999. That price was determined by the exchange rates of the currencies that the euro replaced such as the Deutschmark and the French franc. Between 1999 and 2002, the Euro fell like a rock to $0.85/€. When asked why the euro had fallen, most experts gave seemingly plausible answers such as the uncertainty surrounding a new currency and the excitement generated by the NASDAQ boom in the United States. The dollar-euro exchange rate is pictured in Figure 8.3.

When the euro fell so sharply, I was genuinely puzzled by its fall. As far as I could tell, there was no fundamental reason why this currency

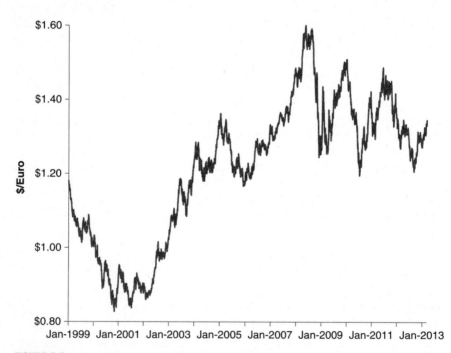

FIGURE 8.3 Exchange Rate for the Euro since 1999
Data source: Federal Reserve Board.

should have fallen by 28 percent, so I believed that it would eventually rebound. Currencies are difficult to forecast, so I did not pretend to know when the reversal of the euro's move would occur. But on a number of occasions, I counseled American investors to do three things, in no particular order. Investors should (1) visit Paris while it was still so cheap, (2) buy as much French (and other European wine) as possible because there was a fire sale on Burgundies and Bordeaux, and (3) buy European stocks and bonds.

Eventually, the euro started to reverse course. It rose back to its starting point at $1.18/€ on the way to an eventual high of $1.60/€. Subsequent events like the financial crisis of 2008–2009 and the Greek default crisis have pushed the euro back from its high, but the general trend since 2002 has been upward. As a result, American investors in European stocks have enjoyed a windfall currency gain on their investments.

In the three years from 1999 to 2001, the dollar return on the European index averaged *minus* 5.0 percent/year because the currency loss of 7.2 percent more than offset the stock return in local currency. The period after 2001 was very different. Currency gains contributed 3.1 percent per year to European stock returns from 2002 through 2012. As a result, European stocks measured in dollars had positive returns of 6.2 percent per year, much higher than the return in local currency during this period.

Currency effects add an extra dimension to investing in foreign stock markets. In the short run, as seen in the euro example, currency gains and losses can significantly change returns as seen from an American perspective. Currencies thus add to the short-run volatility of foreign stock returns. But even in the longer run, currency gains and losses can matter. In the case of the EAFE index, for example, the return in dollars averaged 1.8 percent above the local currency return from 1970 to 2012. The higher returns in dollars reflected the overall depreciation of the dollar that occurred over the period. For investors who think that the dollar will trend downward in the future, this may be another reason to diversify into foreign stocks.

Currencies have another effect on the stock portfolios of Americans. Many U.S. companies have extensive operations abroad. That's particularly true of large "multinational" companies such as General Electric, IBM or Microsoft. Some of these multinationals generate more revenue abroad than in the United States. When foreign currencies rise against the dollar, this raises the dollar value of the foreign earnings of these companies. In many cases, this means that their stock prices rise. So foreign exchange rates can affect stocks of American investors even if they refrain from investing in any foreign stocks. This is an integrated world where foreign exchange rates matter a lot.

IS THERE A SHORTCUT TO INVESTING IN FOREIGN STOCKS?

Americans wanting to invest directly in the shares of a foreign company face a few obstacles. First, investors must send money abroad, then exchange that money into foreign currency, and finally buy shares using that foreign currency. When the stock is sold, the three steps have to be reversed. All three steps can be accomplished by a single bank or brokerage firm, but the transaction is more complicated than the purchase of shares in an American company. Of course, as discussed below, investors could opt to invest in foreign companies via mutual funds or ETFs. But investing directly in the shares of foreign companies is more complicated than investing in U.S. shares.

Since the 1920s, however, Americans have been able to invest in foreign stocks indirectly through the market for American Depository Receipts (or ADRs). ADRs are negotiable certificates issued by a U.S. bank with rights to the underlying shares of stock held in trust at a custodian bank. These ADRs are sold, registered, and transferred within the United States like any share of stock in a U.S. company. Dividends are paid in foreign currency to the custodian bank that converts them to dollars.

American investors find investing in ADRs very convenient compared with investing in shares in foreign stock markets. There are now over 3,000 ADRs available in the U.S. market for firms from virtually every country that has an active stock market, so it's possible to invest in a wide variety of foreign stocks through ADRs. Many ADRs are from markets in the developed countries of Western Europe and Asia, but there are also many from emerging market countries. It is evident that an investor can build a diversified portfolio of foreign stocks with ADRs alone.

Investors in ADRS receive the same returns that they would receive if they invested in the shares of the underlying company. This is true at least for the case of liquid stocks that are widely traded by investors and free of any government restrictions. Someone who invests in the Siemens ADR, for example, will receive the same return (ignoring transactions costs) as an investor in Siemens shares in Germany. If traders notice price discrepancies between the prices of ADRs and the underlying stocks, they will immediately jump on the opportunity to make a profit. They will buy in the cheaper market and sell in the higher-priced market.

Some investors believe that ADRs allow investors to avoid exchange risk because they are priced in dollars whereas foreign shares are priced in local currency. Investors in ADRs, however, will see that all gains and losses in currencies are reflected in ADR prices. A rise in the euro, for example, will raise the price of the Siemens ADR just as surely as it raises the price (in dollars) of the underlying shares in Germany. ADRs and the shares of the same companies listed on their home exchanges should have the same prices and the same returns (when expressed in dollars) unless governments impose restrictions on the purchase and sale of the latter by foreigners.

ADRs make it easy for Americans to invest in foreign stocks. But ADRs are not the only convenient way to invest in foreign stocks. Most investors invest in stocks via mutual funds or ETFs. That's true whether they are investing in U.S. stocks or foreign stocks. The mutual fund managers, in turn, handle any transactions required to buy or sell shares in foreign companies. So the individual investor need not ever face the hassle of buying or selling ordinary shares on foreign stock exchanges. On the other hand, many mutual fund managers invest in ADRs for the same reason as do individual investors. ADRs are convenient. In fact, some mutual fund managers invest exclusively in ADRs.

If there are thousands of ADRs, why would an American investor or an American mutual fund manager ever want to invest in the underlying shares listed on foreign exchanges? The answer is that there are many foreign companies without ADRs, particularly smaller companies without global name recognition. For that reason, some mutual fund managers deliberately invest only in foreign shares so that they can focus on lesser known companies that may be priced inefficiently. Others mix ADRs with foreign shares so as to obtain a more diversified group of foreign companies. ADRs provide a shortcut to American investors, but mutual funds allow these investors to broaden the range of foreign companies they invest in.

CONCLUDING COMMENTS

In the long run, foreign stocks deliver comparable returns to those of U.S. stocks. From year to year and decade to decade, however, there are wide variations in performance across regions of the world. This provides a strong argument for diversification.

It has long been recognized that the relatively low correlation between foreign and U.S. stocks provides a portfolio diversification benefit. That correlation, however, has risen sharply since the late 1990s. Yet there remain two strong arguments for investing abroad. First, even though monthly correlations have risen, U.S. and foreign returns vary widely over time. So why not have some of each in the portfolio? Second, investors need to invest abroad to take advantage of the excellent firms in industries where American firms are not necessarily dominant.

Investors like to find short-cuts to investing in stocks listed on foreign exchanges. Buying ADRs instead of foreign stocks provides an effective way to diversify internationally because returns on ADRs are closely aligned with those of the underlying stocks.

Perhaps the strongest argument for foreign stocks is that there is no reason to restrict a portfolio to the stocks of companies that happen to be headquartered in the United States. There is no way of knowing whether foreign stocks will outperform U.S. stocks in the decades ahead, so there is no reason to restrict investment to U.S. stocks.

NOTES

1. The "decade" of the 2000s actually extends from 2001 to 2012.
2. An EAFE index excluding Japan earned an average return of 7.9 percent per year over this same period, 3.5 percent higher than the index including Japan.

REFERENCES

Standard & Poor's. 2012. *Global Stock Markets Factbook*. New York: McGraw-Hill.

CHAPTER 9

Emerging Markets

"**E**merging markets" may be one of the best marketing phrases ever devised. The phrase seems to describe markets that hold a lot of potential for future economic growth and the promise of future returns for investors. Since this phrase is usually attached to national markets where income is relatively low, a more accurate description would be "the markets of less developed countries." Some countries will have great potential for growth and may actually be growing quite rapidly. Other countries, however, may have either little growth or actually be stumbling backward. Argentina might be a good example of the latter. Its economy has been run so badly in recent years that it has been demoted by the MSCI database from "emerging market" status to a lower-level "frontier market" status.

The investment industry tends to focus on the success stories. In the past few decades, China has captured the imagination of investors with its rapid economic growth fueled by the export of manufacturing goods. Just a couple of decades earlier, South Korea and Taiwan had excited investors for much the same reason. The success of other countries has rested less on manufacturing than on services (India) or commodities (Russia, South Africa, and Brazil). All share one characteristic that interests investors, their potential for good investment returns due to their high rates of economic growth.

This chapter will show that at times emerging markets have provided handsome returns for international investors, especially over the past decade. But the record of returns is uneven, to say the least. In the 1990s attention was focused on East Asian growth, but in 1997 many currencies in East Asia suddenly collapsed in what was later termed the "Asian crisis." Three years prior, Mexico suffered a sharp devaluation of the peso. And one year later Russia defaulted on much of its government debt. Yes, emerging markets are sometimes turbulent.

WHAT IS AN EMERGING MARKET?

How is an "emerging market" defined?[1] The World Bank traditionally used one criterion, gross national income per person or "per capita." Any country that was classified by the World Bank as a low-income or middle-income country was also classified as an "emerging market." In 2012, China had a total gross national income of $7,749 billion, but a per capita income of only $5,740. Singapore, in contrast, had a gross national income of $251 billion, but a per capita income of $47,210.[2] So China is classified as an emerging market even though its total output was many times that of Singapore because its income per capita is so low.

The bulk of the world's income is earned by the high-income countries. Figure 9.1 shows the division of the world's gross national income (GNI) in 2012.[3] Only 36.8 percent of GNI is earned by the emerging market countries even though they represent about 85 percent of the world's population. The developed countries dominate world output and world income. Western European countries (including the euro area and other European industrial countries like the United Kingdom) produce 25.5 percent of world income and the United States another 23.4 percent, while the other developed countries of the world including Japan make up the rest.

Figure 9.2 breaks out the GNI of the five largest emerging market countries. China has the largest economy of any emerging market with a GNI larger than all but one of the developed countries (the United States).

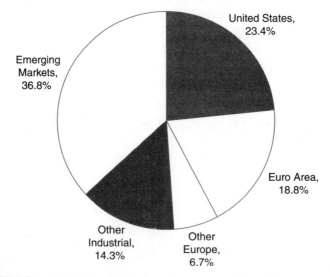

FIGURE 9.1   World Gross National Income in US$, 2012
Source: World Bank, World Development Indicators Database, 2013.

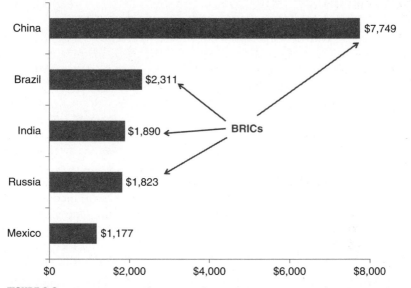

FIGURE 9.2 Gross National Income of Largest Emerging Market Countries, $Billions in 2012
Source: World Bank, World Development Indicators Database, 2013.

With its rapid growth over the last two decades, China's economy is now larger than that of Japan, the next largest industrial country. China is one of the four "BRIC" countries highlighted in discussions of economic development, the others being Brazil, Russia, and India. All four of these countries are among the five economies shown in Figure 9.2. As shown later, the ranking of these five countries would be very different if adjusted for population size. China's huge GNI must be shared by a huge population.

When measuring national income, it's sensible to adjust for the cost of living. That is certainly true within a single country over time. If you want to measure the income of the average American today relative to decades ago, the only sensible way to measure income is to adjust for changes in the cost of living. So we might compare gross national income per capita in the year 1960 versus that of 2012 by adjusting income in 1960 by the lower cost of living in that year. A similar approach might be used in comparing GNI per capita between countries at the same time since there might be substantial differences in the cost of living across countries. A basket of goods might be much less expensive in China than in Japan because prices are so much lower in China than in Japan.

The World Bank and other international agencies adjust the GNI of a country by the cost of a common market basket in that country. The results

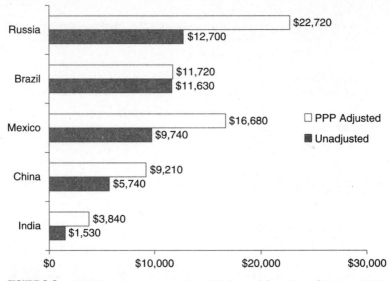

FIGURE 9.3   GNI Per Capita, Actual, and Adjusted for Cost of Living, 2012
Source: World Bank, World Development Indicators Database, 2013.

follow a consistent pattern. Less developed countries have lower costs of living than industrial countries. So the "adjusted" GNI per capita of the less developed countries tends to be larger than the unadjusted GNI. In the case of the industrialized countries, the reverse is true. The adjusted GNI of these countries tends to be smaller than unadjusted GNI.

Figure 9.3 presents the GNI per capita of the five largest emerging market economies using two measures of national income. One measure, labeled "unadjusted," simply converts the GNI per capita of a country into dollars using recent exchange rates.[4] The second measure, called the PPP or purchasing power parity measure, adjusts for the cost of living. The results are quite striking. China's GNI per capita is only $5,740 when measured at current exchange rates. But when it is adjusted for the low cost of living in China, GNI per capital rises to $9,210. Similarly, Mexico's GNI per capita is only $9,740 when measured using current exchange rates, but it rises to $16,680 when adjusted for the cost of living.

To give some perspective on these GNI figures, consider the GNI per capita of some of the major industrial countries. France has a GNI per capita of $41,750 using current exchange rates and $36,720 after adjustment for the higher cost of living in France. The United States has a GNI per capita of $50,120 at current exchange rates and $50,610 after adjustment.[5] The gap between the incomes of emerging markets and industrial economies is wide indeed.

EMERGING STOCK MARKET INDEXES

Emerging stock markets represent 25.5 percent of the world's stock market capitalization of $46.8 trillion. So a block of countries with about 37 percent of the world's national income hosts about one-quarter of the world's stock market capitalization. The bulk of the market capitalization is found in the developed countries with the U.S. stock market representing a little over 33 percent of the total.

The emerging stock markets are divided along regional lines in Figure 9.4. East Asia provides the largest block in terms of capitalization. This region consists of all markets between Indonesia and China except for Singapore and Hong Kong (the latter being measured independently of China). South Asia includes India which accounts for most of the region's market value. (East Asia and South Asia are combined in the "Asia" region in some of the statistics below). The Middle East and Africa region includes two relatively large emerging stock markets, South Africa and Saudi Arabia.

These measures of market capitalizations may be misleading if we are interested in stocks that are actually available to the international investor. Not all shares issued by a firm are available to ordinary investors of that country, and even fewer are available to residents of other countries. There are several issues to sort through. First, some shares may be owned by the government or closely held by other investors. For example, firms in the

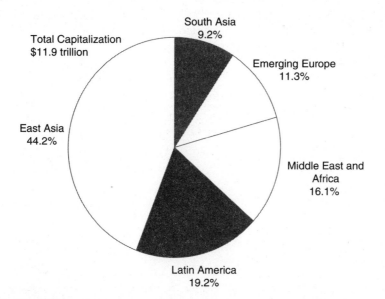

FIGURE 9.4 Stock Market Capitalization of the Emerging Markets
Source: S&P *Global Stock Markets Factbook,* 2012.

same industrial group can cross-hold each other's shares. Second, some or all shares of a firm may be off-limits to foreign investors. Most foreign investment restrictions have been removed by developed countries, but such restrictions are widespread in the emerging countries.

To illustrate how different emerging markets look if we consider only investable indexes, consider Table 9.1, which compares actual (total) market capitalization for the emerging markets with the weights of the same regions or countries adopted by MSCI in its "investable" indexes. China has a 36.3 percent weight in the total market capitalization of the emerging markets, but only a 17.9 percent weight in the MSCI investable index. In contrast, South Korea and Taiwan represent only 11.1 percent of the total market capitalization, but they represent 24.1 percent of the MSCI investable index. (South Korea remains in the emerging market category in the MSCI database even though Standard & Poor's has elevated it to developed country status in the Global Stock Markets Factbook).[6] China has many stocks that are off-limits to foreigners or stocks that are only partially accessible to foreigners. Korea and Taiwan are much more open to foreign investors (even though their markets used to be subject to multiple restrictions).

Because the investable universe is so different from the total emerging market universe, it's imperative for investors to use proper benchmarks for evaluating emerging market managers. Performance should be judged relative to the MSCI indexes, not relative to the broad stock market indexes of a country or region. Shanghai's stock market may have soared 20 percent over a particular period, but that does not mean that the investable indexes tracked by American investors have soared that much. They may have risen more or less than the Shanghai index.

TABLE 9.1   Emerging Market Capitalization Compared with MSCI Weights

Markets	Actual Market Capitalization, 2009	MSCI Weights, 2009
China	36.3%	17.9%
Korea and Taiwan	11.1%	24.1%
Rest of Asia	13.8%	13.8%
Brazil	8.5%	16.9%
Rest of Latin America	6.1%	6.9%
Europe, Middle East, and Africa	24.3%	20.4%

Sources: S&P (2010) for actual market capitalization, MSCI Barra (2009) for MSCI weights.

TABLE 9.2   MSCI Emerging Market Index

Largest Countries	Market Share	Largest Firms
China	17.8%	Samsung (South Korea)
South Korea	15.2%	Taiwan Semiconductor (Taiwan)
Brazil	12.6%	China Mobile (China)
Taiwan	10.6%	China Construction Bank (China)
South Africa	7.8%	Gazprom (Russia)
India	6.6%	Indus & Com Bank of China (China)
Russia	6.0%	America Movil (Mexico)
Mexico	5.1%	Vale SA (Brazil)
Malaysia	3.5%	Petrobras (Brazil)
Indonesia	2.6%	CNO Oil Company (China)

Source: iShares.com, February 2013.

Table 9.2 provides some interesting details about the MSCI Emerging Market Stock Index as reflected in the iShares ETF. The largest countries are given on the left of the table and the largest firms on the right. China is the largest market in the index, but notice that South Korea is almost as large despite having a much smaller economy. (The gap between China and the other countries would be larger if we looked at all shares rather than just shares "investable" by foreigners as measured by MSCI.) The list of largest firms includes two mobile phone operators (China Mobile and America Movil), two electronics firms (Samsung and Taiwan Semiconductor), a mining firm (Vale SA), and three oil firms (Gazprom, Petrobras, and CNOOC).

EMERGING STOCK MARKET RETURNS

Emerging markets tend to be volatile and crisis-prone. But before examining the risks of investing in emerging markets, let's consider the returns earned in the past. The data sets for emerging market stocks do not extend back as far as those of developed countries. There are indexes for individual countries that extend back into the 1970s, but the broad indexes begin in the late 1980s. As in the case of the stocks of industrial countries, MSCI provides stock market indexes for the emerging markets that are widely used as benchmarks for emerging market funds. These indexes start in 1988. There is a composite index for the emerging markets consisting of 21 emerging markets including five from Latin America, eight from Asia, and five from

Europe and the Middle East. There are also regional indexes. The Latin American emerging market consists of Brazil, Chile, Colombia, Mexico, and Peru. The Asian index consists of China, Indonesia, India, Korea, Malaysia, Philippines, Taiwan, and Thailand. The Europe and Middle East index consists of Czech Republic, Hungary, Poland, Russia, and Turkey.[7]

Table 9.3 examines returns on the composite index for the emerging markets as a whole as well as regional emerging market indexes. The table compares emerging market returns with those of the S&P 500 and the MSCI EAFE developed country indexes. Let's summarize the four broad patterns:

1. Emerging market stock returns as a whole exceed those of the S&P 500 and far exceed those of the MSCI EAFE index. Recall that the EAFE index suffered badly from the collapse of Japan beginning in 1990. So any comparison that begins in the late 1980s is bound to show EAFE in a bad light.
2. Over the whole period, emerging market Asia was a disappointment to investors. Returns beginning in 1988 fall far short of the emerging market index as a whole. The reason for this poor performance will be examined below.
3. The Latin America index earns extraordinary returns during this period. No doubt the period studied matters here. Latin America suffered a "lost decade" in the 1980s because of the Latin American debt crisis that began in 1982. From low levels Latin American stock markets (as a whole) have risen sharply.
4. The Europe and the Middle East index has also lagged far behind Latin America.

TABLE 9.3 Emerging Market and Developed Market Stock Returns, 1988–2012

Market	Average Return
Emerging Markets	
MSCI composite	12.7%
Asia	8.4%
Latin America	19.4%
Europe and Middle East	8.7%
Developed Markets	
S&P 500	9.7%
MSCI EAFE	5.5%

Data sources: MSCI and S&P Dow Jones Indices.

As shown in Table 9.3, returns for the Asian region are much lower than those for the other regions as well as emerging markets as a whole. This is a true puzzle because Asia has grown faster than any other region in the world. The largest emerging market economy, China's, has had double-digit growth for much of the period. Shouldn't growth translate into high stock returns? It turns out that the answer is "not necessarily." The evidence is that many emerging market countries that have high growth rates actually have lower stock returns than those with lower growth rates.[8]

Economists do not have a good explanation for why there is no positive relationship between economic growth and stock returns. The economic causation should go from high economic growth to high firm profits to high stock returns. There could be a break in the chain if high expected profits have already priced stocks in that country relatively high. Think of Japan in the 1980s when future growth and future profits appeared to have no upper limit, so price-earnings ratios were sky high. There could also be a break between high growth and high profits. Certainly Soviet Russia had high growth (at least in the 1950s and 1960s), but were profits in this state-controlled economy high? (By profits we mean economic profits since all large enterprises were state owned). In any case, the automatic assumption on Wall Street that a fast-growing country or region will deliver high returns seems unwarranted at best.

To investigate the peculiar case of China in more detail, consider the returns on Chinese stocks beginning in December 1992 (when the MSCI China series begins) through 2012. The average return on China's investable index is *0.0 percent per year from 1993 through 2012*. It is hard to believe that an economy growing as fast as China's could deliver such paltry returns. The MSCI Asia index performed much better than the China index with a positive return of 5.9 percent/annum over the same period. But over the same period, the S&P 500 index earned 7.4 percent per annum. It's important to note that the returns just cited are "investable" returns, so they record what an average foreign investor would earn in these markets. Growth evidently does not reward all investors.

China, however, did have a terrific run late in the period. For the two years prior to the peak of its market in October 2007, the MSCI China index had a return of 306.4 percent! No wonder investors were rushing into this market. From that peak, the Chinese index fell 64.8 percent through October 2008. Through December 2012, it has again risen spectacularly by 98.2 percent. It has been quite a roller coaster ride. The key question is whether China's recent stock market performance is more indicative of the future than the full record of returns since 1992. China will no doubt remain volatile. But will it deliver more than the paltry returns seen *on average* since December 1992?

RISKS OF INVESTING IN EMERGING STOCK MARKETS

Emerging market stocks are inherently risky. Using one common measure of volatility, the standard deviation, emerging market stocks are two thirds more risky than U.S. stocks and almost one third more risky than foreign industrial country stocks. But these conventional measures of volatility may underestimate the risks of emerging market stocks because these markets are so prone to crises.

Consider an investor trying to make decisions about emerging market stocks in early 1997. At that time, there were only nine years of data from the MSCI database. Over the nine years ending in 1996, the compound return on the Asian Emerging Market Index was 16.6 percent per annum. It's true that over the same period, the S&P 500 offered equally hefty returns of 16.5 percent per year. But the correlations between emerging markets and U.S. stocks were low enough to justify large allocations to emerging market stocks.

In early 1997, few investors realized that Asian markets were about to be hit by a financial tsunami that would drive many markets down by 75 percent or more. The crisis first hit the Bangkok foreign exchange market in early July 1997 when the Thai central bank was forced to float the Thai baht. The value of the baht was cut in half almost immediately (with the dollar initially rising against the Baht from Bt 25/$ to Bt 50/$).

The collapse of the baht soon set off speculation against the Malaysian ringgit, the Indonesian rupiah, the Korean won, and other Asian currencies. Why was there such widespread contagion? The most important reason is that firms in all of these countries had loaded up on dollar debt and other foreign currency debt. Once rumors of depreciation spread in the market, these firms rushed to hedge their foreign currency liabilities, which had the effect of driving down their currencies. If a fire breaks out in a ballroom, every one heads to the exits at the same time.

Stock market investors suffered grievously. The Asian emerging markets as a whole returned—32.1 percent per annum in 1997–98. The stock markets of Thailand, Malaysia, and Korea all fell by 60 percent or more (in dollar terms). The contagion even spread to Latin America where markets fell 7.6 percent per annum over the two-year period. Within a few years afterward, emerging markets as a whole had recovered most of their lost ground. But in the case of the Asian stock markets, the index return per annum over the whole period from 1988 to 2012 is still over 8 percent per annum below what it was at the end of 1996!

The Asian crisis is not an isolated incident. Other markets have been prone to crisis. Consider three other important examples: Mexico in 1994, Russia in 1998, and Argentina in 2000–2002.

1. The Mexican crisis was precipitated by a currency collapse just as in the case of Thailand. In December 1994 following the inauguration of President Ernesto Zedillo, the peso depreciated from Ps 3.5/$ to Ps 7.0/$. The depreciation led to widespread bankruptcies among Mexican firms (including major banks) because so much debt was denominated in dollars. The impact on the stock market was dramatic. The Mexican market fell by 60 percent (in dollar terms). It took several years for the Mexican economy to recover from this disaster.
2. The Russian crisis involved a default by the Russian government on its debt rather than currency depreciation. The Russian stock market began a dramatic decline a year before the actual default, which occurred in July 1998. Between September 1997 and a year later, the Russian stock market declined (in U.S. dollar terms) by over 80 percent. The bond default itself precipitated a fall in many bond markets worldwide.
3. The Argentine crisis began as early as 2000 when the long-established peg to the U.S. dollar began to be seriously questioned. In January 2002, Argentina was forced to float its currency and put controls on financial outflows. By that time, the stock market had already plummeted. From February 2000 until June 2002, a few months after the crisis, the Argentine market fell over 80 percent in dollar terms.

Even in the absence of specific crises, these markets tend to be highly volatile. Consider the example of China once again. China's stock market is like a roller coaster. In the two years starting in December 1993, China's market fell 58 percent. It recovered most of this ground by 1997, but in August 1997 it fell sharply again as the Asian crisis hit. Within a year, the Chinese market had fallen by almost 80 percent (measured in dollar terms). Investors must be prepared for volatility if they invest in these markets.

Prior to the 2008 crisis, emerging markets returns soared over 85 percent from December 2005 to December 2007. So it has been hard to convince investors of the risks of investing in emerging market stocks. Of course, the plunge by 53 percent in 2008 may help.[9]

SO WHY INVEST IN EMERGING MARKETS AT ALL?

Investors remain excited about emerging markets despite past episodes of crises and market plunges. One reason is that these markets have done so well recently. Investors seem to pay a lot more attention to recent returns than longer records of past returns. Why else would investors be excited by commodities and, in particular, gold as an investment? But another reason is the inherent belief that high growth will eventually reward investors. Most experts believe that emerging market economies will grow faster than the tired, old industrial economies of Europe, Japan, and the United States, with their aging populations and debt-ridden governments.

Let me not stand in the way of this excitement. After all, the previous section has already warned investors about the risks of emerging markets. In fact, the emerging markets have come alive in recent years. The catalyst, if you believe in magic, was a speech by Jim O'Neill of Goldman Sachs in November 2001 that introduced the term "BRICs" standing for Brazil, Russia, India and China. Shortly after O'Neill's speech, BRIC returns started to soar. But so also did the returns on emerging markets in general.

Figure 9.5 presents the returns in the four BRIC countries as well as emerging markets as a whole. The chart divides returns into two periods: 1995 to 2001 and 2002 to 2012.[10] For the seven years of the first period, only Russia provides attractive returns for investors. China loses 16.8 percent per year over this period, and the emerging markets as a whole lose 4.1 percent per year.

Once the BRICs are introduced, however, the whole emerging markets sector comes alive. For the 11 years ending in 2012, the average return in the

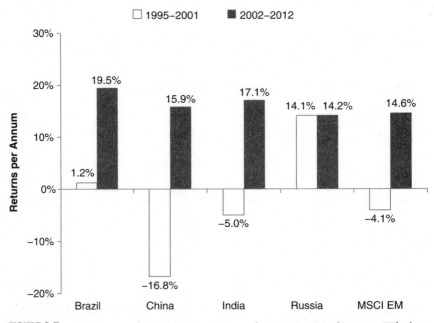

FIGURE 9.5   Returns in the BRIC Countries and Emerging Markets as a Whole
Data source: MSCI.

emerging markets is 14.6 percent. And in Brazil, the top performer among the BRICs, the average return is 19.5 percent. No wonder the term *BRICs* has caught on so well.

Here is the crucial question facing investors: Now that the emerging markets have begun to fulfill their promise, will they continue to thrive? Are we justified in believing that their higher growth rates (compared with those of the industrial countries) will be translated into higher stock returns? One leading investor believes so. In the annual report of the Yale Endowment, David Swensen and his staff always provide estimates of investment returns that Yale expects to receive in the future. The horizon is not measured in years, but decades (as is appropriate for an endowment that has been around for centuries). In the latest report, Swensen estimates that emerging market stock returns will be 1½ percent higher than those in the United States and the other industrial countries. Given the prospect of higher returns, it may make sense for even ordinary investors to have an allocation to emerging market stocks.

CONCLUDING COMMENTS

The world's stock markets are divided into developed and emerging for a good reason—emerging markets are riskier. The dividing line between the countries themselves is somewhat arbitrary, but the division between the assets of these two sets of countries is a meaningful one. Consistent with higher risks, emerging market stocks have delivered stellar returns, especially during the last decade, and promise higher returns in the future.

NOTES

1. The phrase "emerging markets" was introduced by economists at the International Finance Corporation, an arm of the World Bank that aims to promote private investment in the developing countries.
2. All gross national income statistics are from the World Bank, World Development Indicators Database, July 2013.
3. Gross national income (GNI) measures the income side of the national income accounts, while the better known gross domestic product (GDP) measures the production side of those accounts. Emerging market status is based on GNI per capita.
4. The "unadjusted" figure is obtained by using a moving average of the past three years' exchange rates. The World Bank calls this the "Atlas method" for calculating GNI.

5. Unlike most industrial countries, U.S. per capita income rises rather than falls when adjusted for the (relatively low) cost of living in the United States.
6. MSCI has indicated that both South Korea and Taiwan are "under review" for possible upgrade to developed country status. South Korea's per capita income in 2012 had reached almost $22,670 (and almost $31,000 on a PPP-adjusted basis).
7. The three remaining countries are Egypt, Morocco, and South Africa.
8. This evidence is reviewed in Chapter 6 of Marston (2011).
9. That's compared with a 37 percent decline in the S&P 500 in 2008. In 2007–2008, the world learned that even industrial countries can suffer major financial crises!
10. Russia's returns begin only in 1995.

REFERENCES

Marston, Richard C. 2011. *Portfolio Design: A Modern Approach to Asset Allocation*. Hoboken, NJ: John Wiley & Sons.
MSCI/Barra. 2009. MSCI Market Classification Framework (June).
Standard & Poor's. 2010 and 2012. *Global Stock Markets Factbook*. New York: McGraw-Hill.
World Bank, World Development Indicators Database. 2013. www .worldbank.org.

CHAPTER 10

Investing in Bonds: The Basics

Bonds are the bedrock of any portfolio. As with buildings built on bedrock, portfolios with bonds have a solid base. We don't expect to earn high returns with bond investments. After all, bonds provide fixed coupons with little upside, at least in normal times. But we expect our bond investments to be safe.

Unfortunately, bonds have weaknesses. These solid rocks crumble when inflation occurs. In the inflation-ridden decade of the 1970s, bonds lost ground to inflation. So bond investors ended up poorer than at the beginning of the decade. This is something to keep in mind when we examine the history of bond returns. We should also be mindful of credit risk. If a bond provides a much higher yield than offered on U.S. Treasury bonds, the bond probably has credit risk to worry about.

This chapter will study U.S. Treasury bonds, bonds that are free of default risk (despite the views of one rating agency).[1] That will allow us to examine the impact of inflation on bond yields. We will also study how bond yields vary by maturity. In this chapter we will also discuss various strategies for investing in any type of bonds (not just Treasuries). Strategies will include "buy and hold," "laddering" the bond portfolio, and investing in bonds via mutual funds. Then in the next chapter we will study non-Treasury bonds like those issued by corporations. Credit risk is obviously an issue with some of those bonds. Finally, we will examine municipal bonds. The tax advantages of municipals are examined, but so also are the credit risks of this sector of the bond market.

BOND YIELDS AND BOND RETURNS

Bonds are often favored by investors because they provide "fixed income" in contrast to the variable returns offered by equities and by most other assets. A stream of fixed income payments is often viewed as essential to retirees as well as many institutional investors because of their need for steady income. Yet bond yields represent only part of the return on bonds. The variation in yields over time leads to capital gains and losses on existing bonds that sometimes dominate the total return from holding these bonds. In the 1970s, for example, bond *yields* were quite high relative to long-run averages. Yet bond *returns* were quite abysmal because of capital losses. As inflation and interest rates rose over the decade, existing bonds fell in value. So the total return on these bonds, consisting of capital gains as well as coupons, was far lower than the coupons themselves. Returns on bonds in the 1970s were lower still when adjusted for inflation.

How does inflation affect interest rates? In the short run, central banks often play a critical role in setting short-term interest rates. Inflation plays only a secondary role. For example, the Federal Reserve directly controls the Federal Funds interest rate, the rate at which banks borrow in the interbank market. And other short-term dollar interest rates rise in tandem, such as the 30-day Treasury bill interest rate and the interest rate on short-term bank certificates of deposit (or CDs). So if the Fed raises the Fed Funds rate by 25 "basis points," or 0.25 percent, the Treasury bill rate, bank deposit rates, and interest rates on money market mutual funds are likely to rise by a similar amount (in normal times, at least). In the long-run, however, the role of the Federal Reserve is very different. In the long run, U.S. interest rates are *primarily determined by inflation*. And it is the Fed's role in helping to determine the inflation rate that matters.

Recall the history of U.S. interest rates since the mid-1950s as shown in Figure 3.3. Except for a temporary bout of inflation during the Korean War, inflation remained low in the United States throughout most of the 1950s and 1960s. Inflation peaked following two oil price shocks in 1973–1974 and 1979. Beginning in the late 1960s, interest rates slowly but surely responded to rising inflation as inflation expectations became imbedded in bond yields. The 10-year Treasury yield reached double digits by late 1979. The same inflation expectations led to rising wage demands and to downward pressure on the U.S. dollar. To lower interest yields from their highs in the late 1970s, it was necessary for the Federal Reserve to pursue a tight monetary policy. This shift in policy began in 1979 with the appointment of Paul Volcker as chair of the Federal Reserve Board. The low interest rates that we experience today were "made" at the Fed. But in the long run, low interest rates result from low inflation, not from the Fed lowering the Fed Funds rate.

To provide further evidence of the link between inflation and interest rates, consider the bond *returns* earned on long-term Treasury bonds in each decade since 1950 as shown in Figure 10.1 This chart shows the nominal bond return and the inflation-adjusted "real" bond return, both measured per annum. The latter is obtained by deflating the nominal return by the inflation rate. The low bond yields of the 1950s were more than matched by

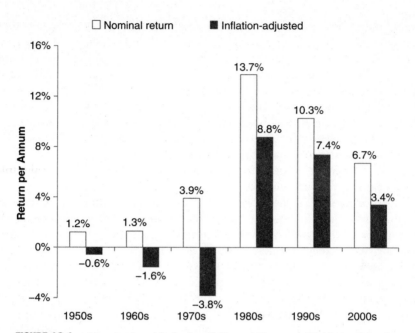

FIGURE 10.1 Nominal and Inflation-Adjusted Treasury Yields by Decade
Data source: Morningstar.

inflation. So the investor actually *lost* money *once inflation was taken into account.* During that decade, the investor earned 1.2 percent per annum on average measured in nominal terms, but inflation averaged 1.8 percent per annum.[2] The value of the investor's bond portfolio was smaller at the end of the decade than at the outset once the rise in the cost of living was taken into account. Over the next two decades, the 1960s and 1970s, inflation expectations evidently lagged behind actual inflation so bond holders earned even larger losses on their bonds with negative *real* bond returns of −1.6 and −3.8 percent (per annum), respectively, in these two decades! Fixed income earners were deceived by the "steadiness" of the coupons on their bonds. The real value of the bonds was being eroded by inflation, and the coupons themselves were being debased by rising price levels.

The terrific returns earned since 1981 are a direct result of the Fed's policy of fighting inflation. Over this period, bond yields and inflation expectations lagged behind actual inflation once again. But in this case, bond holders were surprised by falling inflation and they were rewarded with unusually large real returns on their bonds. In the decade from 1981 to 1990, the compound real return on the long-term (20-year) Treasury bond averaged 8.8 percent/annum. That return was followed by a 7.4 percent/annum compound return in the 1990s. Returns like these can be earned when inflation falls from 13.5 percent to its current level and when bond yields fall from almost 15 percent to less than 5 percent.

The wide range of returns over the 60-year period is of concern in itself. To see decade-long, inflation-adjusted returns ranging from –3.8 to +8.8 percent is quite alarming. But that shows the potential vulnerability of "safe" bond investments to inflation. It's true that the average real return over the full six decades is close to longer-run averages. From 1951 to 2010, the inflation adjusted return on the 20-year Treasury was 2.3 percent. If the period is extended back to 1926, the average return rises to 2.4 percent. But the long-run averages hide a lot of variation.

What influences Treasury returns besides inflation? Treasury yields are certainly influenced by the maturity of the bond. Usually, longer-term bonds earn higher yields than shorter-term bonds. So in most periods, the "term structure" of interest rates is upward sloping, which means that 20-year Treasury bonds, for instance, pay higher yields than five-year Treasuries. Consider Figure 10.2, which shows the "term structure" of yields on U.S. Treasury bonds in three different years, 1985, 1995, and 2005. In all three years the economy was growing, so the term structure of yields had its normal upward slope. (If a recession had occurred in one of these years, the term structure of

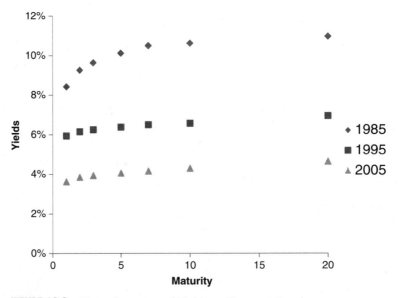

FIGURE 10.2   Term Structure of Yields on Treasury Bonds
Data source: Federal Reserve Board.

yields could have been inverted temporarily, particularly if the Federal Reserve had recently raised short-term interest rates to cool the economy.) Over the three decades shown in the figure, inflation and interest rates were dropping. So the whole term structure of yields fell over time. Thus the figure illustrates two of the three determinants of bond yields: inflation and the maturity of the bond. The third factor, default risk, is negligible in the case of Treasuries.

Bond yields are only one component of bond returns. Bond *returns* reflect both the coupon paid and the capital gain over the holding period of the return. Table 10.1 breaks down the bond return into two components: the income earned on the bond plus the capital gain. The table reports bond returns for two maturities of U.S. Treasuries. The long-term bond is a 20-year Treasury bond, while the medium-term is a five-year Treasury. First consider returns for the 30-year period ending in 2010 (at the bottom of the table). In periods of falling interest rates, such as those in the 1980s until present, long-term bonds should outperform medium-term bonds. That is indeed the case. In the table, the return on the 20-year bond is 2.2 percent higher than on the five-year bond during the period from 1981 to 2010. During this period, the capital gain component of the bond return contributed 3.1 percent to the total return of the 20-year bond.

These results are reversed in the earlier period ending in 1980 when inflation was rising. Even though both Treasury bonds have about the same income during the earlier period, the capital loss on the 20-year bond is much larger than on the five-year bond. So the total return on the longer-term bond is only 2.3 percent compared with a 4.1 percent return on the five-year bond. These are miserably low returns in a period when inflation averaged 4.3 percent/annum. Both returns, as discussed above, would be *negative* if inflation was taken into account.

TABLE 10.1   Treasury Bond Returns: Income and Capital Gains

	Income Return	Capital Gain	Total Return
1951—1980			
Long-term	5.2%	–2.9%	2.3%
Medium-term	5.1%	–1.1%	4.1%
1981—2010			
Long-term	7.7%	3.1%	10.9%
Medium-term	6.8%	1.9%	8.7%

Notes: The long-term Treasury bond has a maturity of 20 years, while the medium-term Treasury bond has a maturity of five years.
Data source: Morningstar.

What are the lessons from this table? *Bond returns are more variable the longer the maturity of the bond.* In periods of falling inflation and falling interest rates, bond returns are maximized if you own longer-term bonds. In periods of rising inflation and rising interest rates, bond returns are worse if you own longer-term bonds. One lesson from the table is that it is best to hold long-term bonds if interest rates are falling. That's the lesson that all investors learned well over the past 30 years. It was a glorious period of falling interest rates. But what if interest rates are likely to rise in the future? *Then you shorten maturities.*

BUT WHAT IF I BUY AND HOLD?

Some investors may decide to avoid capital gains by buying and holding a long-term bond. In that case, so the reasoning goes, an investor can avoid suffering from exposure to market fluctuations. That is, the investor's investment statement will show a constant value for the bond investment (if the statement reports the so-called "book value" of the bonds). But is the investor really protected from the market?

Why is it so important to ask this question? In early 2013, Treasury yields are near all-time lows. Let me go out on a limb to say that these yields will not stay low forever. And if yields do rise, we need to know how investors can best protect themselves. If they buy and hold, will that protect them?

Let's consider a simple example. Suppose that an investor buys a 20-year bond in early 2013 with a yield of 2.5 percent. And let's imagine that bond yields rise to 5 percent within the next five years. That's not too farfetched because *real* (inflation-adjusted) interest rates average about 2.5 percent in the long run. With even moderate inflation, a nominal yield of 5 percent could easily prevail. If new bonds yield 5 percent, then the price of the investor's existing bond will fall. But let's ignore this change in the bond's price. After all, the investor thinks that the book value of the bond and the coupon of the bond are all that matters. In what sense has the investor suffered a loss? Well, until the bond matures, the investor is foregoing the opportunity to earn 5 percent interest rather than 2.5 percent. That's as much of a loss as is suffered by the bond investor who sells the original bond and realizes a capital loss. Buying and holding does not shield the investor from losses when interest rates rise.

It might be helpful to look at actual investment experience during the time of rising interest rates in the late 1960s and 1970s. Suppose that an investor bought a $10,000 10-year bond at the beginning of 1965 with a yield of 4.2 percent. This investor would see a steady income of $4,200 each year for the next 10 years. But in the meantime, yields on new bonds were rising. If the investor paid attention to the value of the existing bond, it fell as yields rose. But let's assume the investor held the bond until maturity. Let's examine the investment performance by comparing the investor's return with that of another investor who held short-term securities (called Treasury bills). Consider Figure 10.3 where the yield on a 10-year Treasury bond in 1965 is compared with a succession of yields on one-year Treasury bills. When the 10-year bond is first issued, the one-year interest rate is below the 10-year. But the interest rate on the one-year Treasury is higher by the time of the first rollover. In fact, as seen in Figure 10.3, the one-year interest rate keeps rising until 1969 and never declines back to the original 10-year Treasury yield.

The potential risks of a buy-and-hold strategy are exacerbated if the real returns on a bond are measured rather than nominal returns. Inflation became a serious problem in the 1960s. Indeed, interest rates were rising because of rising inflation. Over the 10-year period starting in 1965, inflation averaged 5.2 percent. With the investor stuck in a 4.2 percent bond, the average inflation-adjusted return on this bond was actually negative at −1.0 percent. It's true that at maturity the investor was fully paid what was promised by the government. Both principal and interest were paid on schedule. But by the end of the 10-year period, the investor was poorer *in real terms* than when the investment was made. If a 10-year bond had been

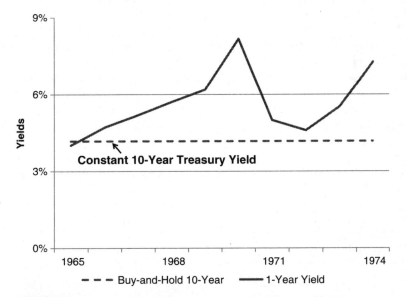

FIGURE 10.3 Buy-and-Hold Strategy for Bonds When Yields Rise
Data source: Federal Reserve Board.

purchased 10 years later at the beginning of 1975, the yield would have been a much higher 7.4 percent. But over the subsequent 10 years, inflation would rise to an average of 7.3 percent per year. So the investor barely broke even in real terms. Of course, if the investor persisted for another 10 years when inflation started to fall sharply, he would have been amply rewarded. But the point is that locking in bond yields does not shield the investor if inflation rises.

It wouldn't be fair to recount experiences with bond investing in the 1960s and 1970s without also examining the past few decades of falling yields and falling inflation. Let's imagine that in 1981 an investor decides to invest in a 30-year Treasury bond yielding 14.5 percent. The investor chooses this bond at a time when inflation is still running at a 9 percent rate (having fallen from over 12 percent in 1980). Paul Volcker, the Chair of the Federal Reserve Board during this period, is busy trying to bring inflation down, but most investors remain skeptical that the Federal Reserve can stick to its anti-inflation policies. Certainly support for Volcker in the Reagan Administration and Congress is lukewarm. Most observers blame Volcker's policies for the double-dip recession that is occurring. (The U.S. economy emerged from a brief recession in July 1980 only to fall back into recession in July 1981. That recession was a deep one that saw unemployment rates peak at 10.8 percent.) Despite uncertainty about whether the Fed's policy would continue, this investor decides to buy the 30-year bond. How will the investor fare?

Now let's imagine that the investor were to "fast-forward" to 2011, the year when this 30-year bond matures. The investor has enjoyed 30 years of high coupons. There is no doubt that this bond investment has been a real triumph. What is the investor's annual return during this period? The answer is simple: in nominal terms, the investor has made 14.5 percent per annum. In real terms, the result is almost as dramatic because inflation has declined so sharply during the period. The average real return is 11.1 percent. This was a very astute investor, or at least a very lucky one. Readers will wish that they had bought the 30-year bond along with this investor. If only we had all known how successful the Fed would be in bringing down inflation and interest rates!

BOND INVESTING WHEN INTEREST RATES ARE AT RECORD LOWS

What are the lessons from these past experiences? The late 1960s and the 1970s were a disastrous period for bond investors. There is no reason to believe that U.S. history is likely to repeat itself. We will probably not see double-digit bond yields anytime soon. Nonetheless, bond investors should be wary about the current environment of record low interest rates. If interest rates were to rise significantly, we could very well experience periods of *negative* bond returns. And, even if nominal bond returns remain positive, investors could see *negative real (or inflation-adjusted) bond returns*. If this is the case, locking in long-term bond yields may not make much sense. Investors in a long-term bond might be able to sleep well at night knowing that their interest payments will be stable (at least in nominal terms). But these investors should be more concerned with their bond returns than their bond yields.

If interest rates are headed higher, what should an investor do? The simplest answer is to shorten bond maturities. Instead of investing in long-term bonds with maturities of 10 to 30 years, investors might choose bonds with maturities less than five years. This strategy would be costly in terms of yield. In May 2013, a five-year Treasury bond provides a yield of only 0.84 percent, whereas a 10-year Treasury has a yield of 1.93 percent and a 20-year has a yield of 2.73 percent. But a five-year bond would be less exposed to interest rate risk.

When I said that investors should pay attention to the maturity of their bonds, I wasn't being precise enough. Investors worried about future increases in interest rates should pay more attention to the duration of their bonds than to the maturity of those bonds. Duration takes into account cash flows that occur prior to the maturity of the bond, so it is a better measure of the average maturity of all of the bond's cash flows.[3] The duration of a bond tells the investor how sensitive is the bond's return to increases in the interest rate. For example, the return on a bond with a duration of three years will fall 3 percent if the interest rate rises by 1 percent. The return on a bond with duration of 15 years will fall by 15 percent in response to the same increase in interest rates. So the latter bond is five times as sensitive to interest rate increases!

In the spring of 2013, it makes sense for investors to keep the duration of their bond portfolios lower than five years. If they do so, investors will still suffer losses if interest rates increase. But the losses will be much smaller than from a long-term bond portfolio.

LADDERING THE BOND PORTFOLIO

Is there an alternative to "buy and hold?" One obvious alternative is to invest in a diversified portfolio of bonds with varying maturities. For an investor with moderate wealth, a diversified portfolio can be obtained through investing in a bond mutual fund. A mutual fund can mix a variety

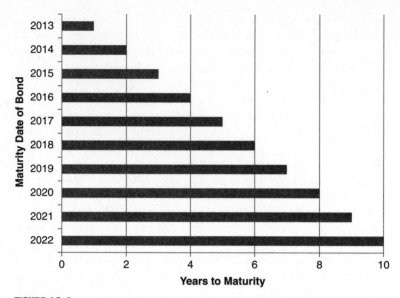

FIGURE 10.4   Bond Portfolio Laddered with 10 Bonds

of maturities. And, jumping ahead to the next chapter's topic, a mutual fund can provide a mixture of different types of credit risk.

Yet many investors want to own bonds directly. Is there a way to invest in bonds without betting on a single maturity? Many investors elect to "ladder" a bond portfolio, buying bonds every year so that there are a variety of maturities in the portfolio at any given time. Consider a stylized bond portfolio as shown in Figure 10.4 consisting of 10 bonds maturing in each of the next 10 years. One bond in this portfolio will mature at the end of 2013. That bond had been purchased nine years ago when 10-year bond yields were 4.1 percent. This bond has just one year of maturity left, but its interest rate is quite different from that of a one-year bond issued at the beginning of 2013 (which bears an interest rate of 0.15 percent). The portfolio also has a new 10-year bond that will mature in 2022 bearing an interest rate of 1.9 percent.

What does a laddered portfolio provide to the investor? It certainly reduces the volatility of yields within a portfolio. Consider Figure 10.5 where the yields on a laddered portfolio are compared with yields on pure 10-year and one-year bond portfolios. Notice how volatile the one-year yield is. As stated earlier, the Federal Reserve controls very short-term interest rates through the Fed Funds rate. But even one-year yields will be significantly influenced by Fed policy. When a recession hits, as in 2000, the Fed drives

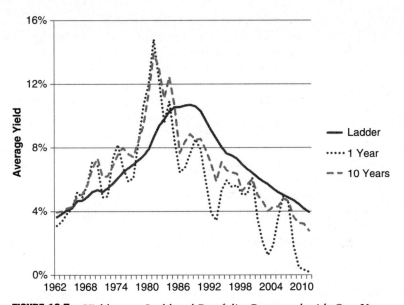

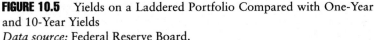

FIGURE 10.5 Yields on a Laddered Portfolio Compared with One-Year and 10-Year Yields
Data source: Federal Reserve Board.

interest rates down with active intervention in the short-term market. So the one-interest rate falls sharply. The 10-year interest rate also might react to the Fed stimulus, but this rate will move much less sharply.

Why is the yield on the laddered portfolio so much smoother? The reason is that this yield is an average of past and current interest rates so changes in yield cannot occur abruptly. In times of rising inflation such as the 1970s, the laddered portfolio will delay the arrival of higher yields. And it will smooth the abrupt changes in yields (as experienced in the late 1970s). The peak for yields on the laddered portfolio actually occurs as late as the mid-1980s. By the same token, a laddered portfolio will delay the decline in yields as inflation falls. That is also seen in Figure 10.5. For the entire period from the mid-1980s on, the laddered portfolio provides higher yields than the 10-year and one-year bonds.

A laddered portfolio does not solve problems posed by current low yields. If interest rates rise from current levels, the longer-term bonds in the portfolio will suffer more than proportionately. So the longer the duration of bonds in the ladder, the worse the portfolio will fare. It's true that a laddered portfolio will suffer fewer losses than a portfolio of long-term bonds held by a "buy-and-hold" investor because the ladder includes shorter-term bonds. But losses will still occur if bond yields rise. If investors fear rising interest rates, they need to keep the average duration of their bond portfolios relatively short whether or not they invest in a laddered portfolio.

Now let's contrast this laddered portfolio with a bond mutual fund. To make the contrast as clear as possible, let's imagine that the mutual fund manager decided to build a laddered portfolio with the same bonds as in the portfolio described in Figure 10.5. (Usually fund managers would have strategies more complex than this one). How would the two portfolios differ?

1. The mutual fund manager would charge a fee for the mutual fund. Fees range from less than 0.10 percent for index mutual funds to over 1 percent for some actively managed funds. The laddered portfolio instead incurs transaction expenses. There may be direct brokerage fees involved. But just as importantly, there will be hidden expenses because the buyer of a bond pays the ask price while the seller of a bond receives a (lower) bid price. And for lightly traded issues, these two prices can be quite different. (It should be noted that an investor can buy a Treasury bond directly from the U.S. government thereby minimizing such hidden expenses). Of course, the mutual fund manager also has to pay an ask price when the manager buys a bond. But because of the large scale of mutual fund purchases, the manager is likely to pay a lower price for the bond than an individual investor. That is, the bid-ask spread faced by a mutual fund manager is likely to be smaller than that facing an individual investor. So don't necessarily assume that the mutual fund route is the more expensive one. In fact, it's hard to beat the cost of some of the index mutual funds.

2. The second difference is that the mutual fund manager would be required to "mark to market" the portfolio, telling the investor exactly how much return was earned each month. So during a period of rising yields, the return on the portfolio would be lower than the yields reported to an investor in the laddered portfolio. Of course, both portfolios have the same return because we are assuming they consist of the same set of laddered bonds. The difference is that the mutual fund investor knows the total return on the bond portfolio (including capital gains and losses), whereas the investor in the laddered portfolio can remain blissfully unaware. Maybe ignorance is bliss, but it's important to understand that gains and losses on the laddered portfolio exist whether or not we acknowledge them.

There is an advantage of mutual funds that is hard to beat with an individual bond portfolio. A bond mutual fund can diversify credit risk and provide the investor with a wide range of different types of bonds. That is a considerable advantage once the investor moves beyond (ultrasafe) U.S. Treasury bonds.

The next chapter considers three types of bonds worthy of attention by investors. First, there are U.S. taxable bonds issued by corporations and other entities. Then there are Treasury Inflation-Protected Securities (or TIPS), a new type of bond begun in the late 1990s. Finally, there are tax-exempt municipal bonds.

NOTES

1. In August, 2011, Standard & Poor's downgraded U.S. Treasury debt from AAA (outstanding) to AA+ (excellent). The other rating agencies, Moody's and Fitch, maintained AAA ratings for this debt.
2. As Chapter 2 explains, the real return is calculated as $(1 + 0.012)/(1 + 0.018) - 1 = -0.006$ or -0.6 percent.
3. The duration of a bond is almost always shorter than the maturity of that bond. The one exception is when the bond is a "zero coupon" bond whose only cash flow is at the maturity of the bond, in which case the duration is equal to the maturity.

CHAPTER 11

Investing in Bonds:
The Wider Bond Market

Chapter 10 introduced investors to the bond market. However, the examples involved only one type of bond, U.S. Treasuries. The reason why we focus so much attention on Treasuries is that they are the purest type of bond. There is virtually no credit risk to these bonds (despite what Standard & Poor's might contend). And Treasury bonds have the most active markets so their prices always reflect current conditions. To study the basics of the bond market, there is no better bond to focus on than Treasuries. Yet the U.S. bond market has many other types of bonds including corporate bonds, mortgage-backed bonds, and tax-exempt municipal bonds. In fact, U.S. Treasury bonds constitute only 28.6 percent of all U.S. bonds.

Investors should consider looking beyond Treasuries for three reasons. First, other bonds may offer higher yields than Treasuries. The attractiveness of higher yields is particularly important in 2013 when Treasury yields are at record lows. Second, investing in other bonds helps to diversify the portfolio. Third, municipal bonds, in particular, offer earnings that are exempt from Federal income tax.

To see the range of bonds available in the U.S. market, consider Figure 11.1, which reports the distribution of bonds outstanding as reported by the Securities Industry and Financial Markets Association. At the end of 2012, the total value of the U.S. bond market was $38.1 trillion. Of that total, 28.6 percent was represented by Treasury bonds, 9.7 percent by municipal bonds, and 23.8 percent by corporate bonds (including so-called high-yield bonds). There are also a variety of other types of bonds that are discussed later in the chapter.

This chapter begins by discussing corporate bonds and other investment-grade bonds. Then high-yield bonds and Treasury Inflation-Protected Bonds (TIPs) are examined in turn. The last section of the chapter discusses municipal bonds in some detail because those bonds are so commonly included in the portfolios of individual investors.

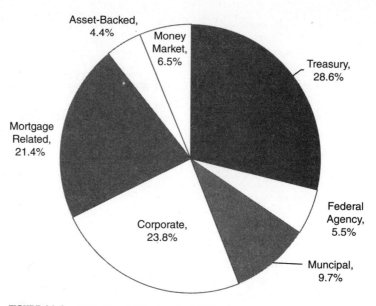

FIGURE 11.1　U.S. Bond Market in 2012
Source: Securities Industry and Financial Markets Association,
2012.

CORPORATE BONDS

Corporate bonds have been issued in the United States for over 100 years, so it is fitting that we begin a discussion of the non-Treasury bond market by focusing on corporate bonds. We have yield data from the Federal Reserve extending back to 1919. There are other historical series reaching back even further in time. It's not that we need to study data from such earlier periods, but it just shows that corporate bonds have long had a prominent place in American portfolios.

Because corporate bonds have higher default risk than U.S. Treasury bonds, their bond yields are correspondingly higher (adjusted for maturity). Consider the default premiums for investment grade corporate bonds. Both Standard & Poor's and Moody's rate the default risk on corporate bonds. According to the classification by Moody's, investment grade bonds are rated in four categories ranging from AAA to BAA. The Federal Reserve has two series for corporate bonds in its database, both provided by Moody's. The series are for bonds rated AAA and BAA. Since these bonds have a maturity of at least 20 years, they should be compared with a 20-year Treasury bond. Over the period from October 1993 to December 2012,[1] the 10-year Treasury bond had an average yield of 5.3 percent. Over the same period, the yield on the highest rated of these corporate bonds, those with AAA rating, averaged 6.2 percent for a premium of 0.9 percent over Treasuries. The lowest-rated investment grade bonds, those with a BAA rating, had an average yield of 7.1 percent, so the premium over Treasuries was 1.8 percent and the premium over the highest-grade corporate bonds was 0.9 percent. These premiums give some indication of the importance of default risk in the pricing of non-Treasury bonds.

Yet there are other differences between corporate bonds and Treasuries that should be noted because they will also influence the premiums found in corporate yields. Treasury bonds are exempt from state and local income taxes, while corporate bonds are not. Corporate bonds may have call provisions that allow a corporation to call in a bond prior to maturity. If such a call provision exists, the yield on the corporate bond has to be high enough to compensate the investor for this risk of the bond being called early. There is also generally less liquidity in the corporate bond market than in the Treasury market. So if an investor has to sell the bond, it will be harder to find buyers for the issue. Everything else being equal, the corporate bond has to have a high enough yield to compensate the investor for higher liquidity risk.

Figure 11.2 displays the yields on AAA and BAA corporate bonds over the past 22 years. Also included in the figure is the yield on 20-year Treasury bonds (beginning in 1993) for comparison. Notice how the yield spreads between the two corporate bonds and between the corporate bonds and Treasuries vary over time. Notice in particular how the yield spreads widen sharply as the financial crisis unfolds in 2008 and early 2009. There is evidently a risk of widening spreads on corporate bonds when financial conditions deteriorate. On the other hand, it is nice to pick up that extra yield available on corporate bonds in normal periods.

What about returns on corporate bonds? Barclays Investment Grade Corporate Bond Index gives the returns on a portfolio of corporate bonds with duration of a little over five years. Table 11.1 compares the return on this series with the medium-term (five-year) Treasury index from Morningstar, the same index discussed in Chapter 10. This table displays these returns over two periods, 1976–2012 (1976 representing the start of the Barclays series) and the 10-year period, 2003–2012. In both periods, the corporate bond outperforms the medium-term U.S. Treasury bond. The premium in returns is only 0.8 percent over the longer period, but the premium is 1.5 percent over the past 10 years.[2]

Higher return premiums can be obtained by accepting more credit risk in issues below investment grade. Before discussing this so-called high-yield market, we will broaden the discussion of the investment-grade bond market.

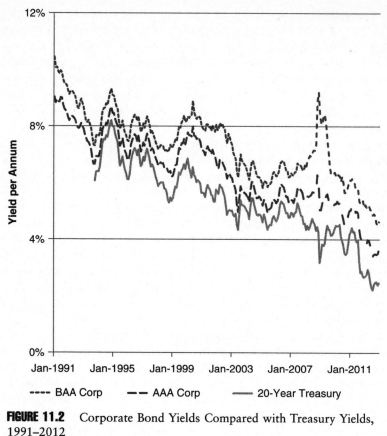

FIGURE 11.2 Corporate Bond Yields Compared with Treasury Yields, 1991–2012
Source for data: Federal Reserve Board.

TABLE 11.1   Returns on Corporate Bonds and Other Bonds

	1976–2012	2003–2012
Corporate Bond Index	8.7%	6.3%
Mortgage-Backed Bond Index	8.3%	5.1%
Barclays Aggregate Investment-Grade Index	8.2%	5.2%
Medium-Term Treasury Index	7.9%	4.8%

Data sources: Barclays for the Aggregate and Corporate Bond Indexes, Merrill Lynch for the Mortgage-Backed Index, and Morningstar for the Medium-Term Treasury Index.

OTHER INVESTMENT GRADE BONDS

After U.S. Treasuries, the second biggest portion of the bond market consists of a type of bond little known 40 years earlier, mortgage-backed bonds. (See Figure 11.1 where mortgage-backed bonds represent 21.4 percent of all bonds). One of the major innovations in financial markets in the past few decades has been the securitization of mortgages, turning individual mortgages into diversified packages of mortgages issued in the form of mortgage-backed bonds. These bonds can be privately issued by banks, for example, or issued by Fannie Mae or Freddie Mac, two agencies of the Federal government that until their collapse during the financial crisis were quasi-private corporations.

Now that this country has experienced a major financial crisis tied at least in part to the mortgage-backed market, it is hard to appreciate the advantages of this financial innovation. Mortgages used to be held by savings and loan companies. These S&Ls would fund 30-year mortgages with short-term bank deposits. All we needed was a rise in interest rates, as occurred in the 1970s, to undermine this model of mortgage financing. To keep deposits, the S&Ls had to raise interest rates. But with the rates on existing mortgages fixed, the profitability of the S&Ls was undermined. In contrast, the market for mortgage-backed bonds allowed banks (including S&Ls) and other mortgage issuers to offload the mortgage assets from their balance sheets. Bond investors assume the risks of these bonds, both interest rate risk and default risk, just like these investors do when they purchase corporate bonds. In addition to mortgage-backed bonds, Figure 11.1 also shows "asset-backed" bonds, packages of credit card receivables, business loans, or other types of assets that have been similarly "securitized." Securitization provides a way for commercial banks to reduce their exposure to all of these assets. (It's not the fault of the securitization process that bank managements figured out other ways to destroy shareholder value).

There is another major type of bond in Figure 11.1, the so-called Federal Agency bonds issued by non-mortgage entities such as Student Loan Marketing Association (Sallie Mae). Securitization thus extends to these non-mortgage agencies as well. Finally, there are money-market funds, another modern invention that allows investors to earn market rates on short-term securities.

In the 1980s, Lehman Brothers developed a widely used index of investment grade bonds called the Lehman Aggregate Bond Index. When Lehman filed for bankruptcy in 2008, Barclays Capital purchased this and other indexes, renaming them Barclays Capital Indexes. The Barclays Capital Aggregate index is a well-diversified mix of investment grade bonds, with about one-third consisting of Treasuries, another third in mortgage-backs, and the rest in corporate bonds and other types of investment-grade securities.[3] So some components of the index have the explicit or implicit guarantee of the U.S. government, while others (such as corporate bonds) are purely private issues.

Table 11.1 reports the returns on the Barclays Aggregate Index along with the Merrill Lynch Mortgage-Backed Bond Index. For the longer period beginning in 1976 as well as the 10 years ending in 2012, both series give returns just a little higher than the U.S. Medium-Term Treasury index. The return differentials are small because both types of bonds involve relatively small default risk—at least in normal times. To earn higher returns, investors have to take on more default risk. That is what the high-yield market provides to investors.

HIGH-YIELD BONDS

Default risk is of utmost importance in pricing high-yield bonds. Until the 1980s, the high-yield market consisted primarily of "fallen angels," bonds that were originally issued as investment grade, but that had fallen below investment grade because of poor financial performance. It was only in the 1980s that investment banks such as Drexel Burnham saw the potential for issuing noninvestment grade (or "junk") bonds to provide financing for firms with weaker credit standing. Since then, the high-yield market has become an important part of the overall corporate bond market in the United States.

High-yield bonds are very sensitive to the business cycle. When the U.S. falls into recession, some firms fail so the default rate on high-yield bonds soars. Figure 11.3 displays the default rates between 1984 and 2012. The average default rate was 4.0 percent/annum during this period, but the default rate varies widely over time. The effects of the Gulf War recession of 1990–1991 and the 2001 recession are evident in the high default rates shown on the graph. Notice that the recession that began in December 2007 saw only a modest rise in default rates in 2008, but then defaults rose over 10 percent in 2009.

The spreads of high-yield bonds over Treasury bonds also vary over time through booms and busts. Figure 11.4 shows these spreads from 1985 through 2012 (measured in percent/annum). The effects of the three recessions during this period are evident in the figure. During the Gulf War recession of 1991–1992, the spread rose to almost 12 percent, while in the 2001 recession, the spread reached about 10 percent (peaking in October

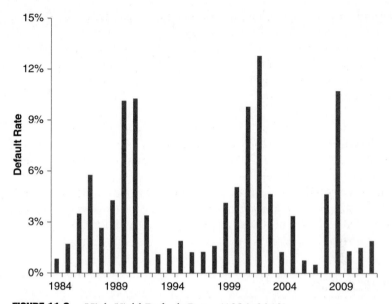

FIGURE 11.3   High-Yield Default Rates (1984–2012)
Source: Altman and Karlin, 2010, updated with data provided by Edward Altman.

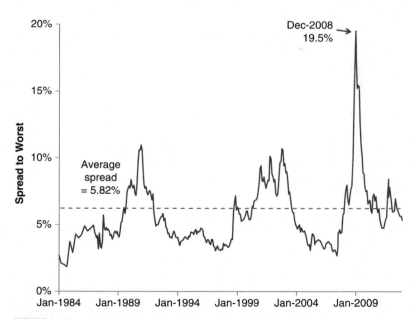

FIGURE 11.4   Spread of High-Yield Bonds over Treasuries
Source: Federal Reserve Bank of St Louis database.

TABLE 11.2   Comparison between High-Yield Bonds and Other Bonds

	July 1983–Dec. 2012	2003–2012
High-Yield Bond Index	9.5%	10.6%
Corporate Bond Index	8.7%	6.3%
Medium-Term Treasury Index	7.7%	4.8%

Data sources: Barclays for the High-Yield and Corporate Bond Indexes, and Morningstar for the Medium-Term Treasury Index.

2002 after the recession had ended). In the recession beginning in 2008, the spread reached almost 20 percent. That's an extraordinary spread. Such a high spread probably reflects as much the illiquidity of the high-yield market during the financial crisis as it does the expectation of future defaults.

High-yield spreads reflect the *ex-ante* default risk of a bond, but do not indicate the *ex post* returns that the investor receives from investing in that bond. These returns are measured using the Barclays Capital High-Yield index, which begins in July 1983. Table 11.2 compares high-yield returns with the Barclays Investment Grade Corporate bond index and the Medium-Term Treasury index described in Table 11.1. High-yield bonds returned an extra 0.8 percent over Investment Grade Corporate Bonds over the period beginning in 1983. Over the past 10 years, however, the excess return is much larger at 4.3 percent. It's this high excess return that has attracted many investors to this market. At a time of miniscule Treasury yields, the high-yield market has attracted many new investors.

It's important to recognize that high-yield bonds provide no free lunch. They are riskier than investment grade corporate bonds not only because a certain portion of them will default (as shown in Figure 11.3). In addition, these bonds suffer large capital losses when recessions approach even if they do not go into default. As Figure 11.4 makes abundantly clear, the yields on these bonds respond very dramatically to the business cycle. When yields rise from 4 percent to 12 percent, large capital losses occur on the bonds even if they don't default.

On the other hand, when recessions end, there are great returns to be made. In Figure 11.4, the yield spread comes down dramatically at the end of the last three recessions. So investors are rewarded with large capital gains. In the two year period from November 2008 (when the rally began) to November 2010, for example, the return on the Barclays High-Yield index was over 92 percent. No wonder investors were pleased. But this is a very cyclical asset. Caveat Emptor!

TREASURY INFLATION-PROTECTED SECURITIES (TIPS)

In Chapters 10 and 11, we emphasize a major drawback of bond invest-ments: their vulnerability to inflation. Since 1997, the U.S. government has offered explicit protection against this risk in the form of securities that compensate investors for inflation. This innovation of the Clinton Admin-istration was long overdue. The British government had introduced similar bonds in the early 1980 s.

Here is how they work. As inflation occurs, the original value of the bond is adjusted upward. In addition, the bond pays a fixed interest rate, but that interest rate applies to the adjusted value of the bond. So the interest payment also rises with inflation. The investor has to pay ordinary income taxes each year on the inflation adjustments as well as on the interest pay-ments. The interest rate itself will be much lower than on an ordinary Treas-ury bond because the investor is being compensated for inflation. In mid-December 2011, for example, the interest rate on 20-year TIPS was 0.5 percent, whereas ordinary Treasuries with that maturity paid 2.5 percent. When the bond matures, the investor receives the adjusted value of the bond reflecting the cumulative inflation that has occurred.

The returns on TIPS have been somewhat higher than those of ordinary Treasuries and other investment grade bonds. Between March 1997 and December 2012, TIPS have provided an average return of 7.1 percent compared with a return of 6.1 percent on medium-term Treasuries and 6.2 percent on the Barclays Aggregate Index. But even if the average return on TIPS was no higher than on other bonds, there may be a very good reason to hold them in a portfolio. TIPS provide a valuable insurance policy against *unanticipated inflation*. Suppose that inflation were to break out in this country as it did in the late 1960 s or 1970 s? TIPS would protect the investor from the capital losses that would hit ordinary bonds. In his book *Unconventional Success* (2005), David Swensen of the Yale Endowment recommends that half of the bond portfolio of ordinary investors should be devoted to TIPS. His reasoning is that the ordinary investor has very few protections against inflation, so it's important to include a sizable allocation to this government-guaranteed inflation hedge. When such an astute investor endorses investment in TIPS, the rest of us have to consider TIPS more seriously than past return performance would justify.

MUNICIPAL BONDS

Many American investors are attracted to the municipal bond market in the United States because most bonds issued by state and local governments are exempt from Federal income tax. Investors compare the yields offered on these bonds with the after-tax yields on conventional bonds. At times in the past, the muni yields have been very attractive, particularly for investors in high tax brackets.

Municipal bonds are the primary source of long-term funding for state and local governments. In 2010, bonds worth almost $500 billion were issued to fund these governments. That's more than double the value of bond issuance 20 years earlier in 1990. Many bonds are issued by state and local "authorities" created for specific purposes. For example, the majority of states have housing authorities that are authorized to issue bonds to finance housing. Table 11.3 presents a breakdown of the issuers into several different categories including state and local governments borrowing directly from the market. State authorities lead the list with 31.8 percent of the issuance over the 10-year period ending in 2009. State governments directly borrow another 10.3 percent of the total.

There are two types of bonds issued in this market. General obligation (GO) bonds are those issued with the full faith, credit, and taxing power of the government issuing the bond. Revenue bonds are issued with specific revenue streams, such as those of the water authority or waste treatment authority, backing the bonds. In 2010, 34.1 percent of new issues were general obligation bonds while 65.9 percent were revenue bonds.[4]

Who holds these municipal bonds? The largest category of holder is the individual household with a 45.5 percent share in the first quarter of 2013.[5] Mutual funds are next with a 28.3 percent share of the market, while banks and insurance companies account for another 23.2 percent. Of course, households are also important investors in mutual funds that specialize in municipal bonds. So households probably constitute well over half of the ownership.

TABLE 11.3   Issuers of Long-Term Municipal Bonds, 2000–2009

Issuers	Issuance (%)
State authority	31.8%
Local authority	18.3%
District	16.0%
City, town, or village	13.3%
State governments	10.3%
County/parish	6.3%
College or university	2.5%
Direct issuer	1.1%

Source: Table 1.2 of SIFMA, 2012; also using data from Thomson Reuters.

Within the household and corporate sectors, tax rates help to determine the attractiveness of this investment. The higher the tax bracket of the investor, everything else being equal, the more attractive are municipals relative to other bonds. The yield on a municipal bond can be converted into a "tax equivalent" yield using the following formula:

$$\text{Tax equivalent yield} = \text{Municipal yield}/(1 - \text{tax rate})$$

So, for example, an individual facing a 33 percent marginal tax rate would consider a 4 percent yield on a municipal bond "equivalent to" a 6 percent yield on a taxable bond. That's because

$$4\%/(1 - 0.33) = 6\% = \text{Tax equivalent yield}$$

Consider the results in Table 11.4 showing the tax equivalent yields by tax bracket. The tax brackets are defined for 2013 taxable income using tax rates prevailing in that year (including the new tax on investment income levied under the 2010 Patient Protection and the Affordable Care Act). The table shows the tax equivalent yields for a muni bond paying 4 percent interest. An investor in the 28 percent tax rate finds a tax equivalent yield of 5.6 percent, whereas an investor in the 33 percent bracket finds a tax equivalent yield of 6.0 percent. An investor in the top bracket naturally has the highest tax-equivalent yield of 7.1 percent.

Many states also give tax exemption to municipal bonds. In most cases, the tax exemption is only for municipals issued by that state's issuers. So if

TABLE 11.4   Tax Equivalent Yields for a 4 Percent Municipal Bond Investor (Married Filing Jointly)

Income (Married Couple)	Tax Rate	Tax Equivalent Yield
$17,851–$72,500	15%	4.7%
$72,501–$146,400	25%	5.3%
$146,401—223,050	28%	5.6%
$223,051–$250,000	33%	6.0%
$250,000–$398,350	33% + 3.8%	6.3%
$398,351–$450,000	35% + 3.8%	6.5%
Over $450,000	39.6% + 3.8%	7.1%

Notes: The 2010 health care law levied a tax of 3.8% beginning in 2013 on investment income for individuals making over $200,000 and married couples making over $250,000.
Source for tax rates: IRS website (www.irs.gov).

you live in California, for example, you can avoid both federal and California income taxes on most municipal bonds issued in California. Thus investors in high tax states often choose mutual funds restricted to that state's municipal issues. These investors have to balance off the tax savings with the higher concentration of risk associated with investing in the bonds of only one state.

Do the tax savings make municipal bonds more attractive than taxable bonds? Many observers compare municipal yields with Treasury yields. But Treasuries have lower default risks than most municipal bonds. So it makes sense to compare municipals with a broader group of bonds. Table 11.5 does just that for three years: 2005, 2010, and 2013 (after taxes were raised). The table examines bond yields on the "20-bond index" of municipal bonds compiled by the Bond Buyer. This index is based on general obligation bonds of 20 issuers with an average rating of AA by S&P. These bonds have an average maturity of 20 years. The table compares the municipal bonds with 20-year Treasuries (with AAA rating from Moody's and AA+ rating from S&P) and with two types of corporate bonds, those rated AAA and BAA. All of these yields are reported by the Federal Reserve. The table then reports the tax equivalent yields on the municipal bonds for two tax brackets, 25 percent for those making $100,000 per year and the top bracket, which rose from 35 percent in the 2005 and 2010 to 43.4 percent in 2013.

TABLE 11.5   Yields on Long-Term Municipal and Taxable Bonds, 2005, 2010, and 2013

	Jan. 2005	Jan. 2010	Jan. 2013
20-Year Treasury Bond	4.8%	4.5%	2.7%
Corporate AAA Bond	5.4%	5.3%	3.8%
Corporate BAA Bond	6.0%	6.3%	4.7%
20-Bond Municipal Index	4.4%	4.3%	3.6%
Tax Equivalent Yields*			
25% Bracket	5.9%	5.8%	4.8%
Top Bracket	6.8%	6.7%	6.4%

Notes: 20-Bond Municipal Index is based on general obligation bonds of 20 issuers as compiled by the Bond Buyer. The municipal bonds have an average maturity of 20 years, whereas the maturity of the AAA and BAA corporate bonds ranges from 20 to 30 years. All data is from the Federal Reserve Board.
*In all three years, the 25% bracket applied to those making $100,000 per year. The tax rate for the top bracket in 2005 and 2010 was 35%. In 2013, it was raised to 43.4%.
Data source: Federal Reserve Board.

The results are quite interesting. For taxpayers in the top tax bracket, municipal bonds have higher tax equivalent yields than any of the other bonds. For taxpayers in the 25 percent bracket, tax equivalent yields are higher than yields on Treasury bonds or AAA-rated corporate bonds. And in the most recent year, municipal bonds have higher tax-equivalent yields than any of the bonds, even corporate bonds with BAA ratings. There is no doubt that municipal bonds deserve a place in the portfolios of taxable investors, at least if they are in the 25 percent tax bracket or higher. And this analysis ignores taxes levied at the state level.

But what about default risk? We have taken default risk into account in Table 11.5 by comparing bonds with different credit ratings. But with the deterioration of the finances of state and local governments since the financial crisis, maybe "this time is different." Maybe in the years ahead we will find that municipal bonds are riskier than they have been in the past. After all, in late 2010, a well-respected financial analyst, Meredith Whitney, predicted on *60 Minutes* that the municipal bond market would suffer hundreds of billion dollars of losses in the years ahead.

We know a lot about past default rates on municipal bonds. Moody's published a study in early 2013 analyzing default rates on municipal bonds over the period from 1970 to 2012. Table 11.6 reports some of the most interesting findings of this study. The table compares the default rates of municipal bonds with those of corporate bonds with the same credit ratings. The results are quite dramatic. Defaults on municipal bonds rated A or higher were negligible over the period. In contrast, over 2 percent of corporate bonds rated A went into default during this period. Municipal bonds rated BBB defaulted at only a 0.30 percent rate compared with a 4.74 percent rate for corporate bonds. You had to dip into the noninvestment grade range for municipals to get a sizable default rate. The Moody's study provides considerable comfort to muni investors. At least in the past, municipal bonds have been very safe investments.

TABLE 11.6 Historic Default Rates (1970–2012)

Rating	Default Rates	
	Municipal Bonds	Corporate Bonds
AAA	0.00%	0.50%
AA	0.01%	0.92%
A	0.05%	2.48%
BAA	0.30%	4.74%
Noninvestment grade	5.67%	33.88%

Source: Moody's, *U.S. Municipal Bond Defaults and Recoveries, 1970–2012*, 2013.

But have things changed? Meredith Whitney's work deserves attention. After all, she was one of the few analysts to sound warnings about banks prior to the financial crisis. Have conditions changed in the muni market? Is it "different this time?"

Two things have changed for municipal bonds. First, the financial crisis undermined the insurance companies that insured many municipal bond offerings. According to the SIFMA (2012) study, 57.3 percent of long-term municipal bond issues were insured in 2005. By 2010, that percentage had dropped to 6.2 percent. In the interim, the ratings agencies had dropped the ratings of the insurers. This in turn made investors in municipal bonds less willing to pay a premium for insurance and made issuers of municipal bonds less willing to pay for insurance. The second change that has occurred is that state and local governments have become more aware of their pension liabilities. Politicians for many years increased the pension and health care benefits of state and local workers without taxpayers paying too much attention. Now the spotlight is on these pension benefits. And in the case of some local governments, the liabilities they face may make default a more attractive option than it has been in the past. So Table 11.6 may not fully reflect future risks of default. At least that is the view of skeptics like Whitney.

What is an investor to do in the face of these risks? The following three steps seem obvious.

1. First, make sure that there is a thorough analysis of the municipal securities chosen for the portfolio. If the investor chooses the mutual fund route to investing, make sure about the reputation of the fund manager for avoiding default risks. If the investor elects to hold municipal bonds directly in the portfolio, make sure that the advisory firm choosing the bonds has a strong municipal bond desk.
2. Think about choosing higher rated issues than in the past. Sure, you will give up some yield, but that may be desirable if we are entering uncharted waters.
3. Most important, it makes no sense to concentrate defaults risks in only a few municipal bonds issues. Diversify municipal bond holdings.

But by all means, keep investing in municipal bonds. The tax savings are attractive enough.

CONCLUDING COMMENTS

This book has devoted two long chapters to bonds. The reason is obvious. Bonds are going to be an important part of every individual investor's portfolio. That's especially true for investors who are in retirement or approaching retirement. (More is said about retirement portfolios in Chapters 16–19).

It's imperative that investors understand the basic characteristics of a bond portfolio. Inflation can lead to capital losses. And if inflation is high, real returns can fare a lot worse than nominal returns. But investors should also be aware of default risk. That means that the bond portfolio should be chosen carefully. Hopefully these two chapters have pointed out some of the pitfalls as well as opportunities in bond investing.

NOTES

1. The Treasury series is not available from 1987 to September 1993, so interest rates are compared beginning in October 1993.
2. The corporate bond return falls short of the return on the 20-year Treasury bond (9.3 percent for the period 1976–2012), but that's primarily because the corporate bond series has a much shorter duration. As explained in Chapter 10, longer term bonds outperformed medium-term bonds over the past 30 years, so it is important to compare bonds with similar maturities.
3. The Barclays Aggregate Index has an average duration of a little over five years.
4. SIFMA (2012).
5. The data are reported on SIFMA's website in a table entitled "Holders of U.S. Municipal Securities."

REFERENCES

Altman, Edward I., and Brenda J. Karlin. 2010. "Special Report on Defaults and Returns in the High-Yield Bond and Distressed Debt Market: The Year 2009 in Review and Outlook." New York University Stern School of Business.

FitchRatings. 2012. "Fitch U.S. High-Yield Default Insight—2011 Review." www.fitchratings.com.

Moody's. 2013. *U.S. Municipal Bond Defaults and Recoveries, 1970–2012.* New York: Moody's Investors Service.

Securities Industry and Financial Markets Association. 2012. *Fundamentals of Municipal Bonds*, 6th ed. Hoboken, NJ: John Wiley & Sons.

Swensen, David F. 2005. *Unconventional Success: A Fundamental Approach to Personal Investment.* New York: Free Press.

www.irs.gov.

CHAPTER 12

Investing in Real Estate: REITs

For ordinary investors, real estate is often the only type of investment that is considered outside of stocks and bonds. Real estate provides equity-like returns that are relatively low in correlation with traditional equity. In his book *Unconventional Success* (2005), David Swensen of the Yale endowment recommends that ordinary investors consider real estate for as much as 20 percent of their portfolios rather than pursue the other, more exotic types of alternatives that Yale and other large institutional investors focus on.

By real estate, we mean commercial real estate such as office buildings, shopping malls, and apartment buildings. The reason why these investments are accessible to ordinary investors is that they can buy real estate investment trusts (or REITs) which in turn invest in a mix of properties. REITs were developed in the 1960s to package commercial real estate properties. The underlying properties usually provide a stream of investment income based on the rents charged to tenants. There may also be capital gains when the properties are sold. So they resemble stocks in their payout structures, although real estate usually provides higher rents than the dividends offered by stocks. Residential homes are not usually considered part of the investment portfolio, though many home owners may regard them as investments. We will discuss homes in the next chapter.

Some investors choose real estate as their *principal* form of investment, not just one asset in a larger diversified portfolio. These investors own apartment buildings or perhaps an office building or even a small shopping mall, counting on the rents from these buildings to provide a steady stream of future income. These investments are the equivalent of a concentrated stock market investment in IBM or AT&T or GM shares. There may be little diversification in the type of real estate that is owned. And, just as important, there may be no diversification across locations. Owning real estate in Nevada prior to the financial crisis, or in Houston in the 1980s, is almost as risky as owning an individual stock. REITs, in contrast, allow investors to obtain extensive diversification.

The total amount invested in commercial real estate can be measured by tracking the sources of capital for real estate, both debt and equity, at least the capital that can be easily measured. According to a 2012 report on commercial real estate by the Urban Land Institute and PricewaterhouseCoopers, there was a total of $3.9 *trillion* invested in real estate in 2011.[1] Of that total, almost 70 percent represents debt, both public and private, rather than equity. That should not be surprising since real estate has always been a highly levered investment. The equity portfolio totals a little less than $1.2 trillion in value. About one-fifth of that equity is provided by REITs, with most of the rest coming from institutional investors, including pension funds, and "private investors" including real estate partnerships.

These figures do not account for all of the commercial real estate in the United States. Instead, they represent the real estate that can be easily tracked because it is owned either by big institutional investors or by REITS. There are doubtless trillions of dollars of commercial real estate that are owned by smaller investors. Think of all of the office buildings, retail space, warehouses, factories, and apartment buildings in any city. Surely only a fraction of these facilities are easily tracked in national figures. Real estate is more important to the economy than these figures indicate.

REAL ESTATE INVESTMENT TRUSTS (REITS)

Real estate investment trusts, or REITs, were developed in the 1960s as a liquid alternative to direct ownership of real estate.[2] REITs own, and in most cases operate, income-producing real estate such as apartments, shopping centers, offices, hotels, and warehouses. REITs are corporations that invest in real estate but are set up to pay little or no corporate income tax. To qualify for tax exemption, the REITs must distribute 90 percent of their income each year to investors.[3] REITs may be publicly or privately held just like other corporations. Publicly traded REITs typically trade on stock exchanges such as the NYSE and NASDAQ.

Prior to the 1990s, the total capitalization of the REIT sector was less than $10 billion. But in the early 1990s, laws were changed to allow long-established real estate operating companies to package properties they owned into REITs. This led to an IPO boom that sharply increased the size of the REIT sector. In 1992, REITs totaled only $11.2 billion, but that total rose to $78.3 billion four years later and to a peak of $400.7 billion in 2006.[4] After falling sharply during the financial crisis, the REIT market recovered enough so that in 2012 the value of REITs rose over $500 billion.

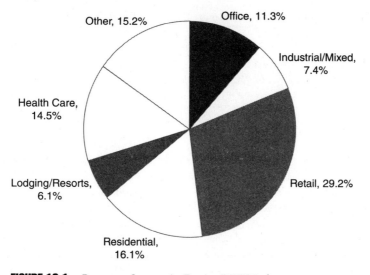

FIGURE 12.1 Property Sectors in Equity REIT Index
Source: NAREIT, 2013.

Since the early 1970s, NAREIT has maintained indexes of REIT returns that are widely used in the investments industry. NAREIT has an index for mortgages, but this chapter will focus only on the equity REIT index. The REITs included in the index must have at least $100 million in capitalization and must have a minimum amount of turnover.[5] Figure 12.1 gives the breakdown of properties included in the equity NAREIT index in 2012. The largest sector is retail with 17.6 percent in regional malls, 8.8 percent in shopping centers, and the rest in freestanding retail real estate. The residential component representing 16.1 percent of the index consists largely of apartment buildings. Health care complexes and office buildings are the next two largest categories. Thus there are a variety of different types of property included in the index.

NAREIT provides monthly returns starting in 1972. Because the REIT market was so small until the early 1990s, we will present REIT returns over two periods, from the start of the series in 1972 to present and from 1992 on. Table 12.1 compares REIT returns with large-cap and small-cap stocks. For the period 1972–2012, small caps are represented by the Ibbotson Small Cap Index. For the shorter period, small caps are represented by the Russell 2000 Index.

The results are quite interesting. Let's focus on the most important comparison, between REITs and the S&P 500. In both periods the NAREIT index has a higher return than large-cap stocks. The difference is particularly

TABLE 12.1   NAREIT Returns Compared with Stock Returns

	1972–2012	1992–2012
NAREIT Index	12.1%	11.2%
S&P 500 Index	10.0%	8.2%
Small-Cap Index	13.0%	8.9%

Data sources: NAREIT, S&P Dow Jones Indices, Russell®, © Morningstar.

striking in the shorter period beginning in 1992. Despite the precipitous decline in the REIT index during the financial crisis of 2007–2009 (discussed below), REITs beat the S&P index by 3 percent over the 21-year period starting in 1992.

Since most REITs are classified as small-cap stocks, it's interesting to compare the NAREIT index with small-cap indexes. Over the full period beginning in 1972, the Ibbotson small-cap stock index beats the REIT index by 0.9 percent. Recall from Chapter 6 that small-cap stocks performed unusually well in the 1970s. Over the period beginning in 1992, however, the REIT index beats the Russell 2000 small-cap index by over 2 percent. So there is no doubt that REITs provide attractive returns. But how do they fit in a portfolio?

HOW WELL DO REITs FIT IN A PORTFOLIO?

As stated at the outset of this chapter, real estate is the one investment alternative to stocks and bonds that is widely held by ordinary investors. Private equity, hedge funds, commodities, and other relatively exotic investments are held by very wealthy families and by institutional investors like endowments and pension plans. But few investors of modest wealth choose these investments (or are eligible to invest in them). Many of these investors instead add real estate to their portfolios. That has been especially true since REITs were introduced over 40 years ago.

How much real estate is appropriate? Judging from the weight of real estate in total stock market capitalization, the answer is not much. REITs constitute only 2.7 percent of stock market as measured by the Wilshire 5000 index. Equity real estate as a whole, as measured in Emerging Trends in Real Estate, totals almost $1.2 trillion, or about 9 percent of the value of the stock market. So if we think of REITs representing all real estate investment, we could justify an allocation equal to 9 percent of the equity portfolio. But if equity constitutes only 50 to 70 percent of most portfolios, then that leaves relatively small allocations to REITs.

Contrast this with the recommendation of David Swensen of the Yale Endowment in his book aimed at ordinary investors entitled *Unconventional Success* (2005). Swenson argues that ordinary investors do not have the luxury of investing in a wide range of assets other than stocks and bonds. Yale and other institutional investors can invest in private equity and venture capital, hedge funds, oil and gas properties, and timberland. But the average investor does not. So Swensen recommends that an ordinary investor devote 20 percent of the entire portfolio to real estate. Why so much?

One reason why real estate is attractive to investors is that it is relatively low in correlation with stocks. The emphasis is on the word "relatively." Different segments of the U.S. stock market, like small-cap stocks versus large-cap stocks or value stocks versus growth stocks, tend to be very highly correlated with one another. Real estate is less correlated. But don't expect real estate to always zig when stocks zag. Both are influenced heavily by the business cycle. When the economy is booming, there is a demand for more office buildings, more malls, more factories and distribution centers. A booming economy also drives up stock prices. The opposite can be said of a recessionary economy.

Yet real estate does sometimes have a life of its own. Consider the recession that followed the collapse of the NASDAQ in 2000. According to the National Bureau of Economic Research (NBER), this recession began in March 2001 and lasted until November 2001. As explained in Chapter 3, the S&P 500 reached its peak in August 2000, seven months before the recession began and reached its trough in February 2003. Over this period, the S&P 500 return totaled –42.5 percent, while the NAREIT return was +24.9 percent. This was fortunate indeed for investors who had diversified their portfolios by adding REITs.

Does real estate always buck the trend of stock markets? The answer is that the recession of 2001 was unusual. In normal recessions, you would expect REITs to suffer along with stocks because both types of investment depend on a healthy economy. Consider Table 12.2, which examines S&P 500 returns and REIT returns in the five recessions from the mid-1970s to the present. In every recession except for that of 2001, REIT returns turn negative along with stock returns. It's true that in the very bad recession of the early 1980s, REITs did not fall nearly as much as stocks did. (If the S&P 500 provides a –16.5 percent return, investors should be grateful that REITs fall only 0.2 percent). But in the three other recessions, REITs either matched the poor performance of stocks or performed even worse. That was particularly the case in the most recent recession brought on by the financial crisis.

Figure 12.2 shows the movement of the S&P 500 and NAREIT indexes during the past two recessions. Notice that the S&P 500 dips down sharply

TABLE 12.2 REITs and Stocks During Recession

Recession	Peak/Trough of S&P	S&P 500	NAREIT
Mid-1970s	Jan. 1973/Dec. 1974	–36.2%	–34.6%
Early 1980s	Nov. 1980/July 1982	–16.5%	–0.2%
Gulf War	June 1990/Oct. 1990	–14.1%	–17.4%
NASDAQ	Aug. 2000/Feb. 2003	–42.5%	+24.9%
Financial Crisis	Oct. 2007/Mar. 2009	–46.7%	–63.4%

Data sources: NAREIT and S&P Dow Jones Indices.

in 2000 while the NAREIT index, having fallen somewhat in 1997, just keeps rising as the NASDAQ and broader stock market indexes decline. This is in sharp contrast with the most recent recession. This recession began in December 2007 (months before Lehman Brothers failed) and ended in June 2009. But the stock market peaked two months earlier in October 2007 and fell until March 2009. Over this period, the S&P 500 returned –46.7 percent. But over this same period, the NAREIT index fell a distressing 63.4 percent. The performance of real estate in this period deserves a closer look.

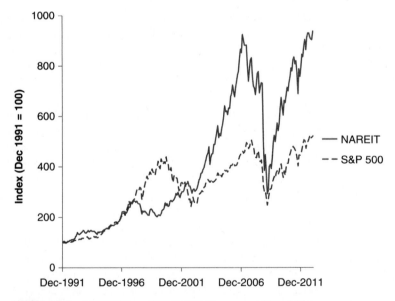

FIGURE 12.2 NAREIT and S&P 500 Returns, 1992–2012
Data sources: NAREIT and S&P Dow Jones Indices.

REITS AND THE FINANCIAL CRISIS

The financial crisis of 2007–2009 began as a real estate bust. It was not only a bust in residential real estate, the first nationwide decline in housing prices since the Depression of the 1930s, but also a bust in commercial real estate. Financing for both types of real estate virtually dried up. During the boom period in mid-decade, commercial real estate came to depend heavily on commercial real estate mortgage-backed securities (or CMBS). After reaching a peak in early 2007, the CMBS market collapsed soon after. Banks are the other major source of funding for real estate transactions. The financial crisis crippled many major banks. So real estate loans dried up overnight. The real estate boom was fueled by readily available financing at bargain basement rates. The end to this financing led to a collapse in real estate values.

All sectors of commercial real estate suffered during the crisis, although the retail and hotel sectors were hurt the most. Property values fell and sales declined sharply. But the size of the reduction in REIT prices caught many observers by surprise. To see returns fall by over 60 percent must have been a shock to many investors. That's the price that investors pay for having marked-to-market pricing of real estate. If investors are spooked by a decline in real estate values, they will sell their REIT holdings. The fall in REIT prices may exaggerate the actual decline in real estate values.

Whether that is the case is a matter for debate. Institutional investors rely on real estate appraisals to judge the value of their holdings. Since the early 1980s, the National Council of Real Estate Investment Fiduciaries (NCREIF) has collected return data on real estate owned by institutional investors (the great majority of which are pension funds). The NCREIF returns consist of two elements: net operating income (gross rental income less operating expenses) and the capital gain on the property. The capital gain measure is based on periodic appraisals using standard commercial real estate appraisal methodology. Since these appraisals are done only periodically, the NCREIF index responds only sluggishly to changes in real estate values. So it's probable that the NCREIF index underestimates the actual decline in real estate values during the crisis.

Figure 12.3 compares the two indexes, NAREIT and NCREIF, starting at the peak of the NAREIT returns in the first quarter of 2007. Notice how the NAREIT return starts to react negatively to the first signs of financial distress in the summer of 2007. At that time, two Bear Stearns hedge funds that were heavily committed to CMBS securities ran into difficulty. In the meantime, the NCREIF index kept rising through the second quarter of 2008. This index based on appraisals kept rising even after Bear Stearns collapsed into the arms of JP Morgan in March 2008. It was only in the fourth quarter of 2008, after Lehman Brothers had failed, that the NCREIF index

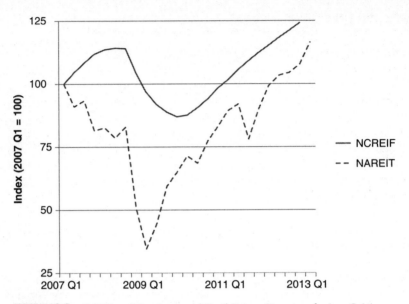

FIGURE 12.3   REIT and Institutional Real Estate Returns during Crisis
Data sources: NAREIT and NCREIF.

started to fall sharply. But the 8.3 percent drop in the fourth quarter of 2008 paled by comparison with the 38.8 percent drop in NAREIT returns in that quarter. Investors in REITs panicked as they saw the financial sector teeter on the brink of collapse.

Although the two indexes behaved differently during the crisis, Figure 12.3 shows that both have rallied strongly since then. By the end of 2012, the NAREIT index was almost 8 percent above its previous peak in the first quarter of 2007, having risen more than 200 percent from its bottom in early 2009. (Recall that if a market falls 65 percent, it must rise almost 190 percent to get back to where it started). Over the same period, the NCREIF index rose by 24 percent. So the worst financial crisis since the Great Depression of the 1930s has not permanently crippled the commercial real estate sector. However, it did give heartburn to many investors.

REITs AS A SOURCE OF INCOME FOR INVESTORS

I have saved one of the best features of real estate for last. REITs pay higher dividends than stocks do. One reason is that they are required to distribute 90 percent of their income so as to avoid corporate income tax. Consider Figure 12.4, which compares the dividend yields of REITs with those of

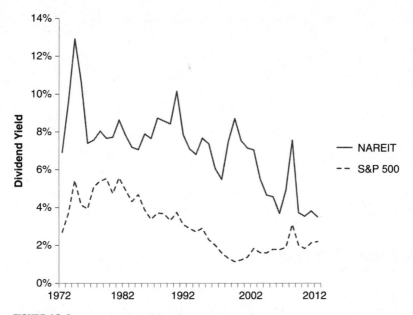

FIGURE 12.4   Dividend Yields of NAREIT and S&P 500
Data sources: NAREIT and Standard & Poor's.

S&P 500 stocks since 1972. At no time during this period were dividends on stocks as high as on REITs. Dividend yields do vary over time. When REIT prices fell during the financial crisis, for example, dividend yields rose sharply. That's not because dividends rose, but because prices fell. After all, the dividend yield is the ratio of dividends to prices. Imagine that you are an investor lucky enough (or astute enough) to purchase REITs at the bottom of the financial crisis. In December 2008, the average dividend yield on the NAREIT index was 7.6 percent! That's a big change from a dividend yield of 3.7 percent in December 2006.

Let's compare dividend yields over time. Table 12.3 reports the dividend yields of the NAREIT and S&P 500 indexes over two periods: the full sample period beginning in 1972 and the past 10 years ending in 2012. Dividend yields have been declining for both stocks and REITs over the longer period. The S&P 500 has seen its dividend yield change from an average of 4.6 percent in 1972–1981 to 3.9 percent in 1982–1991 to 2.0 percent in 1992–2001 and to 2.0 percent in 2003–2012. That is one reason why investors have had so much trouble living off the income from their portfolios. But it's clear from Table 12.3 and Figure 12.4 that REITS have consistently retained their income advantage over stocks. Over the past 10 years, for

TABLE 12.3 Average Dividend Yields of NAREIT and S&P 500 Indexes

	1972–2012	2003–2012
NAREIT Index	7.1%	4.6%
S&P 500 Index	3.1%	2.0%

Data sources: NAREIT website and www.econ.yale.edu/~shiller, which updates Shiller (2000).

example, REITs offered an average dividend yield of 4.6 percent compared with a dividend yield of 2.0 percent for stocks. That's quite an advantage if you are in retirement and need current income.

CONCLUDING COMMENTS

There is a strong case for adding REITs to a stock and bond portfolio. First, REITs offer stock-like returns. In fact, REITs have consistently outperformed the S&P 500, at least over the longer run. Second, REITs offer diversification beyond that provided by choosing different types of stocks for the portfolio. At times in the past, particularly in the recession of 2001, REITs have helped to cushion the impact of stock market declines. Third, REITs have consistently provided investors with higher income than stocks. That's particularly important in today's low rate environment. Investors need to consider allocating part of their portfolio to REITs.

NOTES

1. These figures are from *Emerging Trends in Real Estate, 2012*, an annual report produced by the Urban Land Institute and PricewaterhouseCoopers.
2. In the interests of full disclosure, I am a board member of WP Carey Inc., a company that invests in and manages commercial real estate properties on behalf of several REITs and which recently converted to REIT status.
3. REITs must receive at least 75 percent of their gross income from real estate rents, mortgage interest, or other qualifying income and must invest at least 75 percent of assets in rental real estate, real estate mortgages, or other qualifying real estate.

4. These figures are from the National Association of Real Estate Investment Trusts (NAREIT).
5. The requirements are described in NAREIT and FTSE (2006).

REFERENCES

National Association of Real Estate Investment Trusts and FTSE. 2006. "FTSE NAREIT U.S. Real Estate Index Series: Frequently Asked Questions." www.ftse.com/FAQs.jsp.

Shiller, Robert J. 2000. *Irrational Exuberance*. Princeton, NJ: Princeton University Press

Swensen, David. 2005. *Unconventional Success: A Fundamental Approach to Personal Investment*. New York: Free Press.

Urban Land Institute and PricewaterhouseCoopers. 2012. *Emerging Trends in Real Estate, 2012*. Washington, DC: Urban Land Institute.

CHAPTER 13

The Home as an Investment

For many years, Jonathan Clements wrote an influential personal finance column for the *Wall Street Journal*. One theme he revisited every year or so was the folly in believing that your personal home was a good investment. He argued that an investor would be much better off buying a modest home and investing more in a conventional portfolio of stocks and bonds. Don't buy a $1 million home, he said. Instead, buy a home for half that amount and invest the extra $500 thousand in stocks and bonds. This chapter will show the merits of Clements' argument. Clements will be shown to be right even if we examine housing *prior to its recent collapse.*

For many families in the United States, their home is their largest financial asset. In most cases, home ownership is leveraged with mortgage debt with the latter typically representing the largest financial liability of the family. But even taking into account mortgage debt, home ownership represents a substantial portion of *net worth* for many families. So it's important to study returns on homes as part of a larger study of investing.

Until recently when house prices fell, many families believed that home ownership provided some of the highest returns that they earn in their lifetimes. One of the reasons for this belief is that families often suffer from "money illusion." If your house doubles in value over time, that may or may not be a good return on investment. It all depends on how much the cost of living has risen over the same period. Too often families view the nominal appreciation of their homes as the return on their "investment."

This chapter will examine the real (inflation-adjusted) returns on housing since the 1970s. The primary source of data will be home price indexes maintained by the oversight agency for Fannie Mae and Freddie Mac (the mortgage giants), the Federal Housing Finance Agency (FHFA). The predecessor to FHFA, the Office of Federal Housing Enterprise Oversight (OFHEO), developed these indexes in the early 1990s using series that Fannie Mae and Freddie Mac had developed earlier.[1] Many of the housing series extend back to the mid-1970s. The indexes use a repeat-sales methodology developed by Case and Shiller (1989) that relies on observing sales prices of the same homes over time. The use of repeat transactions for the same house helps to control for differences in the quality or location of houses comprising the sample for any particular area.

The FHFA indexes use data for single-family detached properties that have been financed by mortgages processed by either Fannie Mae or Freddie Mac. These agencies limit their activities to moderate size "conforming" mortgages (up to $417,000 in 2013).[2] So the indexes underweight more expensive homes that require "jumbo" mortgages. This is a particularly important limitation for areas of the country, like California, where average house prices are considerably above national levels with the result that many houses require jumbo mortgages. In addition, FHFA indexes underweight subprime and other lower-rated mortgages. For this reason, we will later consider another set of indexes developed by Case and Shiller now owned by Standard & Poor's. FHFA provides indexes for the country as a whole, all states, as well as most metropolitan areas.

CAPITAL GAINS ON HOUSING BY STATE AND METROPOLITAN AREA

It is interesting to see the differences between housing markets across the country. Some people are lucky enough to live in California. Not only do those people enjoy fresh fruit and sunshine all year long, but they also can watch their houses appreciate (at least, most of the time). Those who live in Pennsylvania (as I do), on the other hand, must contend with cold weather half of the year while watching their home values stagnate. It isn't fair, but at least they don't live in Texas where home values don't even keep up with inflation in the long run. (Of course, these three states all have other attractive features. That's why so many of us are happy to live in Pennsylvania and Texas!)

This chapter begins by looking at the capital gains on housing in the six largest states and ten largest cities. This will give us a broad picture of how much housing varies across the country. The capital gains will be adjusted by inflation (using the consumer price index) so that we can see how much the real value of homes has changed.

Table 13.1 presents real house appreciation for the United States as a whole as well as for the six largest states by population. Two periods are studied, from the second quarter of 1975 (when the series begin) through the end of 2006, roughly 32 years, and 1975 through 2012. The end of 2006

TABLE 13.1   Real House Appreciation in United States and Six Largest States

	1975 Q2–2006 Q4		1975 Q2–2012 Q4	
	Average Real Appreciation	Cumulative Real Appreciation	Average Real Appreciation	Cumulative Real Appreciation
United States	1.5%	59.4%	0.4%	18.0%
California	4.3%	284.7%	2.1%	116.4%
Texas	–0.1%	–1.7%	–0.2%	–8.2%
New York State	2.3%	107.0%	1.3%	60.0%
Florida	1.9%	82.0%	–0.2%	–6.7%
Illinois	1.0%	39.0%	0.0%	–0.6%
Pennsylvania	1.0%	39.3%	0.4%	15.2%

Notes: The real rates of appreciation are calculated using the consumer price index.
Data sources: FHFA and Bureau of Labor Statistics.

was the peak of the housing market, so the shorter period will show housing gains at their best. If housing gains fail to impress us over the shorter period, we will prove Clements right.

The U.S. housing market as a whole provided a real appreciation of 1.5 percent per year through 2006 and 0.4 percent per year through 2012. Those national averages hide tremendous variation across the country. California benefited from a 4.3 percent per year appreciation through 2006. The cumulative rise in California prices over 32 years is 284.7 percent! In contrast, Texas saw a slight drop in house prices (in real terms) through 2006 and Pennsylvania saw only a 1.0 percent/annum appreciation. Clearly "location" matters.

It's interesting to examine real house appreciation by metropolitan areas as well. Table 13.2 shows the real house appreciation in the 10 largest metropolitan areas of the country.[3] Most of the metropolitan area data begins later than the state data, so the table reports returns beginning in the first quarter of 1978. New York City, Boston, and Los Angeles provide the largest appreciations over both periods. Dallas and Houston, in contrast, experienced *negative* real appreciation over both periods. Consider how much location matters. Over the full period from 1978 to 2012, residents of New York City have seen their homes appreciate in real terms by over 130 percent, while residents of Philadelphia have had to be content with a real appreciation of 39 percent, and residents of Houston and Dallas lost ground to inflation.

TABLE 13.2   Real House Appreciation in 10 Largest Cities

	1978 Q1–2006 Q4		1978 Q1–2012 Q4	
	Average Real Appreciation	Cumulative Real Appreciation	Average Real Appreciation	Cumulative Real Appreciation
New York	4.1%	216.7%	2.4%	131.4%
Los Angeles	3.7%	189.4%	1.6%	71.5%
Chicago	1.3%	45.6%	–0.2%	–5.3%
Dallas	–0.1%	–3.9%	–0.4%	–13.0%
Houston	–0.9%	–23.2%	–0.8%	–25.6%
Philadelphia	1.9%	74.9%	0.9%	39.0%
Washington	2.9%	126.2%	1.3%	56.3%
Miami	3.1%	139.8%	0.6%	22.7%
Atlanta	0.8%	24.4%	–0.5%	–16.0%
Boston	4.1%	221.4%	2.6%	141.6%

Notes: Cities are ranked by size of metropolitan statistical areas.
Data sources: FHFA and Bureau of Labor Statistics.

Why are the rates of house appreciation so varied? For house prices to rise rapidly, there must be substantial growth of population in the area, and that requires substantial job growth. But that alone is not enough, since a city like Atlanta has surely seen a lot of growth. In addition, a city (or, more accurately, metropolitan area) must impose limits on land use. Los Angeles certainly qualifies in this regard, while Houston and Atlanta impose few limits on expansion. Scarce land combined with rapid growth lead to the bidding up of home prices.

Figure 13.1 shows the rise in house prices in California and its two largest cities since 1978. At the peak of the housing boom, the cumulative real appreciation of prices was almost 200 percent even for the state as a whole. It's interesting to note that the ascent of prices was interrupted by a substantial decline in the early 1990s. The housing boom of the late 1980s was followed by a prolonged slump with nominal and real housing prices reaching bottom in 1996 or later, nearly seven years after the peak. So Californians experienced a slump in housing more than a decade before the most recent collapse in prices. The country as a whole, however, did not experience a significant decline in either nominal or real house prices until the housing crisis that began in 2007.[4] So for the country as a whole, the recent housing slump was a genuine surprise.

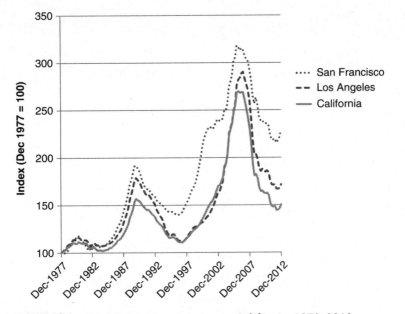

FIGURE 13.1   Real House Appreciation in California, 1978–2012
Data source: Federal Housing Finance Agency.

THE HOUSING BUST

Before considering long-run returns from housing, it's important to discuss the effects of the housing bust that has occurred since 2006. It has been a grueling experience for many families, particularly in the hardest-hit areas of the country.

To study home prices in the recent period, we will use the indexes developed by Karl Case and Robert Shiller, two academic economists, rather than the FHFA indexes used for longer-run comparisons.[5] Unlike the FHFA indexes, the Case-Shiller indexes have the advantage of including houses at all price levels. Since houses with subprime mortgages were particularly hard-hit in the crisis, the Case-Shiller indexes may measure the housing bust better than the more broad-based FHFA indexes.

Consider first the Case-Shiller 20-city index. This index fell by 28 percent between the end of 2006 and end of 2012. That's quite a drop for an asset that hitherto had been considered "safe." Recall that home investments are usually financed with large mortgages. In fact, the average mortgage outstanding at any given time is about 75 percent of the value of a typical house. A 28 percent drop in value is enough to wipe out most if not all of the equity in a home.

How much typical homeowners have lost depends on where they live. Table 13.3 reports the drop in the nominal value of homes between

TABLE 13.3   Changes in Nominal House Prices, December 2006 through December 2012

Housing Market	Change in Nominal Prices
20-City National Index	−28.0%
New York	−23.9%
Los Angeles	−33.8%
Chicago	−32.5%
Dallas	−2.1%
Washington, D.C.	−21.4%
Miami	−45.7%
Atlanta	−27.6%
Boston	−9.6%
San Francisco	−30.7%
Detroit	−32.1%
Phoenix	−43.3%
Las Vegas	−55.9%

Data source: S&P Case-Shiller Indexes.

December 2006 (the peak of the market) and December 2012. Ten of the 12 largest cities are included in the table together with two cities, Phoenix and Las Vegas, that have been particularly hard hit by the bust. Some cities, notably Dallas and Boston, have fared relatively well during the bust, with drops in housing prices of "only" 2.1 percent and 9.6 percent, respectively. At the other extreme, Miami, Phoenix, and Las Vegas have suffered grievously. When home prices fall 40 percent or more, whole neighborhoods are severely affected. Evictions occur and sheriff sales become common. Tax rolls plummet. Even the 30 percent declines in prices that Chicago and Los Angeles have experienced cause great distress.

It's important to remember that individual families fare quite differently depending on their age and other circumstances. Even in cities with sharp declines in prices, the impact of the bust depends partly on where a family is in their life cycle. If the family bought its home in the late 1990s or earlier, perhaps because children were born at that time, it is likely to still be sitting on capital gains. On the other hand, if the family bought near the peak of housing in the mid-2000s, the house is now probably underwater. The level of distress also depends upon whether the family took advantage of rising house prices to refinance. If at the time of refinancing, the family took some of the equity out of the house, then the pain is all the greater. As stated at the outset of this chapter, the home is often the largest asset of a family as they near retirement. For that reason, the housing bust has severely impacted many families' financial statuses.

Because the bust is such an unusual event, it's important to examine housing in the period before the bust. So the next section of the chapter will examine the returns to housing through 2006, the peak of the housing boom. If housing is not a desirable investment prior to the bust, then Jonathan Clements will be proven right. We also will show returns that include the bust period, but that is only to emphasize the dangers of viewing "house ownership as an investment."

RATES OF RETURN ON HOUSING

Rates of appreciation do not represent *rates of return* on housing, so they cannot be compared directly with stock returns or the returns on other assets. First of all, rates of appreciation do not take into account the leverage provided by mortgage financing. Second, the rates of appreciation do not take into account either the benefits of living in a house or the expenses of maintaining it. Returns on stocks and REITs, in contrast, take into account leverage as well as the dividends paid to investors.

The rate of return should depend on the capital gain on the house less the cost of mortgage financing. There is also the benefit of living in the house as well as the tax shelter provided by the favorable treatment of property taxes and mortgage interest in the tax code. But most experts believe that those benefits are offset by the property taxes, maintenance expenses, and other expenses of living in the house.[6] In that case, the return on the house depends only on the *capital gain less the cost of the mortgage*. Of course, the greater the proportion of the purchase price that is financed, the higher the potential rate of return on the house. Leverage helps to raise returns, at least on the upside.

The purchase price of the house is usually financed by a combination of debt and equity. At the time of purchase, the equity in a house is the difference between its price and the debt used to finance it. The rate of return on the house depends on the capital gain on the house minus the cost of the mortgage.[7] Consider a house that has a 12 percent capital gain but pays a 6 percent mortgage rate. Suppose that the house costs $600 thousand, but it has a $450 thousand mortgage. That means that the house has $150 thousand in equity. Then its rate of return is going to be:

$$\text{Rate of return} = [\$600k \times 12\% - \$450k \times 6\%]\,/\,\$150k = 30\%!$$

TABLE 13.4 How Capital Gains on a House
Affect the Rate of Return

Capital Gain on House/Annum	Rate of Return on House
12%	+ 30.0%
9%	+ 18.0%
6%	+ 6.0%
3%	−6.0%
0%	−18.0%

Assumptions: 75% mortgage and 6% mortgage interest rate/annum.

Because the house appreciated so much faster than the mortgage rate, the investor made a huge return. After all, this investment is heavily leveraged.

Suppose instead that the house appreciated by only 6 percent. With a 6 percent mortgage rate, the house will still have a positive rate of return because there is equity in the house. The $150k equity invested in the house will earn a return of 6 percent. But what happens if the rate of appreciation is less than 6 percent? Table 13.4 shows what happens. This table is drawn up under the assumption that the house investor has a 75 percent mortgage and that the mortgage rate is 6 percent. If appreciation is only 3 percent per year, then the rate of return falls to −6 percent per year. And if the appreciation stops altogether, then the rate of return falls to −18 percent![8] Leverage has vicious effects when houses stop appreciating.

Readers may object to these examples on two grounds. First, perhaps the mortgage rate is too high. Second, perhaps the mortgage ratio is too low. (Keeping the mortgage ratio at 75 percent at least limits the damage on the downside). Well, it turns out that the average mortgage on a house is just about 75 percent. Homeowners often start out with a larger mortgage, but they gradually pay off the mortgage over time. The FHFA publishes tables showing average mortgage ratios since the mid-1970s. The average ratio is close to 75 percent over the full sample period as well as more recent periods. FHFA also publishes tables of average mortgage rates. These have fallen over time. From 1975 to 2006, the average mortgage rate was 9.1 percent. Over the six years ending in 2012, the average mortgage rate nationwide was only 5.2 percent. And the average rate in 2012 was only 3.8 percent. If mortgage rates are low as in 2012, the returns from owning a house improve, but leverage continues to lead to huge gains on the upside and grim losses on the downside.[9]

Now let's look at the actual rates of return on housing. Here is the strategy. We will look at nationwide returns as well as returns from owning homes in California. After all, if returns are not great in California, they certainly won't be great in Pennsylvania or Texas. We will calculate the returns assuming an average mortgage ratio of 75 percent. But we will use average mortgage rates for the particular period examined. All returns will be adjusted for inflation using the consumer price index.

We will consider four different periods for study:

1. The 32-year period from 1975 to 2006 (the latter being the peak of the housing boom)
2. The full sample period from 1975 to 2012
3. Ten years of boom ending in 2006
4. Six years of bust ending in 2012

The reason why we want to examine a decade of boom is that we want to understand how the myth of home ownership gets perpetuated. It's great to be able to brag about an investment, whether it is gold in 2010, NASDAQ stocks in 1999, or California real estate in 2006. All you have to do is to bail out "just in time." Then you will be able to regale your friends with tales of your investment prowess.

Table 13.5 presents the rates of return for the U.S. housing market as a whole as well as for the California market. The table reports the nominal rate of appreciation, the average mortgage cost, and the real rate of return based on a 75 percent leverage ratio. Consider first the two long-run periods starting in 1975. During the 32-year period ending in 2006, U.S. housing had a *negative* 7.5 percent per annum real return while California real estate

TABLE 13.5   Real Returns on Housing in United States and California

	1975*–2006	1975*–2012	Boom Years 1997–2006	Bust Years 2007–2012
Nominal House Appreciation				
United States	6.0%	4.5%	6.8%	−2.8%
California	9.0%	6.2%	12.2%	−7.2%
Mortgage costs	9.1%	8.5%	6.7%	5.2%
Real Rate of Return				
United States	−7.5%	−10.9%	4.2%	−28.3%
California	4.0%	−4.4%	25.1%	−45.6%

Note: Rates of return based on 75% mortgage.
*1975 data begins in second quarter.
Data Sources: FHFA, Federal Housing Board, and Bureau of Labor Statistics.

TABLE 13.6 Real Returns on Housing and Other Assets

	1975*–2006	1975*–2012	Boom Years 1997–2006	Bust Years 2007–2012
Housing:				
United States	–7.5%	–10.9%	4.2%	–28.3%
California	4.0%	–4.4%	25.1%	–45.6%
REITs	11.2%	9.3%	11.8%	–0.6%
S&P 500	8.2%	6.9%	5.8%	0.1%

*1975 data begins in the second quarter.
Data Sources: Table 13.5 for housing rates of return. NAREIT, and S&P Dow Jones Indices for other returns.

earned a *positive* 4.0 percent/annum. When six more years are added to this sample period, so that the period from 1975 to 2012 is examined, even California housing has a negative real return.

Should we be impressed with California's positive return in the earlier period? Recall Jonathan Clements' discussion. The alternative to buying a big house in California is to buy a smaller house and invest the rest in a normal portfolio. Table 13.6 compares the real returns on housing with those on the S&P 500 stock index and the NAREIT index over these same two periods. In the period ending in 2006 before the bust begins, the positive real rate of return on housing in California of 4.0 percent is totally swamped by the 11.2 percent real return on REITs and 8.2 percent real return on stocks. If the period ends in 2012 instead, all assets perform worse. But real return on housing in California is now negative at –4.4 percent and the real return for the United States as a whole is an astoundingly large –10.9 percent/year. This is over a period when REITs are earning 9.3 percent in real terms and stocks are earning 6.9 percent. So it's clear that Jonathan Clements was right when he described housing as a poor investment.

What if we look only at the boom period for housing, the 10 years ending in 2006? Guess what? If you lever any asset during a period when it is going to boom, you will become rich! The real return on California housing is 25.1 percent per year during this period. Of course, not all of us can be lucky enough to live in California. If we invested during the boom period in the United States as a whole, we would earn a 4.2 percent real return per year. That is easily swamped by the returns on REITs and stocks. So even during the boom period, you had to live in California (or some other high-flying state) to beat conventional assets.

What if you lever up in a bust period? That's a very relevant question, especially at the present moment in 2013 as housing remains severely depressed.

Borrowing 75 percent of the purchase price leads to a 28.3 percent loss/year in the United States as a whole. (How can it be that large? It's because leverage is brutal on the downside. You are losing 2.8 percent per year on the nominal price of the house. And you are paying an average mortgage rate of 5.2 percent. Look at Table 13.6 again to convince yourself of the brutal effects of leverage). And if you are lucky enough to live in California, you can build up losses of 45.6 percent per year. So much for the belief that the home is a safe long-run asset!

There is a surprising gap between perception and reality when it comes to investment in home ownership. No doubt part of the reason for this gap is that homeowners look at their house appreciation without taking into account inflation. But it's also because home owners do not primarily regard their home as being an investment. It's a place to live. It's only after periods of appreciation of home prices that many individuals begin to regard their homes as investments. And they come to believe that the home provides higher, and more stable, returns than "risky" investments. So it's important to consider the strong evidence to the contrary.

CONCLUDING COMMENTS

There is a huge contrast between the returns on investable real estate and homes. Since their introduction in the early 1970s, REITs have delivered returns even higher than those on the S&P 500. Home ownership is another story. The returns on home ownership are disappointing in most periods compared with investment in REITs or stocks. It's true that with high leverage, home ownership can deliver spectacular returns when house prices are rising (as they did in the ten years through 2006). But that same leverage can lead to spectacular losses when home prices fall. Fortunately, when house prices fall, investors do not mark their homes to market (unless they are in the unfortunate position of having to sell). So they can ignore price trends knowing that there is no investment statement coming in the mail to jolt them back to reality. They simply sit in their houses waiting for the next boom to occur. If only stock investors had the good sense to be as patient.

NOTES

1. The FHFA was established by legislation signed into law in July 2008. It merged two agencies, the Office of Federal Housing Enterprise Oversight and the Federal Housing Finance Board.

2. There is a higher limit of $625,500 (originally $729,750) established for higher cost areas by the Economic Stimulus Bill of 2008.
3. Metropolitan areas in some cases are substantially larger than the cities they contain. Dallas, for example, is the fourth-largest metropolitan area (because it includes Fort Worth and surrounding areas), but it is the ninth largest city.
4. Between 1989 and 1995, there was a decline of about 7 percent in real housing prices nationwide, but no decline at all in nominal housing prices.
5. The Case-Shiller indexes begin only in 1987. Other differences between the two indexes are discussed in OFHEO (2008).
6. A formal model of housing returns is presented in Himmelberg et al. (2005). They estimate that property taxes and maintenance together add up to 4 percent of the value of the house.
7. The total return on the house is equal to the value of the house at purchase times the capital gain on the house minus the mortgage times the mortgage rate. The *rate of return* is the total return on the house divided by the equity invested in the house.
8. How can the return be *negative* 18 percent? With no capital gain on the house, the rate of return is based on the mortgage cost. If you have $150,000 of equity in the house and $450,000 in debt, your rate of return equals: $-\$450\text{k} \times 0.06/\$150\text{k} = -18\%$.
9. If there is no house appreciation and mortgage rates are 3.8 percent rather than 6 percent, for example, the return on a house with a 75 percent mortgage is −11.4 percent rather than −18 percent.

REFERENCES

Case, Karl E., and Robert J. Shiller. 1989. "The Efficiency of the Market for Single-Family Houses." *American Economic Review* (March): 125–137.
Himmelgerg, Charles, Christopher Mayer, and Todd Sinai. 2005. "Assessing High House Prices: Bubbles, Fundamentals, and Misperceptions." *Journal of Economic Perspectives* (Fall): 67–92.
OFHEO. 2008. "Revisiting the Differences between the OFHEO and S&P/Case-Shiller House Price Indexes," (January). www.fhfa.gov/webfiles.

PART
Three

Wealth Management

CHAPTER 14

Choosing a Portfolio: Fitting the Pieces Together

Once an investor understands the basic asset classes, how does that investor choose a portfolio? What mix of assets is appropriate to an investor? I believe that this is one place where many investors go wrong. But choosing a portfolio should not be that difficult.

Some investors choose very "safe" assets like money-market funds for their 401(k) or other investment accounts. Or they invest solely in bonds. This "safe" portfolio may have relatively little volatility during their accumulation years. But, 30 or 40 years later when the investor retires, the safe portfolio *makes their retirement risky* because they have not accumulated enough for retirement. In the long run, bonds don't normally earn enough to fund a retirement portfolio.[1] Neither do other "safe" investments like money market funds or bank CDs.

At the opposite extreme, there are those investors who are sure that they can do better than their peers by concentrating on one risky asset. They focus on real estate alone (and invest in only one location in the United States). Or they load up on their own company's stock. Or they swing from one "hot" investment to another. Today it's MLPs, master limited partnerships that invest in energy infrastructure. Two or three years ago, it was gold. Seven years ago, it was any type of real estate including condos in Las Vegas. A few years earlier, it was tech stocks.

Diversification pays. It may be boring, but it offers an investor a conservative way to accumulate wealth. "Boring" beats "exciting" when an investor's financial future is at stake. Prudent investors will never be able to brag to their friends that they have loaded up on the latest "hot" investment. They may include such an investment in their portfolios, but it will be such a small fraction of their wealth that it won't matter too much to them.

So investors should choose a portfolio that is diversified. But what mix of assets should be in the portfolio? We begin with the most basic portfolio decision faced by every investor—how much to invest in stocks versus bonds. Because stocks and bonds are low in correlation, a mixture of them makes sense for most investors. But which mixture is best? Portfolio strategies will differ depending on an investor's age. Investors can afford to take more risks when they are young, so they tend to hold more stocks than bonds. When they are retired, they choose a more conservative mixture. We will discuss how portfolios vary over a lifetime later in the chapter.

WHY MIX BONDS AND STOCKS?

Bonds and stocks are very different assets. Consider corporate bonds and stocks. Both assets draw upon the same cash flows of the corporation. But corporate bonds provide steady coupons to be paid out of these cash flows before stockholders receive anything. Once an investor buys the bond, the coupon is locked in. If the investor owns stocks, then any increase in corporate profits is owned by the shareholders. Higher profits may lead to higher dividends or may be plowed back into investments in order to raise future stock values. Government bonds share many of the same characteristics as corporate bonds. The difference is that future tax revenues finance these bonds rather than future profits. But like in the case of corporate bonds, the coupons are set in advance.

Let's imagine what happens to bonds and stocks in different economic environments. If the economy grows more rapidly than normal, causing corporate profits to rise, then stocks may thrive. Bonds will not necessarily do any better than normal (and may perform badly if interest rates rise). If inflation rises unexpectedly, then bonds and stocks alike will suffer. But bonds may suffer more because coupons are fixed, while dividends and stock prices may increase in nominal terms. If inflation falls unexpectedly, then bonds will thrive. It is important to understand how stocks and bonds respond to different economic conditions because we see a lot of different conditions over our lifetimes. Just since 1950, we have seen decades when the U.S. economy thrives and stocks surge and other decades when the U.S. economy falters. And since 1950, we have seen periods of inflation when bonds suffer and other periods when inflation falls and bonds thrive. Wouldn't it be sensible to have a portfolio that can weather these different environments?

If we only cared about the long, long run, we would load our portfolios with equities when we are young. After all, the evidence in favor of an "equity premium" presented in Chapter 2 is quite compelling. Yet it is interesting to note that a diversified stock and bond portfolio also fares quite well in the long run. Table 14.1 compares four portfolios over the 62-year period beginning in 1951. The four portfolios are (1) an all-bond portfolio

TABLE 14.1   Real Returns on Portfolios

Portfolio	1951–2012	2001–2012 ("Lost Decade")
Bonds only	2.6%	5.6%
50% bonds/50% stocks	5.1%	3.5%
25% bonds/75% stocks	6.0%	2.1%
Stocks only	6.8%	0.3%

Notes: Portfolios consist of long-term (20-year) Treasury bonds and S&P 500 large-cap stocks.
Data source: Morningstar.

consisting of long-term U.S. Treasury bonds, (2) a diversified portfolio with 50 percent invested in stocks and 50 percent in bonds, (3) a second diversified portfolio with 75 percent invested in stocks and the rest in bonds, and (4) an all-stock portfolio consisting of U.S. large-cap stocks. Table 14.1 reports the real returns on these four portfolios. The two diversified portfolios do underperform the all-equity portfolio, but not by that much. A portfolio invested entirely in the S&P 500 earns 6.8 percent per year in real terms. But a portfolio with 75 percent in stocks, which is the portfolio that I recommend for younger investors, earns 6.0 percent per annum. The portfolio with 50 percent invested in bonds earns almost twice as much as an all-bond portfolio. The equity premium rewards the long-run investor.

If the equity premium is so large, why not invest *only in stocks* during the accumulation years? The answer is evident to any investor who has lived through the past decade of miserable stock returns. This last decade might be called the "lost decade" for stock market investors. The last column of Table 14.1 examines the real returns on the four portfolios during that "decade" (which is measured over twelve years from 2001 to 2012). While bonds were earning average real returns of 5.6 percent per annum, stocks were earning only 0.3 percent per year on average.

How did diversification fare during the "lost decade?" Portfolios split between bonds and stocks earned real returns of 3.5 percent per annum. Portfolios tilted 75 percent toward stocks earned only 2.1 percent returns, but bond holdings cushion the decline in stocks even in this portfolio.

Stocks alone are just too volatile. Consider the sharp movements in nominal stock returns over the past 12 years. Between the peak of the market in August 2000 and the trough in October 2002, the market fell 47.2 percent![2] Then the market rose for five years from October 2002 to October 2007. (For readers interested in odd results, the market reached its bottom on October 9, 2002, and reached its peak on October 9, 2007). From its new peak, the market fell 51.7 percent during the financial crisis through February 2009.[3] Wouldn't it be better to have some bonds in the portfolio at times of market turbulence? That's what most investors believe.

During this lost decade, stocks barely recovered from two bear markets. By December 2012, the S&P 500 is up only 3.25 percent relative to its value in December 2000 (measured as a total nominal return including dividends). In real terms, moreover, the S&P is down by a depressing 21.8 percent during this lost decade. If the investor had allocated 25 percent to bonds, in contrast, the portfolio would be up 27.6 percent over this same period (and down only 3.3 percent in real terms). Because bonds did so well during this lost decade, a 50/50 portfolio would have fared even better with a 51.9 percent gain (up 15.1 percent in real terms). Few investors regret having allocated part of their portfolios to bonds during this lost decade.

LONG-TERM "STRATEGIC" ASSET ALLOCATION

The stock-bond decision is the most important "asset allocation" decision that investors make. But usually, asset allocation involves more than that. Most investors want to choose a mix of different types of stocks and perhaps a mix of different types of bonds. The portfolio chosen is called the "strategic asset allocation." Many institutional investors, such as endowments or pension funds, choose a specific strategic allocation mix after lengthy discussion and review. The allocation will depend in part on the spending needs of the institution, but also on other factors (such as the potential to raise additional funds if markets go awry). In theory, the strategic allocation should remain fixed indefinitely if the institution has chosen wisely. In practice, institutions do change their strategic allocations over time. For example, most institutions invest much more in foreign stock markets today than they did in the 1980s or earlier.

Individual investors should also choose a strategic allocation. But, unlike institutions, individual investors have a good reason to change this allocation over time. That's because most individual investors have one major investment goal—to save enough for retirement. Spending out of their portfolio is usually minimal in the years when they are working. Then spending becomes essential at the time of retirement. For this reason, there is a *life cycle* to investing. In the years when wealth is being accumulated, the stock-bond allocation is more aggressive than when the investor nears retirement.

LIFE-CYCLE INVESTING

In the last few years, investment firms have begun to formalize this process by which asset allocation changes over time. These firms have created *target retirement funds* that change continuously as the investor gets closer to retirement. The funds are usually defined relative to the year of retirement. So in 2012 a 54-year-old might invest in a 2025 retirement fund because that investor intends to retire at 67 years of age (for full Social Security benefits).[4] The "target" of investing is retirement because this is the primary reason why investors save.

Target retirement funds are designed to model the life cycle of investing beginning with the early years of working when very aggressive allocations are called for. Figure 14.1 shows the evolution over time of the Vanguard allocations in their target retirement funds. Up until the investor reaches 25 years before retirement, Vanguard chooses a 90/10 stock/bond allocation. Then the retirement fund begins to increase its allocation to bonds until the investor finally reaches the retirement age (denoted R in the figure) when the stock/bond allocation is 50/50. Even after retirement, the allocation continues to shift. Five years after retirement, the stock/bond allocation is at 41/59. Experts can debate whether these specific allocations are optimal, but the

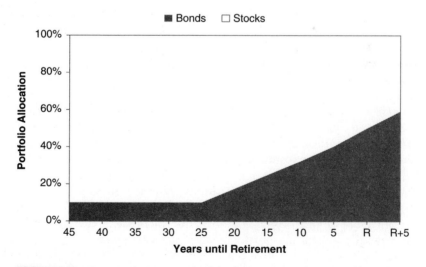

FIGURE 14.1 Vanguard's Target Portfolio Allocations Determined by Years to Retirement
Source: www.vanguard.com.

figure shows clearly how the proportion of riskier assets depends on the distance from the age of retirement.

Vanguard is only one of the firms that offer such target retirement funds. The asset allocation differs somewhat from one target fund to another. Consider the 2025 fund offered by three major firms. Vanguard allocates 70.8 percent of the portfolio to stocks, Fidelity allocates 67.5 percent, and T. Rowe Price allocates 76.1 percent. Yet the basic philosophy motivating each fund remains the same. The target fund starts with an aggressive allocation to stocks when the investor is far from retirement because at that point there is little risk from short-term fluctuations. After all, retirement is years in the future. Then the allocation gradually shifts toward bonds as the investor comes closer and closer to retirement. The target retirement fund is an important innovation for the investment industry because it reminds all advisors of the need to shift asset allocations as the investor gets closer to the retirement spending stage of life. Risks appropriate to a 30-year-old investor are simply different from those of a 70-year-old who is counting on retirement savings.

A MODEL PORTFOLIO

In later chapters, I will discuss portfolios for those already in retirement. In this chapter I will ask what should be in the portfolio of the individual investor when that investor is many years away from the date of retirement. I will describe that investor as a "younger investor" although I believe that the portfolio would be appropriate even for someone only 15 years from retirement. Because the investor is still far from retirement, that investor should devote 75 percent to stocks and only 25 percent to bonds.[5] That's the stock-bond allocation that I chose throughout most of my career. Some observers will argue that the stock allocation should be even higher, but bonds play an important role in balancing the higher risks of stocks in the portfolio.

The bond and stock allocations should each be well diversified. As far as bonds are concerned, the investor should make sure to choose a mix of different types of investment-grade bonds, perhaps including corporate bonds, mortgage bonds, as well as Treasuries and the bonds issued by U.S. government agencies. The bond portfolio might also include TIPS as well as high-yield corporate bonds. (All of these bonds are discussed in Chapter 11.) Depending on the income tax bracket of the investor, there should also be municipal bonds in the portfolio (but not in the investor's tax-deferred account). All of these types of bonds can be accessed conveniently using mutual funds. For example, some bond mutual funds invest in the broad mixture of investment grade bonds represented in the Barclays Aggregate Bond Index.

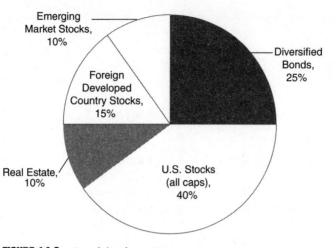

FIGURE 14.2 Portfolio for a Younger Investor

Similarly, the stock portion of the portfolio should be broadly diversified. Figure 14.2 shows the weights I recommend for U.S. stocks, foreign stocks, and REITs. U.S. stocks warrant the highest allocation at 40 percent of the portfolio. Some of this allocation should go to small-cap stocks, but as explained in Chapter 6, small caps represent only 10 percent of all U.S. stocks. Thus most of the U.S. stock allocation should be in large-cap stocks. 25 percent of the portfolio is allocated to foreign stocks, including 10 percent in emerging markets and 15 percent to the stocks from the foreign industrial countries, thereby opening the portfolio to the rest of the world. The 10 percent allocation to REITs gives the investor an exposure to commercial real estate. It's not a fancy portfolio, but it's well diversified. Such a portfolio can be chosen by investors at any wealth level because there are mutual funds open to investors who invest in each of these assets.

Why is there so much diversification into foreign markets and REITs? The simple answer is that diversification gives the investor the opportunity to earn returns even when the U.S. stock market falters. Foreign stocks often have different returns from U.S. stocks. The same is true of REITs. No doubt there is high short-term correlation between all of these types of stocks. But that still allows for varied returns.

Consider Figure 14.3, which examines returns on four different types of stocks over the past three decades. The four types of stocks are as follows:

1. U.S. stocks represented by the Russell 3000 all-stock index
2. Foreign industrial country stocks represented by the EAFE index

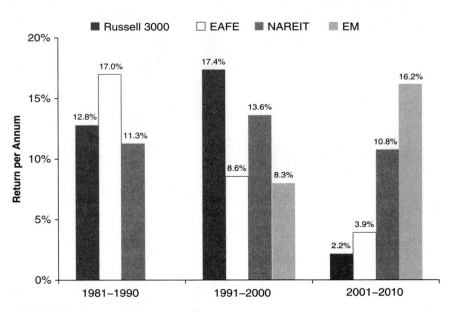

FIGURE 14.3 Returns by Decade on Four Assets
Data sources: Russell, MSCI, and NAREIT.

3. Emerging market stocks represented by the MSCI Emerging Markets Index
4. REITs represented by the NAREIT equity index

The returns are reported as annual averages in percent/annum. Emerging market returns don't begin until the end of the 1980s, so returns for only the last two decades are reported.

Figure 14.3 shows quite a range of returns across these four assets. In the 1980s, foreign stocks outperformed both U.S. stocks and REITs by more than 4 percent per year. That was the decade when Japanese stocks reached their peak. But in the 1990s, U.S. stocks led both foreign stocks and emerging market stocks by about 9 percent/annum. What a glorious decade for American investors. And more recently, emerging markets and REITs have led U.S. and other developed country stocks by a wide margin. Isn't it sensible to have investments in such a wide range of assets? Investors never know which markets will be the next to outperform.

The portfolio in Figure 14.2 is designed for an investor who is still 15 or more years from retirement. The chapters on retirement to follow presume that the investor's portfolio at retirement has only 50 percent in stocks. Why is there such a major change in allocation at retirement? It's because the investor is switching from *accumulating* to *spending*. A market setback when you are 15 years from retirement causes heartburn, but little else. A market setback in the first few years of retirement is hard to cope with because the portfolio has to fund retirement spending. Any dollar spent has no chance to grow as the market swings back. Retirement is a watershed event in more ways than one.

How does the investor get from the young investor's portfolio depicted in Figure 14.2 to a retirement portfolio? I don't think that it is necessary to follow a rigid plan to shift assets away from stocks every year until retirement. But it makes sense to gradually shift toward a higher allocation to bonds as retirement gets closer. By the time an investor is five years from retirement, for example, the allocation might be 60 percent to stocks and 40 percent to bonds.

There should be a similar shift from aggressive to more conservative allocations in college savings funds. But the shift is even more dramatic because spending for college takes place over such a short period of time. It would be folly to have a large allocation to stocks when tuition payments are a few months away. Let's consider a simple plan for investing college funds from birth until college.

INVESTING FOR COLLEGE

This book focuses on retirement saving and investing because that's so important for those many Americans who have no old-style pensions. But investors have other objectives for saving and investing. Those with children or grandchildren often save and invest in order to help pay for college. Surely the cost of American colleges is high enough to warrant attention in a book on investing.

Let's imagine that your child or grandchild was born just yesterday. (That is almost literally the case for this grandfather, writing in January 2013.) What would be a sensible asset allocation for the education account of your child or grandchild? Let's use the insights drawn from target date investing to help us design the portfolio. College won't begin for another 18 years perhaps, so the initial allocation should be more like that of a 45-year-old saving for retirement than for a 60-something nearing retirement. As shown in Figure 14.4, perhaps 75 percent of the portfolio should be allocated to stocks (and stocklike investments such as REITs) and 25 percent to bonds. That would be a sensible portfolio allocation until the grandchild is 10 years of age or so. Then as the child gets closer to college, the allocation shifts more and more toward bonds. At the start of college, at

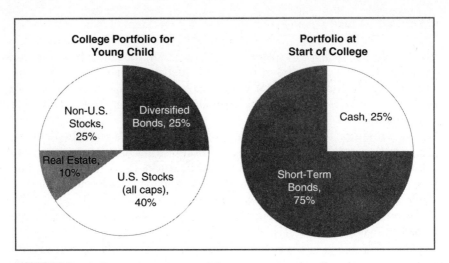

FIGURE 14.4   College Education Portfolios

least 25 percent of the portfolio should be in cash and cashlike instruments such as money market funds. The rest should be in short-term bonds. After all, tuition for senior year is due in only three years!

Why is the allocation so aggressive at first? The portfolio with 75 percent devoted to stocks is designed to keep up with the skyrocketing cost of college tuition. Recall that Chapter 5 described how much faster college costs are rising than the general inflation rate. To try to ensure that the college fund keeps up with college costs, it is allocated relatively aggressively when the child is young. Then as the child gets closer to college, the allocation is shifted toward bonds. Once the child nears the date for beginning college, the family must make sure that enough cash is available for initial college costs, much as a retiree must make sure that cash is available for immediate spending needs. This is all common sense.

Since 2001, families can set aside college funds in so-called 529 plans. The future returns on these funds are exempt from Federal income tax as long as all the funds are used for approved educational expenses like tuition. So parents can begin to save for the college expenses of their children in accounts that can grow without the extra drag of Federal income taxes—much like 401(k)s can grow without taxes on their dividends and interest payments. Those who contribute to the 529 plans must do so with after-tax dollars,[6] but no additional taxes are due when the child attends college. In creating 529 plans, Congress wanted to provide some help for American families facing the burden of college tuitions. Every little bit helps, but families (and children) have to do the heavy lifting of saving enough to make college education possible.

REBALANCING DEFINED

Besides shifting allocations as the date of retirement draws nearer (or college bills loom ahead), an investor also has to make sure that the allocation doesn't "drift" too much over time. That's because markets can push particular assets up or down. When stocks boom, as they did in the 1990s, then the portfolio becomes overweighted with stocks. So any subsequent stock market bust does even more damage to portfolio returns than it should. Similarly, when stocks decline, as they did in the financial crisis, the portfolio becomes overweighted with bonds. When stocks rally later on, the investor misses out on some of the gain. The investor needs to consider "rebalancing" the portfolio to reverse the effects of any "drift" away from the strategic allocation.

Rebalancing sounds so sensible in theory. You rebalance in order to keep investments in line with your original allocation. In practice it is very difficult to carry out. Consider how hard it has been to rebalance during the ups and downs of the past decade.

Rebalancing When Times Are Good

Consider the experience of investors in the five-year period from October 2002 (the trough of the market) through October 2007.[7] Normally, stock markets bottom out prior to the end of a recession. But in the recession following the NASDAQ collapse, stock markets were still falling when the recession ended in November 2001. It was only in October 2002 that markets finally reached bottom.

Suppose that in October 2002, an investor chose the diversified portfolio shown in Figure 14.2. Over the next five years, stock markets boomed. EAFE rose 189.8 percent while the MSCI EM index rose 443.9 percent, and the NAREIT index rose 181.5 percent. Bonds, in contrast, limped along with a 24.1 percent total return over five years. An investor who never rebalanced would find that the portfolio had "drifted" to a much riskier allocation. Figure 14.5 shows the drift of this portfolio. Even though the investor left the portfolio alone, the bond allocation drifts down from 25 percent in bonds to 13.1 percent by October 2007. Where did the money go? The rise in most stock markets lifted the emerging market allocation from 10 percent to 23 percent, lifted the foreign stock allocation from 15 percent to over 18 percent, and lifted the REIT allocation from 10 percent to almost 12 percent. Investors ended up with a lot more risk than they bargained for.

In the case of a booming market, the failure to rebalance increases the risk profile of the asset allocation unnecessarily. Some investors like to ride a good wave. That may be really enjoyable for a while. But a rocky shore may loom ahead.

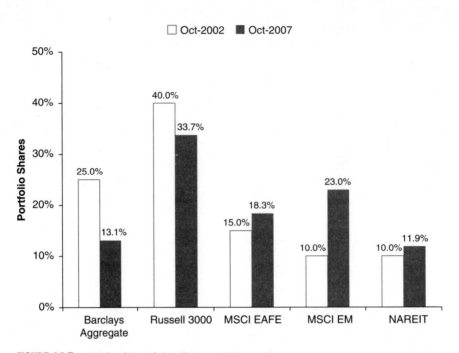

FIGURE 14.5 Drift of Portfolio Shares in Boom
Data sources: Barclays Capital, Russell, MSCI, and NAREIT.

Rebalancing When Times Are Bad

If it seems difficult to rebalance when markets are soaring, it is even more difficult to do so when markets are tumbling. Consider the experience of investors during the bust from October 2007 through February 2009.[8] During that period, the S&P 500 fell by about 51 percent as did the Russell 3000. Foreign stocks fell even more, EAFE by 56.4 percent and MSCI Emerging Markets by 61.4 percent. REITs topped them all by falling 64.8 percent.

Figure 14.6 shows how these sharp losses distorted the asset allocation. The bond allocation drifted upward from 25 percent of the portfolio to over 44 percent. The U.S. stock allocation plummeted by over 7 percent, foreign stocks by over 4 percent. REITs fell from 10 percent of the portfolio to a little less than 6 percent.

What should the investor have done in that bleak winter of 2008–2009? If the investor followed a disciplined approach to asset allocation, the portfolio should have been rebalanced at the trough or, perhaps more realistically, early in 2009 when annual returns were reported for 2008. But what tremendous discipline would have been required! The United States and the world as a whole had just gone through the worst financial crisis since the

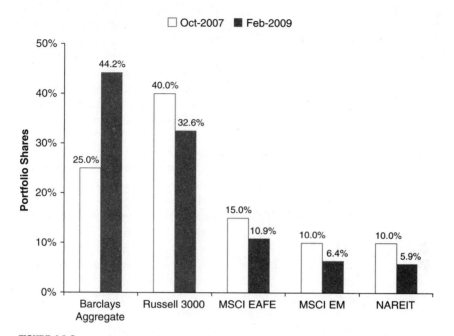

FIGURE 14.6   Drift of Portfolio Shares in Bust
Data sources: Barclays Capital, Russell, MSCI, and NAREIT.

1930s depression. Several major financial institutions had failed or had been saved by mergers and government bailouts. The economy was already in one of the deepest recessions since World War II. It takes a hardy soul to rebalance in such circumstances.

Yet consider the cost of not rebalancing. An investor who had meant to have 75 percent allocated to stocks has only 56 percent in stocks as the market starts to rebound. And the shortfall is due to inaction, not to deliberate investment policy. This just illustrates how hard it is to follow a consistent asset allocation strategy. And that is why, at the end of the day, an investor has to really believe in asset allocation to match the long-term returns that have been reported in this book.

CONCLUDING COMMENTS

It takes a lot of discipline for an investor to choose an appropriate asset allocation and then stick to it. How many investors abandoned their stock allocations after the NASDAQ collapsed in 2000 or after the financial crisis drove down stocks in 2008?

Many investors believe that they can *time the market*. It's not just the aggressive investors who adopt an investment philosophy built around entry and exit from the market. A much larger group of investors are willing to adopt a long-run asset allocation strategy *as long as markets behave themselves*. But when the stock market swoons, as it periodically does, these investors will abandon that strategy. And once they do that, it will be very difficult for them to wade back into the market. After a sharp downturn like we experienced recently, it's seldom clear when to reenter the market. And by the time the rally is in full swing, the investor has missed most of the rebound. Chapter 3 discussed investor experience during the 10 recessions since 1951. On all but one occasion, the market reached bottom before the end of the recession. And in all 10 recessions, the rise in the market was very rapid once it reached bottom. Few investors react quickly enough if they time the market.

Investors also abandon asset allocation in boom times. When unusual investment opportunities present themselves, as in the case of the NASDAQ bubble in the late 1990s or the real estate bubble earlier this decade, investors will often jump into the bubble blindly. If they do it soon enough, they will make some money and perhaps feel confident enough to double up. But investors are often late to the party. In the NASDAQ boom of the late 1990s, many investors piled into tech stocks or into venture capital partnerships only after substantial gains had already been made. And in the recent real estate boom, investor enthusiasm peaked shortly before prices started to turn down.

This chapter has outlined an alternative to these tactical moves. Choose a sensible allocation and leave it alone. It's that simple.

NOTES

1. As shown in Chapter 2, the long-run real return on bonds is only about 2.5 percent.
2. The returns cited are total monthly returns for the S&P 500 including dividends from the end of August 2000 through the end of September 2002.
3. The market index reached its bottom on March 9, 2009.
4. The full retirement age for a 54 year-old in 2012 is actually 66 years and 8 months. See http://ssa.gov/pubs/ageincrease.htm.
5. The investor is assumed to keep cash balances for current spending in an account separate from this portfolio. As explained in the chapters on retirement to follow, an investor once retired must keep part of the portfolio in cash and other liquid investments in order to fund current spending.

6. Some states exempt 529 college fund contributions from state income tax.
7. As mentioned earlier, the trough for the S&P 500 occurred on October 9, 2002. It reached a peak five years later on October 9, 2007.
8. The S&P 500 peaked on October 9, 2007, and reached bottom on March 9, 2009.

CHAPTER 15

Best Practices for Investing

It's all well and good to discuss portfolios of stocks and bonds or individual assets like foreign stocks and real estate. Yet how do investors make sure that investment returns on their portfolios are as good as they should be? How does an investor monitor the performance of fund managers over time? How does the investor track how well the portfolio as a whole is doing over time? Are there some asset classes where active managers should be replaced by index funds? This chapter will discuss these and other aspects of the actual investment process.

Let's begin with an unpleasant subject—the drags on returns with which all of our portfolios contend. Returns lag behind market averages because of the fees and expenses incurred in investing and because our managers often underperform the market averages.

DRAGS ON RETURNS

Investors saving for retirement have to pay attention to investment returns. Of course, they are at the mercy of markets. The market will go up some years and down others. That's as true of the bond market as it is of the stock market. All that investors can do is to make sure that they earn market returns. There are at least two ways that returns can fall short. First, investors may be invested in funds that *underperform* the market indexes. Second, investors may find their returns are dragged down by *fees or other investment expenses*. Let's begin this chapter by showing how these two factors matter.

Suppose that an investor is aiming to earn the same long-run returns on stocks and bonds that we discussed in Chapter 2. Recall that we were measuring real returns or those adjusted by inflation. The returns we assumed in that chapter were 2.5 percent for bonds and 6.5 percent for stocks. These were the long-run real returns that we found in the historical data. A portfolio with 75 percent invested in stocks and 25 percent invested in bonds

TABLE 15.1 How Much Fees Matter: Wealth Accumulated from $100,000 Compounded at Historical Real Rates of Return (in $ thousands)

	No Fees	Drag 1% per Annum	Impact of Drag
10 years	$170.8	$155.3	–9.1%
20 years	$291.8	$241.2	–17.3%
30 years	$498.4	$374.5	–24.9%

Notes: The $100,000 portfolio is assumed to consist of 75% in stocks and 25% in bonds. Before fees, stocks are assumed to earn 6.5% real returns and bonds 2.5% real returns. The drag on returns due to underperformance or fees is assumed to be 1% per year.

would earn a return of about 5.5 percent per year in real terms. An investor with $100,000 to invest would see that sum swell to $170,800 within 10 years, to $291,800 in 20 years, and to $498,400 in 30 years. Remember that these accumulations are in constant dollars. So wealth in real terms is actually rising quite substantially over time. These results are shown in the first column of Table 15.1.

Now let's consider what happens if the investor chooses managers who underperform and if there are fees and expenses dragging down returns. Table 15.1 shows what happens to wealth accumulation if the returns are dragged down by 1 percent per year. In that case, an investor with 75 percent in stocks and 25 percent in bonds earns 4.5 percent per year rather than 5.5 percent. If the account is left invested for 20 years, the resulting accumulation of wealth is reduced by 17.3 percent. Over 30 years, the reduction in wealth is 24.9 percent.

Why would a portfolio underperform by 1 percent or more? One important reason is that the fund managers underperform by that much. That is easy to do. If a fund manager earns the same return as the stock market before subtracting fund fees, then the fund would necessarily underperform *net of fees*. Investors hope they can find the managers who are able to earn *gross returns* above that of the market. Since the market as a whole cannot outperform itself, it's unlikely that the universe of active fund managers can outperform the market in terms of gross returns. Some will. But those managers have to outperform enough to offset their own fees.

A second reason that the portfolio might underperform is because of the fees charged at the portfolio level by the investment advisor. An advisor can play a critical role in the investing process: helping the investor choose an appropriate asset allocation, selecting managers for each asset class, providing reports on portfolio performance, reminding the investor to rebalance the portfolio, and so forth. But the advisor needs to be paid for this effort. In many cases, the fees charged by the managers and the investment advisor are lumped together in a single "wrap" fee expressed as a percent of all assets under management.

The important lesson to keep in mind is that the investment returns that matter to the investor are those that are calculated *net of all fees*. And as Chapter 5 suggests, the returns are even more meaningful if we calculate them net of taxes as well.

MEASURING MANAGER PERFORMANCE

It's the task of the investment advisor to recommend good managers. That task is not an easy one. There are thousands of investment managers to choose for any of the broad asset classes. Past performance has to be examined carefully. Has the manager performed well over the past year, past three years, past five years, and so on? How much risk has the manager taken on to achieve those returns?

A good advisory firm will have a research group (or groups) to search for managers. Such a group will typically screen a large number of managers using proprietary software. Then the group will narrow in on a subset of managers for in-depth research. The research team will compare the (risk-adjusted) returns generated by a fund manager with those of other fund managers investing in similar types of stocks or bonds. The returns will also be compared with the relevant stock or bond market indexes. The research team will also investigate who are the principals in the fund management company, what is their background and expertise, what is their methodology, and how consistently do they follow that methodology. So it's not just the performance numbers that count.

Once a manager has been chosen, the research group has to make sure that performance keeps up over time. If returns slip for a year or two, is there a reason for this slippage? Has there been a change in management at the firm? Does the fund manager have a sensible explanation for underperformance? A good advisory firm will be able to explain to an investor why performance has been good or bad. But how does the investor keep track of all this? How do investors judge how well fund managers are performing?

In some years, stock or bond markets do well. In other years, they disappoint. But in any type of market, funds can underperform or outperform. It's the job of investors to keep track of the performance of the funds we invest in. Investors can't control what the markets do, but they can insist that their funds do as well as the markets. In order to monitor the performance of the funds, they must insist on having the right *benchmarks*.

I am going to describe the type of investment reporting that I look for in my role as an advisor to wealthy families. For every type of investment in their portfolio, the family (or family office) asks the investment firm to choose a benchmark index. And every investment statement has to report the return on this index. If the family is investing in a large-cap stock fund, for example, the investment statement has to report the performance of the index along with that of the fund.

Table 15.2 provides a template for such an investment statement. In this table, there are four bond and stock funds whose performances are reported. These are actual funds that a family has invested in (but I have replaced the actual fund name by a generic one). The fund returns are reported *net of fees*. For every fund, there is a corresponding index reported for the same time period. For example, Foreign Stock Fund D is compared with the MSCI EAFE foreign stock market index. The investment statement gives returns over the past year as well as over preceding periods. If the

TABLE 15.2   Benchmarking Funds: Model Investment Statement

Mutual Fund/ Benchmark Index	2011	2010	2009	2008	2007	5-Year Average
Municipal Bond Fund A	*6.7%*	3.2%	8.4%	*2.9%*	*4.6%*	*5.1%*
Barclays 1–10- Year Municipal Bond Index	7.6%	3.1%	7.2%	*4.5%*	4.9%	*5.5%*
U.S. Large-Cap Stock Fund B	7.7%	*10.0%*	*20.8%*	−27.8%	12.8%	3.1%
S&P 500 Index	2.1%	*15.1%*	*26.4%*	−37.0%	5.5%	−0.3%
U.S. Small-Cap Fund C	5.6%	*25.1%*	30.5%	−27.4%	+5.2%	5.7%
Russell 2000 Index	−4.2%	*26.8%*	27.2%	−33.8%	−1.6%	0.1%
Foreign Stock Fund D	−9.9%	13.3%	*30.5%*	−37.9%	15.9%	−0.8%
MSCI EAFE Index	−11.7%	8.2%	*32.5%*	−43.1%	11.6%	−4.3%

Notes: All returns are expressed in percent/annum. The fund returns (with names disguised) are from the investment statement of a family office. Returns for years when the fund underperformed are italicized.
Sources for index returns: Barclays, S&P Dow Jones Indices, Russell®, and MSCI.

statement is issued at mid-year, then the returns would include figures for year-to-date (YTD) performance. If there have been cash flows into or out of the portfolio, then the returns on these indexes have to be calculated in exactly the same way as the returns on the funds. (This is not so easy to accomplish, but investment firms have software to do this properly.)

By reporting the returns of each fund in this manner, it's easy for the investor to judge how well the manager is doing. For example, the Municipal Bond Fund A underperformed the muni index in 2011 by 0.9 percent. But it outperformed the index by 1.2 percent in 2009. Large-cap Stock Fund B outperformed the S&P 500 index by 5.6 percent in 2011, but underperformed by 5.1 percent in 2010. Over the five years as a whole, this fund outperformed the index by an impressively large 3.4 percent per year. In years when the bond or stock market does badly, the manager is still judged in relative terms. For example, in 2008 all stock markets fell. The three stock managers in this portfolio, however, performed well *relative to their benchmarks.* U.S. Large-Cap Stock Fund B lost 27.8 percent. That's terrible news to the investor, but it's a lot better than the S&P 500 Index losing 37.0 percent. Similarly, the Foreign Stock Fund D lost 37.9 percent, distinctly better than the MSCI EAFE Index, which fell 43.1 percent.

What does this investment statement accomplish? The investor has an easy way to judge the performance of each manager. If the "market" (as measured by the benchmark) has gone down, how well has the manager fared relative to the market? If the market has soared, has the manager captured this upside?

The harder task is trying to judge whether the fund has done badly enough to be replaced. There is more art than science in that decision. Let's take an example from the period prior to the financial crisis. A value stock manager in 2005 and 2006 may be underperforming because he or she has underweighted banks in the portfolio. Only in 2007 and 2008, when bank stocks imploded, do we learn how smart that decision was! Do we tolerate two or three years of underperformance? Perhaps we do, but only if we believe that there is a good reason for the underperformance.

Some investment firms may quarrel with this approach by pointing out that investors cannot actually earn the index returns used as benchmarks. There are index funds for almost every benchmark index, but these funds charge fees. This is certainly true, but index funds can be very cheap. The Vanguard S&P 500 Index Fund charges a fee ranging from 0.17 percent for small accounts to 0.05 percent for accounts over $10,000. The fees would be higher for more specialized funds such as the Vanguard Emerging Market Stock Index Fund where fees range from 0.33 percent for small accounts to 0.20 percent for larger accounts. Alternatively, the investor could choose to buy exchange-traded funds (ETFs) that follow market indexes. The SPDR

S&P 500 ETF offered by State Street, for example, tracks the S&P 500. The investor pays an initial brokerage fee plus an annual expense of less than 0.10 percent. The important point is that index funds and their ETF counterparts are very cheap. If the investor were to subtract the cost of index funds from the benchmark index returns, the results of benchmarking would still be much the same as was shown above.

Some bond and stock funds may be hard to match to indexes. Some foreign stock managers, for instance, invest in both developed and emerging market stocks. At a time when emerging markets are outperforming, benchmarking against the MSCI EAFE index of developed stocks will make the manager look terrific whether or not that manager is a good stock picker. So a weighted benchmark index might have to be employed. But benchmarking works for most investment funds.

TO INDEX OR NOT

Setting up an investment statement in this manner leads naturally to an interesting question: Should we simply invest in index funds and not search for active managers who can outperform indexes? This is a question that many sophisticated endowments ask. And the answer is interesting. *It depends on the asset class.* There are some asset classes where you can't find many managers who consistently outperform. For other asset classes, because returns differ so much across funds, manager performance may be the key determinant of performance.

To illustrate, let me examine a broad asset class, U.S. stock mutual funds, where we already have some data. In Chapter 6, we discuss a dataset of mutual funds assembled by Dickson and Shoven (1995) for their study of tax efficiency. This data set consisted of 147 stock funds measured over the period from 1982 to 1992.

Let's break up the funds in this dataset into different quartiles of performance. The first quartile has an average after-tax return of 12.5 percent over the 10-year period from 1982 to 1992. (Don't be surprised by the high returns. This was the beginning of the bull market of the 1980s and 1990s). The third quartile, in turn, had an average return of 9.9 percent. So there was a moderately large 2.6 percent gap between the first and third quartile returns. The bigger the gap, the more rewarding is the search for good managers.

David Swensen of the Yale endowment reported the results of a study of manager performance for the second edition of his book, *Pioneering Portfolio Management* (2009). Swensen studied a dataset of active managers for conventional and alternative asset classes for the 10 years ending in

June 2005. He found that the gap between the first and third quartile returns of U.S. fixed income managers was only 0.5 percent![1] For U.S. large-cap managers, the gap widened to 1.9 percent, somewhat smaller than that found in the Dickson-Shoven dataset. But as you get into markets with less market efficiency, the gap between the best managers and others widens a lot. For U.S. small-cap managers, the gap is 4.0 percent. And for international equity managers, the gap is 4.8 percent. So the reward for choosing good managers is greatest in the small-cap and international portions of the portfolio. It should be mentioned that Swensen found far larger gaps among managers of hedge funds and private equity. For that reason, the Yale endowment devotes many of its resources to finding good managers for the alternative asset classes. Why should it focus on finding good bond managers when the rewards are so limited?

This suggests a possible approach to indexing: the investor chooses index funds for the asset classes where there is little difference between the top managers and the average managers or where there are relatively few top managers. For example, there may be little difference between the top managers and the average managers of investment-grade bond funds. So the investor chooses index funds for that category. On the other hand, high-yield bonds may require active managers because it's important to pick and choose among these riskier types of bonds. Similarly, large-cap stocks may be more efficiently priced than small caps. So the investor may choose index funds for large caps. A more sophisticated strategy involves the "core and satellite" investing done by many large institutional funds. These funds invest some of their large-cap allocation in "core" index funds and thereby save on management fees. But the funds also choose to allocate some funds to "satellite" value or growth managers in an attempt to pick up some extra performance. Figure 15.1 illustrates this strategy for a diversified stock and bond portfolio.

The portfolio illustrated has allocated 25 percent to cash and bonds and 75 percent to stocks. The bulk of the fixed income investments are in cash and investment-grade bonds. The investor has chosen to index those investments for the reasons already discussed. But high-yield bonds are actively managed, perhaps because the investor wants a manager to closely monitor credit risks. The allocation to U.S. large-cap stocks is divided into core investments that are indexed and satellite investments that are actively managed. In this portfolio, the rest of the stock market allocation is actively managed, including small caps.

If some investors (and investment advisors) prefer to choose active managers for every asset in the portfolio, this may be a reasonable choice as long as all of the active managers are benchmarked against indexes. The investors can monitor whether the decision to actively manage everything is costing

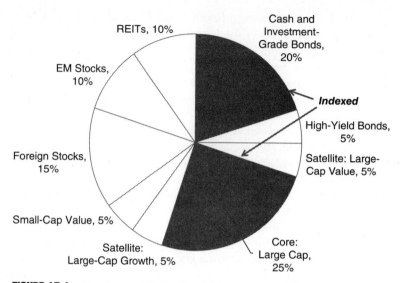

FIGURE 15.1   Passive and Active Fund Management: The Core and Satellite Model

them money. The decision to index or not is an investment decision, not a philosophical choice. Proper monitoring of performance keeps the decision as clear-cut as possible.

OVERALL PORTFOLIO PERFORMANCE

So far we have focused on how well individual managers are performing relative to their benchmark indexes. It's equally important to keep track of how the portfolio as a whole is doing. A portfolio may be underperforming for several different reasons:

- The managers as a whole may be underperforming relative to their respective benchmarks. For example, you may find that Managers A and B are doing well, but Managers C and D are doing badly enough to more than offset the successful managers.
- The weights in the portfolio may have drifted away from the strategic allocation so that some assets are overweighted relative to the strategic allocation. For example, a portfolio overweighted with stocks would have been extra hard hit during the financial crisis when stocks fell sharply.

▪ A third reason is that the investor may have tactically shifted in the wrong direction at the wrong time. For example, a tactical shift into equities in 2007 would have hurt performance a lot.

How does an investor measure the performance of a portfolio?

What I recommend is that an investor measure the performance of a benchmark portfolio that (1) has the same asset weights as in the investor's strategic portfolio and (2) earns the index returns on each asset. The investor compares the returns on this portfolio with returns on the actual portfolio. Table 15.3 presents such a calculation for the year 2011 using the index returns of Table 15.2. To simplify the analysis, the actual portfolio is assumed to have the same weights as the strategic portfolio, so returns on the two portfolios differ only because of manager performance. The investor's strategic portfolio is a simple one with 25 percent in municipal bonds, 50 percent in U.S. stocks, and 25 percent in foreign stocks.[2] According to Table 15.3, the portfolio using *index* returns should have had a small loss of 0.3 percent. The negative returns on small-caps and foreign stocks more than offset the positive returns on large-cap stocks and bonds. The *actual* portfolio earned 2.9 percent, so this portfolio *outperformed* its benchmark by 3.2 percent.

As stated above, in this example the actual portfolio weights were identical to the model portfolio weights. In actual practice, this almost never happens even if the investment firm avoids tactical positions. As explained in the last chapter, actual portfolio weights often drift away from model weights simply because some asset classes perform better than others. Only an aggressive rebalancing policy can limit this drift. Because of this drift, returns on the actual portfolio can differ from the returns on the benchmark

TABLE 15.3   How Much Should the Portfolio Have Earned in 2011?

Asset Class	Weight	Index Used	Index Return	Actual Return
Municipal Bonds	25%	Barclays 1–10-Year Municipal	7.6%	6.7%
U.S. Large-Cap Stocks	45%	S&P 500	2.1%	7.7%
U.S. Small-Cap Stocks	5%	Russell 2000	–4.2%	5.6%
Foreign Stocks	25%	MSCI EAFE	–11.7%	–9.9%
		Portfolio	–0.3%	2.9%

Sources for index returns: Barclays, S&P Dow Jones Indices, Russell®, and MSCI.

portfolio for two reasons: (1) the actual portfolio allocation has departed from the strategic allocation, and/or (2) the managers as a whole have underperformed or outperformed their respective indexes. It's possible to distinguish the two sources of performance.[3] But for most purposes, it's sufficient for an investor to know how well the portfolio is performing relative to its benchmark.

Let's go one step further to examine performance over a longer period. Judging investment performance based on one year's returns alone is not enough. Table 15.4 continues our example by examining relative performance over a five-year period. The actual portfolio underperforms in 2010 and 2009, but over the five-year period the actual portfolio outperforms its benchmark by 1.8 percent per year. If this is the case, the investor should be pleased with the performance. This is true even though the portfolio has had a miserably low return of 3.2 percent per year. The low return is due to market performance over which the investor has no control.

A reader may object that the investor would have been better off investing in bonds alone during this five-year period. That is undoubtedly the case. Municipal Bond Fund A earned an average return of 5.1 percent over this period, almost 2 percent above that of the diversified portfolio. If you find an investment advisor who can shift you into bonds (or any other asset) just at the right time, you have a better strategy than I can offer. Toss away this book. But before you do so, ask the advisor whether he or she shifted into stocks in October 2002 and out of them in October 2007. And ask the advisor whether he or she shorted residential and commercial real estate in early 2007 or at least sold off all holdings. And, finally, ask the advisor why he or she is handling your account rather than getting rich running a big macro hedge fund.

Financial advisors often play a crucial role in guiding investors' decisions as they build wealth before retirement and as they manage that wealth during retirement. Advisors can help investors to understand why they need to build portfolios that are well diversified. Advisors can help guide investors to choose capable managers, and alert investors when managers need

TABLE 15.4 Portfolio Performance over 5 Years: Actual versus Index Performance

	2011	2010	2009	2008	2007	Five-Year Average
Index return	−0.3%	11.0%	23.2%	−28.0%	6.5%	0.9%
Actual return	2.9%	9.9%	20.6%	−22.6%	11.1%	3.2%
Excess return	3.2%	−1.1%	−2.6%	5.3%	4.6%	1.8%

to be changed. Perhaps most important, a good financial advisor can help investors to weather the bad times. When markets fall precipitously as they did in 2008, it takes a good advisor (and a sensible investor) to keep a cool head and to stick to a long-term strategy. If an advisor fails to give you the latest advice about which way to weave in and of assets, don't be disappointed. That advisor has your long-run interests in mind.

CONCLUDING COMMENTS

Investors have responsibilities. First, they have to monitor the performance of their individual fund managers. To do this effectively, they must insist that their investment advisors benchmark each manager to an index. Good practice requires that the investment statement list all fund returns right next to the equivalent index. Second, investors have to monitor portfolio performance as a whole. I have suggested that they do this by calculating the returns they would earn if the portfolio was always at its long-term strategic weights and if the portfolio earned index returns in each asset class. Third, investors have to be aware of the fees and expenses of investing. In the long run, they can make a big difference to wealth accumulation.

NOTES

1. Swensen (2009), Table 4.4.
2. This is a simple hypothetical portfolio used for illustration purposes only.
3. Most investors compare the actual return on a portfolio with the return on a portfolio that kept to its strategic weights and earned index returns: (Actual weights × actual returns) − (strategic weights × index returns). It's possible to break up these calculations into two components: (1) gap due to manager performance = (actual returns − index returns) × actual weights minus (2) gap due to the drift in portfolio weights = (strategic weights − actual weights) × index returns.

REFERENCES

Dickson, Joel M., and John B. Shoven. 1995. "Taxation and Mutual Funds: An Investor Perspective." *Tax Policy and the Economy 9.*

Swensen, David F. 2009. *Pioneering Portfolio Management: An Unconventional Approach to Institutional Investment,* 2nd ed. New York: Free Press.

CHAPTER 16

Investment Income for Retirement

Some employees are lucky enough to have a defined benefit pension that provides a steady stream of income in retirement. Those fortunate employees include most state and local government workers as well as those working for the minority of corporations that have maintained defined benefit plans. Most employees, however, must be content with defined contribution retirement plans like the 401(k) plus Social Security. The savings made within defined contribution plans plus whatever other savings the employees make outside of these plans provide the basis for their retirement. This chapter will discuss whether these savings can replace the steady stream of income of old style pensions.

Baby boomers will find the new retirement system quite challenging. How do they replace the guaranteed income provided by the old system? Will income from investments suffice? After all, interest rates are at all-time lows and stock dividend yields are miserably low. To give readers fair warning, our search for income will come up short. But we will explore what is available in today's markets.

Before we begin to explore sources of income, it's important to explain what I regard as "best practice" in retirement planning. It's not wise to base retirement spending entirely on income generated within the portfolio. Instead, retirees should fund their spending out of the *total return* on the portfolio. Spending the income from the portfolio might mean that retirees are spending too much or too little.

Overspending scenario: If retirees spend the income from the portfolio, they are potentially spending *too much*. Consider a portfolio consisting only of long-term bonds paying 4 percent. If retirees spend the entire income from the bond, they will not be allowing the portfolio to keep pace with inflation. A million-dollar bond portfolio will generate $40,000 the first year of retirement and the same amount for every year until the bond matures. But even modest inflation will undermine retirement spending. An inflation rate of 2.5 percent, for example, raises the cost of living by 28 percent in 10 years and more than 60 percent in 20 years. Wouldn't it be better to spend less initially so that spending could be increased later to keep pace with inflation?

Underspending scenario: On the other hand, spending the income on the portfolio may mean that you are spending *too little*. If retirees are invested in stocks, the dividend yield is on average only a small fraction of the total return on the stock. The capital gain is there to help retirees keep spending in line with inflation. If they don't tap part of the capital gain, their spending in retirement may fall short.

Yet many retirees feel uncomfortable spending any of the capital gain on their portfolio. So they are forced to search for sources of income generated by their investments. I am ready to explore some of these sources of income. But I will caution investors against taking on too much risk in order to find yield. I will provide four solutions for finding income in retirement. None of them will be entirely satisfactory, but all will be essential ingredients of a successful retirement strategy.

SOLUTION 1: BOND INVESTMENTS—MATURITY AND CREDIT RISK

Retirees have traditionally relied on bonds to provide much of their current income. This was very easy to do back in the 1980s when yields were so high. The 20-year Treasury averaged 11 percent in 1985. If only investors of that time had had the good sense to lock in these rates! Over the succeeding decades, yields have declined markedly. That's good news for this country in one sense because the lower yields have resulted from lower inflation. Because the Federal Reserve under Paul Volcker and his successors managed to lower inflation from its peak over 13 percent in 1980 to its current level today, interest rates have also fallen sharply. Consider Figure 16.1 showing Treasury yields at different maturities in four different decades. Yields at every maturity have fallen from one decade to the next. In 1995, the 20-year Treasury paid 7.0 percent. A decade later, it paid only 4.6 percent. Then in early May 2013, the 20-year Treasury yielded only 2.7 percent.

The other significant change that has occurred, but only recently, is that there is a very large gap between the yields on short-term bonds and longer-term yields. Consider interest rates on different Treasury maturities in May 2013 as shown in Table 16.1. An investor willing to buy a five-year Treasury receives a yield of only 0.84 percent! Federal Reserve policy keeping short-term interest rates low may explain these low yields, but that is little comfort to an investor who is trying to live off "fixed-income" securities.

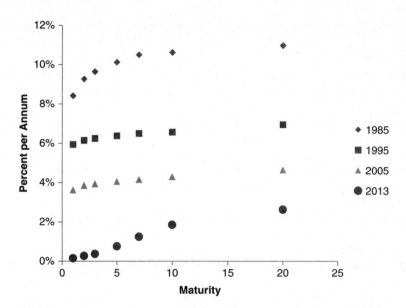

FIGURE 16.1 Treasury Interest Rates by Maturity
Source: Federal Reserve Board.

To obtain a Treasury yield higher than 3 percent, it's necessary to invest in a 30-year Treasury bond.

What is wrong with buying a 30-year Treasury bond? The answer is "nothing at all," as long as the current level of interest rates prevails. But what if interest rates rise? Let's consider a simple example. Suppose that newly issued Treasury bonds with 30 years maturity are yielding 3 percent. What

TABLE 16.1 Impact of Bond Maturity and Credit Rating on Yields, May 2013

Treasury Yields by Maturity		Corporate Yields by Credit Rating	
Maturity	Yield	Credit Rating	Yield
1 year	0.12%	Corporate AAA	3.89%
2 years	0.25%	Corporate BAA	4.73%
3 years	0.40%		
5 years	0.84%		
7 years	1.31%		
10 years	1.93%		
20 years	2.73%		
30 years	3.11%		

Source: Federal Reserve Board.

happens if interest rates on new bonds next year rise to 4 percent? What would happen to the current value of your 30-year bond? The answer is that a bond originally costing $1,000 would now be worth only about $825.[1] If interest rates rise to 5 percent, the price of the bond would fall below $700.

Many investors would have an answer to that: "I don't intend to sell the bond. I will hold the bond to maturity, so it doesn't matter what happens to its price." Well, as explained in Chapter 10, these investors are neglecting the opportunity cost of locking in 3 percent yields. If investors were to wait longer, a 4 or 5 percent yield might be available. Suppose, for example, that interest rates rose by next year. In that case, for the next 29 years the investor could have earned a higher return than on the 3 percent yielding bond. So that investor loses even if the 3 percent bond is held to maturity. "Buying and holding" does not shield the investor from losses due to rising interest rates.

The bottom line is that today's extremely low yields for shorter maturities are forcing investors to make a tough choice. Do I maximize current yield by choosing longer maturities or do I try to limit interest rate risks by choosing shorter maturities? Every investor is facing this tough choice even if he or she is many years from retirement.

How does an investor increase yield in this environment? One answer is to assume some *credit risk*. Treasuries are the safest asset in the world (regardless of what the S&P rating agency says!). If an investor is willing to choose AAA-rated corporate bonds, the interest yield increases about 0.8 percent over 30-year Treasury bonds. (It should be noted that corporate bonds are subject to state income tax whereas Treasury bonds are exempt from these taxes). Choosing a lower-rated corporate bond will increase yields further. Consider the corporate yields reported in Table 16.1 for May 2013. At a time when the 20-year Treasury was paying 2.73 percent and the 30-year Treasury 3.11 percent, the AAA corporate bond was paying 3.89 percent, and the BAA corporate bond was paying 4.73 percent. Bonds below investment grade were paying even higher yields. So it's possible for an investor to earn higher yields by taking on more credit risk.

Does the higher yield translate into higher total return for the investor? Remember that higher credit risk usually means some losses from bonds that go into default. And even in the absence of default, the prices of lower-rated bonds may fall if the economy seems to be faltering. Certainly during times of recession, the prices of riskier corporate bonds fall sharply. So it's important to look at the total return on bonds. Over the 20-year period ending in December 2012, the Barclays High Yield bond index (for corporate bonds with credit ratings below investment grade) provided a return of 8.2 percent compared with a return of 7.1 percent on the Barclays Investment Grade bond index and a return of 7.1 percent on the Barclays 7- to 10-Year Treasury index. So over the long term at least, higher credit risk translates into higher return.

Yet credit risk should be taken in small doses. An investor in retirement certainly would not want to load up too much on credit risk in order to maximize yield. In the recession beginning in December 2007, the Barclays High Yield bond index fell 31.4 percent over the next 11 months! Investment-grade corporate bonds also suffered. The Barclays Corporate Investment Grade Bond Index fell by 11.0 percent over the same 11-month period. That's not very good news for an investor looking for safety in fixed income. So we had better not confine the portfolio to bonds with high credit risk.

SOLUTION 2: MUNICIPAL BONDS

Many retired investors are attracted to municipal bonds because of their exemption from Federal income taxes. This is particularly true of investors in higher tax brackets. The tax exempt status of many of these bonds makes them an attractive alternative to corporate bonds.

To compare municipal with taxable bonds, it's important to adjust municipal bond yields to obtain "tax equivalent" yields (as explained in Chapter 11). Consider a simple example. If a corporate bond pays 4 percent and the tax rate is 50 percent, then a municipal bond that pays 2 percent would have an equivalent after-tax yield. An investor should be indifferent between these two bonds as long as they have the same risks.

In May 2013, corporate bond yields ranged from 3.89 percent for AAA bonds to 4.73 percent for BAA bonds, while the municipal yield averaged 3.72 percent for general obligation bonds. To compare the municipal bond with the taxable bond, we must first calculate the tax-equivalent yield. That is done by dividing the municipal yield by (1 – tax rate). Table 16.2 calculates the tax equivalent yields for four tax rates.[2] For example, if an investor is in the 33 percent tax bracket, a 3.72 percent yield on a municipal bond is equivalent to

$$3.72\%/(1-0.33) = 5.55\%$$

A taxable corporate bond would have to pay a yield of that much to match this aftertax yield. No wonder many higher-income Americans prefer to invest in municipal bonds. It should be noted that state governments in many cases exempt municipal bonds issued in that state from state and local income taxes. But we will ignore state and local taxes in this analysis.

There is one drawback to municipal bonds that should be considered. Just as in the case of taxable bonds, an investor has to choose a longer-term bond to pick up decent yields. In May 2013, the five-year municipal bond had a coupon that was about *2.0 percent lower* than that of the 20-year municipal.

TABLE 16.2   Yields on Municipal and Taxable Bonds, May 2013

Bonds	Yields
Corporate AAA	3.89%
Corporate BAA	4.73%
Municipal Bond	3.72%

Tax Rates	Tax Equivalent Yields on Municipal Bond
39.6% + 3.8%	6.57%
35% + 3.8%	6.08%
33%	5.55%
28%	5.17%

Notes: The Municipal Bond series is a Bond Buyer index for general obligation bonds with 20 years to maturity. The tax rates include the 3.8% tax to fund the Affordable Care Act. That tax applies to the investment income of married couples with taxable income above $250,000 (singles above $200,000). The 33% tax bracket includes taxpayers who are not subject to this 3.8% tax, so this tax is ignored in the calculations for that tax bracket.
Source: Federal Reserve Board.

To obtain a more reasonable yield, the investor has to choose a much longer maturity. As in the case of taxable bonds, a long maturity exposes an investor to considerable interest rate risk if the general level of interest rates were to rise.

Besides yield, there is another important factor that should be considered in evaluating municipal bonds: default risk. But as Chapter 11 showed, default risk for municipal bonds has never matched that for comparably rated corporate bonds. A well-diversified municipal bond portfolio should be able to keep default risk in check. If investors have taken the types of precautions outlined in Chapter 11 to limit default risk, they should worry more about interest rate risk than default risk. Investors should keep their bond maturities shorter than normal, but then interest income will fall short of that shown in Table 16.2.

SOLUTION 3: STOCKS WITH HIGHER DIVIDEND YIELDS

In earlier decades, investors looked to dividends for current income to a greater extent than they do today. That's because dividend yields used to be much higher. In the 1970s, for example, the dividend yield for the S&P 500 stock market index averaged 4.12 percent, and in the 1980s the dividend yield averaged 4.05 percent. But in the 1990s the dividend yield plummeted

TABLE 16.3 Dividend Yields and Price-Earnings Ratios, May 2013

Stock Market Sector	Dividend Yield	Price-Earnings Ratio
Large-cap value	2.36%	15.3
Large-cap growth	1.75%	19.4
Small-cap value	2.05%	17.0
Small-cap growth	0.68%	22.6

Source: Russell.com.

to 2.20 percent. In the decade just past, the average yield was 1.87 percent. Clearly, stocks don't provide the current income that they used to provide.

How can investors find stocks with higher dividends? One answer is to examine the "style" of the stock investment, whether growth or value. Generally speaking, value stocks have higher dividends than growth stocks. (As Chapter 7 explains, growth stocks are those with relative high price-to-book ratios and relatively high earnings growth. Value stocks are those with the opposite characteristics.) Consider the dividend yields reported in Table 16.3 for May 2013. In the large-cap sector, value stocks have a dividend yield about 0.6 percent higher than growth stocks. In the small-cap sector, the differential is even larger at almost 1.4 percent. Tilting the portfolio toward value stocks thus increases dividend yields, although the gain in yields in quite modest.

It's possible to increase dividend yield even further than shown in Table 16.3 by deliberately screening stocks for their dividend yields. Several mutual fund companies do just that. Such a dividend-heavy stock portfolio might be attractive to an investor on a fixed income. But always keep in mind that it's important not to concentrate the stock portfolio too much.

It's also possible to earn higher dividends by investing in foreign stocks. In May 2013, the MSCI EAFE index of foreign industrial country stocks had an average dividend yield of 2.9 percent. That is in contrast to an average dividend yield of only 2.2 percent for stocks in the S&P 500 index. Individual countries have even higher yields. Higher dividend yields provide yet another reason to invest in foreign stocks. Not only does investing in foreign stocks help to diversify the stock portfolio, but it also increases the average dividend yield on that portfolio.

SOLUTION 4: REAL ESTATE INVESTMENT TRUSTS (REITS)

Real estate investment trusts (or REITs) have always paid higher dividends than ordinary stocks. As explained in Chapter 12, REITs are companies that invest in commercial real estate such as office buildings, factories and distribution centers, and shopping malls. One major reason why REITs pay

TABLE 16.4   Average Dividend Yields on REITs and Stocks Compared, 1973–2012

Period	NAREIT Dividend Yield	S&P 500 Dividend Yield
1973–1982	8.61%	4.60%
1983–1992	7.99%	3.59%
1993–2002	7.04%	1.88%
2003–2012	4.69%	1.98%

Sources: NAREIT and Robert Shiller's website, www.econ.yale.edu/~shiller/data.htm.

higher dividends is that they are required to pay out 90 percent of their income in order to avoid having to pay corporate income tax on their profits. Ordinary corporations, in contrast, must pay corporate income tax, but can adopt any dividend policy including a no-dividend policy. So dividends on REITs tend to be considerably higher than those on ordinary stocks.

Consider Table 16.4, which compares dividend rates for REITs and stocks over the past four decades ending in December 2012. In every decade, average dividend yields are roughly twice as high for REITs compared to S&P 500 stocks. For example, over the decade from 2003 to 2012, REITs paid an average dividend of 4.69 percent whereas stocks paid a dividend a little below 2 percent. Dividends on REITs, like those on stocks, have declined markedly over the past 40 years. But they remain much higher than those on stocks.

As Chapter 12 discusses, REITs have also provided higher returns than stocks. Over the 21-year period ending in December 2012, for example, the NAREIT index returned 11.2 percent, whereas the S&P 500 index returned only 8.2 percent. The differential in returns is over 2 percent if the period is extended back to 1972 when the NAREIT series begins. So along with the much higher dividend, the investor has also received a higher return.

Still REITs are a relatively narrow asset class, so an investor should not devote too high a proportion of wealth to this asset class. It's true that REITs provide an entryway to the larger commercial real estate market. (As shown in Chapter 12, REITs represent a little less than 20 percent of the commercial real estate market.) But investors should not concentrate too much risk in REITs any more than they should take on too much risk in corporate bonds or dividend-paying stocks.

LIMITS OF INCOME STRATEGIES

What does this all mean for the average retired investor? The investor could choose to invest in high income assets such as lower-graded, longer-term corporate bonds and high dividend paying stocks as well as REITs. But it wouldn't be prudent to load up too much on the assets with the highest

TABLE 16.5   Income from a Retirement Portfolio, May 2013

Asset	Portfolio Weight	Coupon or Dividend Yield
Cash	5%	0.15%
Municipals	35%	5.55%
Corporate bonds (BAA)	10%	4.73%
U.S. stocks	25%	2.17%
Foreign stocks	18%	2.91%
REITS	7%	3.51%
Portfolio		3.74%

Notes: The cash yield is for a 30-day CD. The municipal yield is a tax-equivalent yield based on a 3.72 percent coupon yield and a 33 percent tax rate. The U.S. stock dividend is for the S&P 500 Index, the foreign dividend for the MSCI EAFE Index, and the REIT dividend for the NAREIT Index.
Data sources: Federal Reserve Board, S&P Dow Jones Indices, MSCI, and NAREIT.

income. So what would happen if the investor chose a well-diversified portfolio? Many experts recommend that investors choose a 50/50 bond/stock portfolio at the time of retirement. Table 16.5 outlines one such portfolio. The portfolio includes a hefty allocation to municipals because their tax equivalent yields are so attractive. And it includes both domestic and foreign stocks as well as REITs.

Table 16.5 reports the yields on each asset as of May 2013. Overall, the portfolio provides a modest income of 3.74 percent per year. It's evident from the table that the bulk of this income comes from the municipal bonds (at least on an after-tax basis) and corporate bonds, although income from REITs almost pulls its own weight. And the high muni- and corporate-bond yields are due to the fact that we have chosen long-term maturities. For the reasons discussed earlier, the 20-year bond has a lot of interest rate risk.

What if the retiree confined municipal and corporate bond investments to five-year maturities? The municipal yield declines by about 2 percent (and by almost 3 percent in tax-equivalent terms) and the corporate yield declines by 2.5 percent. The overall portfolio now earns only 2.44 percent. So you can see that the investor seeking income has to accept a lot of *maturity risk* to earn even a 3.74 percent yield. Bonds are just not paying much unless they are long-term. And stocks no longer pay the dividends seen in the past.

WILL INCOME BE HIGH ENOUGH IN RETIREMENT?

This chapter has explored four options for earning income on a retirement portfolio. To be honest, the income generated is disappointing. It's hard to earn enough income in today's environment of low interest rates and low dividend yields. But a careful blend of bonds, stocks, real estate, and annuities can provide a good portion of the income needed in retirement. That's especially true if we keep spending at the 4 percent rate recommended by retirement experts.

Any one source of income can be too risky for a retiree. With record low interest rates, it makes no sense to invest too much in long-term bonds, even those with high credit ratings. Interest rates won't stay this low forever. And too much credit risk is never a good thing. With record low dividend yields, it might be tempting to invest only in high dividend stocks. But diversification within the stock portfolio is always preferable to too much concentration. Fortunately, REITs and foreign stocks provide more attractive yields than domestic stocks, so diversifying in those dimensions is doubly rewarding in providing higher yields and a reduction of portfolio risk.

NOTES

1. The price of the bond falls because the discount rate has risen. In practical terms, the investor has lost out because newly issued bonds now pay a higher coupon.
2. Table 16.2 includes the new 39.6 percent tax rate on incomes above $400,000 ($450,000 for married couples) passed on January 1, 2013. The table also includes the 3.8 percent tax on investment income for incomes above $200,000 ($250,000 for married couples) to fund the Affordable Care Act. This tax was passed in 2010, but became effective in 2013.

REFERENCES

Marston, Richard C. 2011. *Portfolio Design: A Modern Approach to Asset Allocation.* Hoboken, NJ: John Wiley & Sons.

CHAPTER 17

Spending in Retirement

ow much do you need to retire? That's a very important question that every investor asks when retirement looms ahead. In Chapter 4, I suggested that the savings goal of many investors is to have enough money to keep the standard of living in retirement as high as it was during their working years. That's a reasonable aim. Unfortunately, it may be not possible for many Americans. That's particularly true of those Americans who do not have the defined benefit pensions so common to earlier retirees. Without the steady income provided by old-style corporate pensions or state and local pensions, many Americans may find their standard of living dropping sharply when they retire.

Isn't it possible to live more cheaply in retirement? Some living expenses that we incur during our working years disappear in retirement. Those may include commuting expenses, meals, dry cleaning, and other expenses directly related to work. But, as Michael Stein (1998) recounts in his book, *The Prosperous Retirement*, retirees often find new ways to spend now that they have no work commitments. Many retirees, for example, want to take trips—trips that they have postponed during their working years.

Stein observes that retirees want to spend the most when they first retire. That's because retirement often occurs in three stages:

1. Active phase "go-go"
2. Passive phase "slow-go"
3. Final retirement phase "no-go"

Early in retirement, the retiree is often in good physical shape, so the retiree will want to spend a lot on physical activity—travel, golf, and so forth. In many fortunate cases, this phase may last 10 or 20 years, particularly given how early many people retire. The passive phase begins to occur when aging makes it difficult to be as active as before. Spending therefore drops. In the final phase, there are often large medical expenses that increase spending sharply.

This pattern of spending is a cruel aspect of retirement. Most people want to spend a lot early in retirement. But the more they spend early on, the greater the chance of running out of money before they die. For that reason, many retirement experts favor keeping spending at a steady rate in retirement. As explained in Chapter 4, a "spending rule" is recommended. Naturally, this spending rule is designed to keep up with the cost of living.

In the last chapter we discussed various investments that might provide income in retirement. In today's environment of low interest rates and low dividend yields, an income-based retirement strategy will not work by itself. The only way retirees can find enough income to keep spending high enough is to take risks that are unacceptable for someone on a fixed income. Retirees would need to load up on high-yield bonds and tilt too heavily toward high-dividend-paying stocks and REITs. And the bonds would have to be long-term, thereby exposing retirees to too much interest rate risk. Instead, retirees need to choose a balanced, diversified portfolio of stocks and bonds. And they need to stick with a rate of spending that is sustainable throughout a retirement.

A SPENDING RULE FOR RETIREMENT

As Chapter 4 explains, such a rate of spending is called a spending rule. In that chapter, we discussed the conventional wisdom that a retiree can spend 4 percent of investable wealth each year. This spending rate assumes that the retiree invests in a diversified portfolio of stocks and bonds. The spending rate is kept low so that spending can rise in future years as inflation raises the cost of living for the retiree. Some of the 4 percent spending can be generated by the interest earned on bonds and dividends paid on stock. The rest of it would have to come from harvesting capital gains. In other words, spending would be generated by the total return on the portfolio, not just the income.

Some readers may believe that the 4 percent rule is too high. Their argument might be that such a rule is based on past historical returns, not the lower returns we are likely to earn in the future. More specifically, if the "New Normal" of lower returns described in Chapter 3 were to prevail, a 4 percent spending rule might not be feasible. In that case, savings goals would have to be even more aggressive than those I describe in Chapter 4.

I would bet that there are more readers who argue the opposite: The 4 percent rule is too stingy. If an investor has accumulated $1 million, surely it is possible to spend more than $40,000 a year in retirement!

Let's review the rationale given in Chapter 4 for this rule. The spending rule is low because it is based on real returns, not nominal returns. The long run real returns on bonds and stocks are about 2.5 and 6.5 percent, respectively. A 50/50 portfolio should earn about 4.5 percent in the long run. The spending rate is kept even lower than that to minimize the chance of running out of money in the event that market returns are below average. The 4 percent rule is based on simulation experiments with returns as high as they have averaged in the past, but *with markets as volatile as they have been in the past.*

However, I am not sure that simulations alone will convince readers of the need to keep spending low. Past experience may be more persuasive. Here is what I plan to do. I will look at the fate of retirees retiring in past periods by examining how their investing and spending fares over time. So, for example, I will ask how an investor who retires in 1985 fares over the next 25 years using actual investment returns. The four assumptions that I will make are as follows:

1. The investor retirees with $1 million to fund retirement.
2. The investor chooses a 50/50 stock/bond portfolio.
3. The investor spends 4 percent of the initial retirement portfolio. Spending thereafter is kept constant in real terms, rising with the cost of living.
4. All calculations are done in real terms (so we are dealing with constant dollars).

The results of this experiment are shown in Table 17.1.

TABLE 17.1 How 4 Percent Spending Fares by Retirement Date (in constant dollars)

| Retire at End of Year | Wealth in 20 or 25 Years ($ Thousands) | |
	20 Years Later	25 Years Later
1950	$1,357.3	$1,069.8
1955	$525.2	$311.1
1960	$362.0	$296.7
1965	$110.6	−$79.5
1970	$553.7	$682.3
1975	$1,711.8	$2,579.7
1980	$4,228.4	$4,485.5
1985	$2,844.3	$3,131.2
1990	$2,353.5	

Notes: $1 million is invested in a 50/50 stock/bond portfolio, 50% in the S&P 500, and 50% in long-term Treasury bonds. The portfolio is rebalanced annually. Spending is 4% of initial wealth ($40,000). Withdrawals take place at the beginning of the year. Spending is adjusted each year to keep pace with inflation. All values are in constant dollars.

Data source: © Morningstar.

An investor retiring in 1950 benefited from the strong stock market of the 1950s and early 1960s even though bonds were losing value in real terms. So a retiree living another 20 years saw the portfolio rise to $1,357,300 despite a spending rule of 4 percent per year. If the retiree lived 25 years, the portfolio was hit by the poor stock returns of the early 1970s. So the portfolio in 1975, or 25 years later, fell to $1,069,800. Nonetheless, this retiree coasted through retirement because stocks did so well in the 1950s. Contrast that result with that of an investor retiring in 1965. The table shows that this investor saw the portfolio fall from $1 million to $110,600 in 20 years. And if this poor investor kept spending 4 percent per year, he or she would have been wiped out in the next five years.

How could an investor retiring in 1965 have done so poorly? Remember that the 1970s saw negative real returns for both stocks and bonds. As Table 3.1 showed, stocks had an average real return of –3.2 percent and Treasury bonds had an average real return of –3.4 percent between November 1968 and July 1982. The wealth of this investor is tracked in Figure 17.1. Wealth falls sharply in some years, particularly in the early 1970s. In 1973

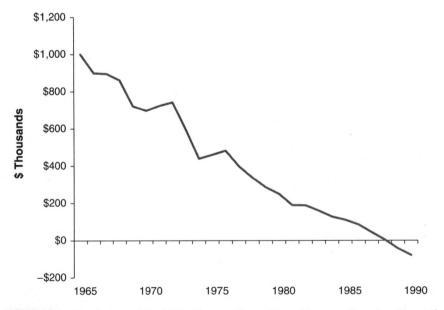

FIGURE 17.1   Evolution of Real Wealth over Time: How 4 Percent Spending Fares if an Investor Retires in 1965
Source for data: © Morningstar Standard & Poor's.

and 1974, for example, the real returns on this investor's 50/50 portfolio were −15.3 percent and −20.7 percent, respectively. But these weren't the only bad years. This investor suffered sizable losses on the portfolio in real terms in 1969, 1977, 1979, and 1981. And, in the meantime, nominal spending had to rise sharply to keep pace with inflation. No wonder this investor's retirement plan was a disaster.

Table 17.1 also shows precipitous declines in wealth for investors retiring in 1955, 1960, and 1970. Investors who think that 4 percent rules are too conservative should remember what the rules meant for those investors who retired in time to suffer from the bad returns of the late 1960s and 1970s.

Investors retiring in 1975 or later fared much better. Consider the luckiest of cohorts—those retiring in 1980. Remember that this cohort had to save enough to accumulate $1 million (in today's dollars) despite very bad markets in the 1970s. But if they had saved $1 million by 1980, they were to enjoy two decades of bull markets in stocks and three decades in bonds. What a fortunate group. A 4 percent spending rule would have allowed them to accumulate over $4.2 million by 2000, 20 years later! That just shows you how sensitive retirement plans are to market performance.

It's useful to update Table 17.1 with a partial report on more recent retirees. Those investors retiring in 1995 have had less than 20 years of experience with spending in retirement. Those retiring in 2000 or 2005 have even fewer years of experience. None of these cohorts are doing as badly as those who retired in the 1950s and 1960s. Figure 17.2 shows the variation in wealth experienced by these investors. As in Table 17.1, the investors start out with $1 million and spend 4 percent of their wealth each year. The investor who retired in 1995 has a portfolio with $1,531,900 (in constant dollars) at the end of 2012. No doubt the splendid stock returns in the late 1990s helped them a lot. Those retiring in 2000 have seen their wealth decrease, but only to $901,000. Those retiring in 2005 are slightly ahead at $1,060,000 million as of the end of 2012. All of these cohorts should thank their lucky stars that they did not have to experience retiring in the 1960s.

The reason why spending rules are so low is that we don't know what returns we will face in retirement. So we err on the side of caution. Guess what? Some cohorts retiring during a time of bull markets will leave far too much to their heirs. Others will run out of money. That's the risk that market volatility brings to retirement.

Is there any way to improve on these results? Spending rules could be more flexible. Consider two alternative models where the retiree begins by spending 4 percent of initial wealth. If the retiree starts with $1 million, he or she spends $40,000 in the first year of retirement.

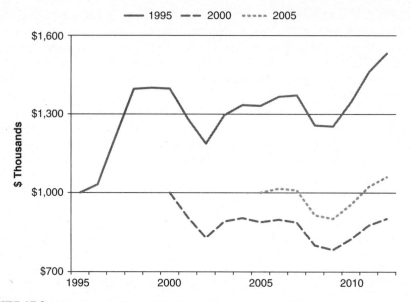

FIGURE 17.2 Evolution of Real Wealth for Investors Retiring in Recent Years with 4 Percent Spending and 50/50 Portfolio
Source for data: © Morningstar, Standard & Poor's.

- **Fixed rule:** Under the fixed rule that I have assumed so far, spending is then increased each year to keep pace with inflation. So if the inflation rate the first year is 3 percent, then the next year the retiree will spend $41,200 (i.e., $40,000 × (1 + 0.03)). Notice that spending remains tied to the level of wealth at retirement. That seems sensible because it is at that time that retirement plans are made. But a fixed rule takes no account of what is happening to portfolio returns during retirement.
- **Proportional rule:** The retiree again starts by spending at a rate of 4 percent. But spending in future years is proportional to the value of the portfolio at the end of the previous year. So if the portfolio rises by 10 percent in the first year, spending rises in proportion. On the other hand, if the portfolio falls by 10 percent in the first year, then spending has to fall in proportion. Many endowments follow such a proportional rule, but they typically smooth out changes in spending by using the average size of the endowment over the previous three years or so. It's harder for a retiree to follow this type of spending rule because it's tough to reduce spending abruptly as markets falter.

The proportional rule reduces the risk of running out of money. If market returns are poor early in retirement, for example, the proportional rule leads the retiree to cut back spending. So naturally there is a better chance for 4 percent spending to be sustainable.[1]

How would this work in practice? For investors retiring in 1965, for example, the fall in wealth would trigger cutbacks in spending that could easily prevent the retiree from running out of money. But notice that this means the retiree still suffers. Suppose the portfolio drops to half of its initial size. Instead of spending $40,000 each year in retirement, the retiree would cut spending to $20,000. That's better than running out of money, but the markets are making this retiree miserable.

Contrast the fate of the 1965 retiree with one retiring in 1980. As the portfolio rises to $3 million, this retiree can raise spending to 4 percent of $3 million, or $120,000 per year. That makes sense if the retiree wants to consume more rather than leave most of the estate to heirs. But it shows once again how vulnerable retirement plans are to future markets.

TWO ISSUES WITH IMPLEMENTING SPENDING RULES

There are two tricky issues affecting spending rules that need to be mentioned. Both involve taxes. The first issue stems from the fact that spending rules refer to *pre-tax spending*. A 4 percent spending rule means that 4 percent of the investor's wealth can be spent, but some of the 4 percent may have to be used to pay taxes on the assets being liquidated. Those taxes may be quite sizable if investors have most of their wealth in tax-deferred accounts. Spending out of a tax-deferred account will usually provide the investor with *much less after-tax spending*.

Let's assume that an investor who is about to retire has part of his or her wealth in a tax-deferred account and the rest in a taxable account.[2] And let's assume that the investor is facing a 40 percent income tax rate on the tax-deferred account. Every $1,000 withdrawn from the tax deferred account nets the investor only $600 for after-tax spending. It's true that dollars withdrawn from the taxable account may also be subject to taxes (in this case on capital gains), but capital gains tax rates are currently far below those on ordinary income. And capital gains taxes are levied only on increases in the value of the assets sold relative to the original tax basis, not on the entire value of these assets. To summarize, drawing from tax-deferred accounts usually yields fewer after-tax dollars for spending than drawing from taxable accounts.

The second issue also concerns taxes. Once an investor reaches 70½ years of age, the IRS requires that distributions be made from the tax-deferred accounts. The distributions start at 3.65 percent of the tax-deferred account at age 70 and rise to 5.35 percent at age 80 and to 8.77 percent at age 90.[3] The rate of withdrawals rises because the investor has a shorter life expectancy the longer he or she lives. These distributions *should not guide spending during retirement*. The distributions are merely designed to ensure that the IRS gets paid. The distributions do require that the investor keeps enough liquidity in the portfolio to pay the taxes that are due. But that's all they are—a schedule to make sure Uncle Sam gets his due.

ADDING ANNUITIES TO ENHANCE SPENDING

We have seen that spending 4 percent in retirement is sometimes too risky for the retiree if markets do badly as they did in the 1970s. But, on the other hand, a spending rate of 4 percent leaves many retirees with insufficient spending in retirement. If the retired investor wishes to find ways to spend more, is there any other investment that could help? The answer is provided by a product with the awkward name, "immediate fixed annuity."

An immediate fixed annuity provides the retiree with a guaranteed income much like in a defined benefit program. The income stream is usually higher than income from bonds because part of the income stream represents the return of some of the capital that the retiree has invested. This capital can be consumed because the income stream is guaranteed to last through the lifetime of the retiree. In return for the income stream, however, the investor gives up the right to that fraction of wealth that is invested in the annuity.

The basic logic behind such an annuity is not understood by most investors. Investors without guaranteed pensions face a serious risk in retirement that is not fully understood by most of them. This is *longevity risk*, the risk that the resources set aside for retirement may not last a lifetime.[4] Longevity risk is due both to the uncertainties of *investing* and the uncertainties of *death*. Let's start with the latter uncertainty. Investors may know when the average person of their sex is likely to die. But the life expectancy distribution is all spread out. Recall Figure 1.2 where the life expectancies of 65-year-olds were examined. A man knows that the median age of death is 83, but 10 percent of his cohort will die by 70 and another 15 percent by 76. On the other hand, 10 percent of the cohort lives to be 94. Women face similar uncertainty, the main difference being that their whole life-expectancy distribution is lengthened by two to three years. Longevity risk also stems from uncertainty about investment returns due to the volatility of markets. We may retire when markets are performing badly. Investors who retired in 2007 may have believed that they were reliving the experience of their grandparents in the 1930s. As it turned out, markets rebounded quickly. But I imagine there are many retirees out there who are still shell-shocked by the recent crisis. For them, longevity risk must have loomed large when their stocks were down 50 percent, as they were early in 2009.

The uncertainty about the time of death forces us to spend less than we would otherwise. To see why, let's imagine that we knew when we would die. Suppose that a 65-year-old single man knows that he will die when he turns 83. This knowledge will allow him to spend much more than he could otherwise. Why? The reason is because he can use up his capital systematically over time. He only needs to set aside enough for his charitable bequests and gifts to his heirs. There is still some uncertainty in his spending as long as the portfolio's returns are uncertain. But that uncertainty is much more manageable because he knows how long the money must last.

How can investors try to duplicate this experience if they don't know the time of their death in advance? What investors can do is to join a *pool of investors* their age. The investors don't know when any one of them will die, but they can predict with some accuracy the age at which the *average person* in the pool will die. Some of the investors will live longer than expected, but the pool of assets will provide for lifetime security. Other investors will die sooner than expected and not collect as much as the rest of the pool. But even for those who die early, the pooling of assets will have served its purpose—to insure everyone in the pool against longevity risk. This is the essential feature of all annuities. They allow us to pool our risks so that we can ensure that we never run out of money in retirement. It's so simple, and yet many investors fail to understand this logic.

It's difficult for a group of individuals to organize the pooling of assets. That's where insurance companies come in. These companies organize the pool and guarantee the annuity contracts in case the pool as a whole lives longer than expected. An individual does not know when he or she will die, but the insurance company can estimate fairly accurately when the pool of investors will die. As a result, payments from the immediate fixed annuity are much higher than from bond investments.[5] Actual annuities are often much more complicated than I have described them. But almost all of them pool the resources of a group of investors so that longevity risk is reduced if not eliminated. Because the insurance company knows the mortality distribution of the pool of investors in the annuity, it can pay back some of the capital invested in the annuity without running the risk of depleting the assets in this pool.

There are three drawbacks to annuities of this type. First, the immediate fixed annuity normally specifies a fixed *nominal* payment. As explained earlier in this chapter in connection with bond investments, inflation can quickly erode the purchasing power of any nominal payment. This certainly would have been the case for investors in the 1970s. And less dramatic erosion can happen even with relatively moderate inflation. The solution to this problem is to choose an *inflation-indexed* (or *real*) immediate fixed annuity. It is possible to find such annuities, but by their very nature they would have lower payment rates (for the same reason that Treasury inflation-adjusted securities have lower yields than conventional Treasury bonds). So most immediate fixed annuities leave the investor with inflation risk, just like the inflation risk faced by investors with traditional defined benefit pensions (at least those that aren't indexed to inflation).

A second drawback is that investors have to worry about the possibility that the insurance company defaults on the annuity contract. Defaults by major insurers are low in probability, but not inconceivable. And if an investor has handed over a large proportion of retirement savings to a company, a default could be disastrous for this investor.[6] A solution to this problem is to diversify annuity contracts among several insurance companies.

A final important drawback is that with annuities, *two are forced to live more cheaply than one.* That is, annuity contracts are less attractive if they insure the longevity risk of a married couple rather than an individual. And the contracts provide lower payouts for women than for men. Insurance companies base the contract terms on life expectancies. Since women live on average longer than men, they receive less from an annuity. And since the joint life expectancy of a married couple is longer than for either one individually, that couple receives even less from an annuity than a single woman.

Consider the rates quoted for immediate annuities in March 2013.[7] These rates are shown for illustration only. Table 17.2 reports these rates for a single man, a single woman, and a married couple, all at the age of 66. If a single man buys a $250,000 immediate fixed annuity, he can obtain an annual payment of $17,400 or a 7.0 percent return. (Of course, that "return" includes a repayment of some of the capital he has invested.) A single woman receives 0.7 percent less. And a married couple receives 1.2 percent less than a man. So it's true that "two (must) live more cheaply than one."

It is important to emphasize that the annuity payments reported in Table 17.2 are for ordinary immediate fixed annuities, not inflation-indexed

TABLE 17.2 Payments for a $250,000 Immediate Fixed Annuity for a 66-Year-Old Individual or Married Couple

Investor	Annual Payment	Payment as a % of Investment
Single man	$17,400	7.0%
Single woman	$15,900	6.3%
Married couple	$14,500	5.8%

Source: www.immediateannuities.com.

annuities, so they will stay fixed through time. If a married couple receives $14,500 in year one of retirement, that nominal sum will remain fixed throughout retirement. In this respect, an immediate fixed annuity is a lot like an old-style defined benefit pension.[8] In fact, you might think of such an annuity as being *a defined benefit pension that you purchase when you retire.*

How should investors integrate annuities into a larger retirement strategy? Let's consider the case of a married couple that is about to embark on retirement. The couple has to worry about the likely event that one will outlive the other. So the portfolio has to last long enough until the survivor dies. For a married couple who are 65 years old, the median age of death of the *surviving spouse* is over 90 years of age! So the money has to last a long time. The couple is trying to rely as much as possible on income from the portfolio. To enhance income, the couple might decide to invest a quarter of the portfolio in an annuity. The rest of the portfolio is invested in ordinary stocks and bonds.

Let's use the couple's plan to address a big issue with annuities. Many investors insist on a *death benefit* for the annuity investment. After all, without a death benefit, "If I die, my heirs get nothing." This couple has taken care of that problem. Three-quarters of their portfolio, the portion invested in bonds and stocks, remains in their estate for their heirs. It's only the one-quarter that is allocated to an annuity that will be removed from the estate. The point is that the annuity itself *need not have a death benefit* because the rest of the portfolio provides one.

Let's explore this point a little more extensively. Earlier in the chapter, we discussed how an investor could plan on spending 4 percent or so of the stock and bond portfolio each year. The reason that the 4 percent rule is suggested is that this level of spending lowers the risk of running out of money to 10 percent or less. But as discussed in Chapter 5, if there is a 10 percent risk of running out of money, this means that there is a 90 percent chance of dying without exhausting retirement savings! So there is a very high probability that retirees will *leave their heirs with more than they intended.* That is, the new "defined contribution" retirement system will provide too large a death benefit. The retiree's children will be pleased, but what about the retiree? So retirees should not worry about whether the annuity has a death benefit. The remainder of the portfolio provides one. If there is no such benefit from the annuity itself, the payout from the annuity will be that much larger.

As explained above, the immediate fixed annuity is a simple product designed to address a major risk in retirement: longevity risk. Other types of annuities, such as "variable annuities" and "equity-indexed annuities," also address longevity risk. But they add complex features that are costly to the investor, including the "death benefits" just discussed.[9] I prefer simplicity to complexity. Immediate fixed annuities provide a steady income stream for life, thereby helping to solve the problem of longevity risk.

THE BEGINNINGS OF A RETIREMENT PLAN

We have begun to assemble the ingredients of a retirement plan for those investors who don't have defined benefit pensions. Those ingredients include a spending rule to govern how much is spent out of any wealth that has been accumulated. This wealth includes whatever has been saved in 401(k) or other defined contribution pension accounts. This chapter has provided rationales for such a spending rule, but the chapter has also shown that the rule is at the mercy of markets. Sometimes retirees will spend too much and sometimes too little.

If only investors could be reborn with an old-style defined benefit pension! Yet this chapter has also shown how we can create a pension ex post. Investors can invest some of their wealth in an annuity and obtain a guaranteed income stream for the rest of their lives.

In the next chapter, we pull together these two elements and add a third ingredient, Social Security. It's time to try to put together a full retirement package.

NOTES

1. In Chapter 14 of Marston (2011), I show how a flexible spending rule that makes spending proportional to recent levels of wealth lowers the risk of running short of money later in retirement.
2. The tax-deferred account, for example, could be a 401(k) or IRA. A Roth IRA, in contrast, is free of tax because it was funded with after-tax dollars.
3. The withdrawal rates are framed in terms of a "distribution period" in years. You are supposed to divide the amount in the tax-deferred account by the distribution period to find out how much you must withdraw. For a 70-year-old, the distribution period is 27.4 years. If an investor has $100,000 in an account, then the withdrawal is $3,650 (or $100,000/27.4). $3,650 is 3.65 percent of the $100,000.
4. Most Americans do have Social Security as a backstop. Chapter 18 discusses how Social Security fits into a retirement plan.
5. Beginning finance students learn an "annuity" formula that is the basis for payments on an immediate fixed annuity. A 20-year-bond with a 4 percent coupon will pay the investor 7.4 percent if it is enhanced with

the payback of the capital invested. An immediate annuity will not pay back as much because of the expenses incurred and profits earned by the insurer.

6. Note that many states have guarantee programs that protect annuity holders against losses (up to a limit) if an insurance company fails.
7. These rates are quoted on the website, www.immediateannuities.com.
8. Most defined benefit pensions are fixed in nominal terms.
9. For a discussion of some of these costs, see the chapters on annuities in Jason (2009) and Solin (2009), as well as the SEC study of variable annuities (U.S. SEC, 2011).

REFERENCES

Jason, Julie. 2009. *The AARP Retirement Survival Guide*. New York: Sterling Press.

Marston, Richard. 2011. *Portfolio Design: A Modern Approach to Asset Allocation*. Hoboken, NJ: John Wiley & Sons.

Solin, Daniel R. 2009. *The Smartest Retirement Book You'll Ever Read*. New York: Penguin, 2009.

Stein, Michael K. 1998. *The Prosperous Retirement: Guide to the New Reality*. Boulder, CO: Emstco Press.

U.S. Securities and Exchange Commission. 2011. "Variable Annuities: What You Should Know." www.sec.gov/investor/pubs/varannty.htm.

CHAPTER 18

Retirement: Putting Together a Plan

A major goal of savings is to provide for a comfortable retirement, one where retirees can maintain the standard of living that they enjoyed during their working years. Retirees don't necessarily need the same income as in their working years since they no longer have to save for retirement. But most retirees would like to keep spending as much as in the past. In his book *The Prosperous Retirement* (1998), Michael Stein emphasized that if retirees don't have enough resources to come close to their past standard of living, they find a way to live within their means. That is most likely true of most people just by necessity. But surely retirees would like to continue to live the way they have in the past.

What are the key ingredients necessary to maintain this standard of living? In earlier chapters, we emphasized that drawing resources from past savings was crucial for those who do not have the luxury of a defined benefit pension. And many of those who do have defined benefit pensions need to supplement them by drawing on savings. But in addition to past savings, retirees also have the Social Security system guaranteeing them payments for the rest of our lives. Social Security is a key element of any retirement plan for most Americans. It is only if you have substantial wealth that Social Security payments can be almost ignored. So before we put together a financial plan for retirement, it's important to investigate the key features of the Social Security system.

THE ROLE OF SOCIAL SECURITY

Since the 1930s Americans have had a backstop for their retirement. Once they reach the eligible age, they can collect a steady stream of payments from the Social Security system. The payments are tied to the inflation rate, so they rise with the cost of living. (Some retirees may complain that the payments don't rise fast enough to offset increases in their *personal* cost of living, but the inflation adjustments are nonetheless important.)[1] Social Security therefore provides most Americans with an annuity that will last as long as they live. And the annuity is indexed to inflation.

As part of the 1983 Social Security reform, the "full retirement age" (FRA) was gradually raised from 65 for those born in 1938 or later. For example, those born between 1943 and 1954 receive full Social Security benefits if they retire at 66. Those born in 1960 or later must wait until age 67. Waiting for these full benefits makes a great deal of difference. Assuming that an individual has a sufficient history of earnings, however, Social Security payments can begin as early as age 62. If they retire at 62 rather than full retirement age of 66, retirees born between 1943 and 1954 receive 25 percent lower benefits *for the rest of their lives*. If you wait another four years to retiree at 70, the benefit rises 32 percent above that received at 66.

Consider the Social Security benefits of individuals retiring in 2013 at the age of 62 or 66 or 70. Let's assume that these individuals have recently earned $100,000 per year (like the individuals we studied in Chapters 4 and 5). Here is how the benefits offered to this individual vary depending on the age of retirement:[2]

Retire at 62: $19,500/year

Retire at 66: $26,000/year

Retire at 70: $34,300/year

The Social Security system has designed these benefit levels so that they are actuarially fair. That is, they are set so that the average person receives the same lifetime benefits no matter what age of retirement is chosen. Nonetheless, the differences in benefits are huge. An individual who retires at 70 rather than 62 receives over 75 percent higher benefits per year for the rest of his or her life!

Despite these incentives to work longer, many Americans start taking Social Security as soon as they are eligible. Table 18.1 reports (for the year 2011) what percentage of Americans began collecting Social Security at 62 or older. 41.4 percent of men and 46.5 percent of women began collecting at 62, while 66.4 percent of men started collecting prior to the full retirement age of 66. Only 5.8 percent of men and 6.2 percent of women delayed Social Security past FRA. It's useful to compare these Social Security figures with those from the year 1980, at a time when defined benefit pensions were more common than they are today. In 1980, 51.7 percent of men filed for Social Security prior to FRA (which was then 65). 63.9 percent of women

TABLE 18.1 Percent Distribution of Initial Social Security Awards in 2011

Age	Men	Women
62	41.4%	46.5%
63 to full retirement age (FRA)	25.0%	25.1%
Full retirement age = 66	27.8%	22.1%
Older than FRA	5.8%	6.2%

Source: Social Security Administration, *Annual Statistical Supplement*, 2012, Table 6B5.

filed early (compared with 71.6 percent in 2011). So Americans are retiring earlier than they used to at a time when the retirement system is shifting away from traditional pensions. This section will evaluate whether retiring that early makes financial sense.

The decision about when to retire is driven by many factors. Many individuals are unable to work much beyond their early sixties. Some retire then because they are physically unable to work longer. This might be true of someone in a construction trade requiring physical stamina. Others retire because it's difficult to stay employed in their line of work. Companies often push workers out when they reach their early sixties. Some might even offer incentives to retire early. But there are other Americans who have discretion about when they retire from their line of work. And there are those who have the option of turning to another field of work or working part-time in their original occupation. The following discussion is aimed at them.

It should be clear from the discussion of spending rules that it is difficult to finance a comfortable life style in retirement. Investors save all of their lives in order to afford to retire, but it's difficult to keep their "income" in retirement as high as it was during their working years. If they adopt a 4 percent spending rule for their savings, they have to have a lot of wealth to finance a reasonable level of spending in retirement. Worse still, they have to worry constantly about whether their spending rule might be undermined by a bad investment environment. It has happened in the past. Wouldn't it be nice if they could fund an annuity that continues to pay their bills no matter what has happened to their investments?

Social Security provides just such an annuity. What a splendid system it is. If someone retires at the full retirement age of 66, he or she could receive over $30,000 per year if he earned the maximum income subject to Social Security taxes ($113,700 in 2013). As explained earlier, moreover, married couples receive even more. A married couple with only one spouse who has qualified for Social Security receives 50 percent more than a single person. (A married couple with each qualifying for separate benefits may earn considerably more as well, depending on how large their incomes were during their working years.)

But notice that there is a way to increase the size of this annuity—*delay applying* for Social Security. By delaying Social Security from 66 to 70, benefits increase by 32 percent. Richard Thaler (2011) and others have suggested viewing this option as a cheap way to purchase an immediate fixed annuity. That is, by delaying Social Security for four years, investors can raise their benefits forever. And these benefits adjust to higher inflation, so this annuity is an unusual one with an inflation "escalator."

Let's focus on this inflation escalator. Suppose that a 66-year-old retires with a $26,000 Social Security benefit and a similar size old-style corporate pension. Most corporate pensions are fixed in nominal terms at retirement. Now let's follow the two pensions through retirement until the retiree turns 86 years of age. And let's assume that the inflation stays at 2.5 percent per year. The Social Security pension increases to $42,600 over the 20-year period until the retiree turns 86. That is, the Social Security pension increases 63.9 percent in nominal terms. The corporate pension, in contrast, stays fixed at $26,000 in nominal terms. But the cost of living has in the meantime risen by over 60 percent. It's the Social Security benefit that buttresses the later stages of retirement. And, like a regular annuity, this benefit never disappears even if the retiree lives many years before normal life expectancy.

Not many Americans are convinced by arguments like this one. As mentioned earlier, Americans are retiring at an earlier age than they used to. Consider participation in the labor force by workers 65 or older. Table 18.2 tracks labor force participation rates since 1950. Among men, participation has fallen from 45.8 percent in 1950 to 21.5 percent in 2008. How strange this

TABLE 18.2 Labor Force Participation for Workers 65 Years or Older

Year	Men	Women
1950	45.8%	9.7%
1960	33.1%	10.8%
1970	26.8%	9.7%
1980	19.0%	8.1%
1990	16.3%	8.6%
2000	17.5%	9.4%
2008	21.5%	13.3%

Notes: Figures show percentage of population 65 years old or older still participating in the labor force.
Source: Purcell, "Older Workers: Employment and Retirement Trends," 2009, Table 2.

is. Men are retiring much earlier as life expectancy increases and as defined benefit pensions become rarer. Participation rates among women reflect the results of two opposite trends. In the last few decades, women have raised their labor force participation at any age. But women also tend to retire earlier than in the past. The net effect is that labor force participation by women 65 or older has risen modestly from 9.7 percent in 1950 to 13.3 percent in 2008.

As stated earlier, there are very serious practical problems in postponing Social Security beyond 62 or beyond the full retirement age (66 for those born between 1943 and 1954). Many individuals find it difficult to continue working into their 60s even if they are physically able to do so. As mentioned earlier, in many fields retirement is expected when you reach your early 60s. But I believe that there are many individuals who *elect* to retire early. It has become the norm. And the key question is whether those who retire early have really *done the math*. Have they determined that they have enough money to retire?

In any case, let's salute the Social Security program. Social Security is an essential support for the retirement of most Americans. Given the poor state of Social Security finances, it is likely that there will be changes to the program in the years ahead. But there is so much voter support for the program that it is unlikely that the program will be undermined by these changes. And it is doubtful that most existing retirees will see any change in their benefits.[3] So we will assume that it can remain part of the retirement plan to be discussed below.

PUTTING TOGETHER A RETIREMENT PLAN: SPENDING OUT OF SOCIAL SECURITY AND SAVINGS

Now that we have discussed Social Security, it is time to put together a retirement plan. By a retirement plan, I mean a financial plan to support spending in retirement. Let's begin by listing possible sources of income in retirement:

Social Security payments

Defined benefit pension or pensions

Withdrawals from savings or from defined contribution pensions like 401(k)s or IRAs

Distributions from annuities

Other income such as earnings from occasional work or deferred payments for past work

Many Americans will have to depend on Social Security as their sole source of support in retirement. But even those who are fortunate enough to have other sources of income in retirement may come up short in their retirement plans.

Let's consider that fortunate investor whom we have followed through much of the book, the investor earning $100,000 throughout most of his or her life. Remember that this $100,000 income stays fixed because we are measuring everything in real terms. Because the investor has earned so much throughout the working years, he or she qualifies for about $26,000 per year at the age of 66. This income will increase each year because it is indexed to the consumer price index. If the investor is married but the spouse has not qualified for separate Social Security benefits, then the couple will receive 50 percent more than the single man or woman who has earned the same income. So the bedrock of the retirement plan for a couple will consist of $39,000 the first year with inflation adjustments thereafter.

The investor is also assumed to have savings, both taxable and tax-deferred. As noted in Chapter 17, taxable and tax-deferred savings are not equivalent. Taxable accounts may have some imbedded capital gains in them for which taxes are due when the assets are sold. But tax-deferred accounts like a 401(k) require that income taxes be paid at withdrawal. (If the investor has saved within a so-called Roth account, using after-tax dollars, then no further taxes are due at withdrawal.) To simplify the discussion, we will ignore deferred taxes.

Let's assume that the investor has saved consistently throughout his or her working years. In Chapter 5, it was shown that an investor earning $100,000 (in constant dollars) and saving 15 percent of that income could have saved almost $1.1 million over 30 years. That $1.1 million will provide income in the form of dividends and interest. But as explained in the last chapter, spending in retirement should not be based solely on the income received currently. Instead, the investor with savings should adopt a "spending rule" out of savings. And that spending rule should be based on long-run expected real returns, not just on investment income or on nominal returns. We will assume that the investor spends only 4 percent, or $44,000, of his or her wealth each year. Like Social Security, this spending rule is indexed to inflation, thereby allowing for upward adjustments in response to increases in the cost of living.

The two pillars of this investor's retirement provide a sizable level of spending in retirement. Table 18.3 reports the level of spending provided by Social Security and savings to a single man or woman or to a married couple. A single investor is able to spend $70,000 in retirement, or 70 percent of lifetime income. Many investors would be very satisfied with this outcome. Yet the result is somewhat disappointing since this investor has saved diligently throughout his or her working years. Remember that this investor has been diligent enough (as well as fortunate enough) to have accumulated

TABLE 18.3 Spending in Retirement: A Retirement Plan Based on Social Security and Savings

Source of Spending in Retirement	Individual	Couple*
Social Security benefits	$26,000	$39,000
Spending out of portfolio	$44,000	$44,000
TOTAL	$70,000	$83,000
Percent of previous income ($100,000)	70.0%	83.0%

Assumptions: Retirement occurs at full retirement age (66 in 2013). Retiree has accumulated $1.1 million by the time of retirement and has adopted a 4% spending rule.
* Married couple where one spouse earns $100,000 income and other spouse qualifies for maximum spousal benefit.

$1.1 million. If the investor had saved at a lesser pace, or if the investor had had other expenses to absorb savings, or if the investor had suffered worse than average returns, spending in retirement might have fallen far short of $70,000.

The married couple (where one spouse has not worked) earns 50 percent more in Social Security benefits than the single individual. So spending totals $83,000 rather than $70,000. That's much closer to the ideal of matching preretirement income, particularly when you remember that the couple no longer has to save for retirement!

What if the married couple earned $100,000 together rather than singly? After all, the majority of both men and women receive Social Security based on their own work histories rather than as the spouses of workers.[4] Surely this married couple should get the same Social Security payment as a married couple with only one worker. Sadly, this is not the case. To explain this, let me introduce some Social Security jargon. The "Primary Insurance Amount" or PIA of a worker is the retirement benefit available to a worker when reaching "Full Retirement Age" or FRA (66 for workers retiring in 2013). The spousal benefit is equal to 50 percent of the difference between the PIA of the higher earning worker and the PIA of his or her spouse. The spousal benefit is maximized when there is *only one breadwinner* in the household.

Let's consider an extreme case. Suppose that each of the spouses earned $50,000 throughout their working years (in real terms). Each individual would be eligible for the same PIA if each retires at 66. But neither individual would be eligible for any spousal benefit (since the difference between their PIAs is zero). The two spouses will each receive what they would have received if they had been single. Suppose instead that one person earns $60,000 and the spouse earns $40,000. Then the spousal benefit of the latter would be 50 percent of the difference between the PIAs of the higher and lower earning spouses. So that couple's Social Security payments will be enhanced by spousal benefits. But their combined Social Security benefits will not be as large as that of the couple with one spouse earning the entire $100,000 (the couple shown in Table 18.3). The spousal benefit is maximized for families with a single "breadwinner" relative to families with the same income coming from two spouses.[5] It's not my place to pass judgment on the wisdom of this feature of Social Security law, but the Social Security benefits of a married couple depicted in Table 18.3 are the maximum available based on a $100,000 family income. Couples splitting a $100,000 income will have lower Social Security benefits depending on how the income is split between the spouses.

HOW DOES THE PLAN CHANGE IF I RETIRE EARLIER OR LATER?

The discussion has centered on an individual or married couple that decides to retire at the age of 66. What happens to the retirement plan if the investor decides to retire earlier or later? I will describe how the plan changes for an investor retiring at 62 or 70 years of age.

There are two changes that occur if the retirement age is changed:

1. First, as explained above, Social Security payments depend on the age at which the worker retires. Payments are 25 percent lower for those who retire at 62 rather than at the "full retirement age" of 66, and 32 percent higher for those who postpone retirement until 70. If an individual would have received $26,000 in benefits at age 66, he or she will have to get by with $19,500 if retirement is at 62.

   Spousal benefits are also reduced for those who retire early. Assume that the spouse is the same age as the working beneficiary. Spouses of those retiring at 62 receive only 35 percent of the worker's full retirement age benefit rather than the 50 percent spousal benefit of those retiring at 66.[6] Thirty-five percent of $26,000 is only $9,100 (rather than $13,000 for the spouses of those retiring at 66). So if both spouses are 62, they will receive only $28,600 together rather than the $39,000 available at 66.[7]

2. Second, retiring at 62 cuts short the savings process. Those last four years of savings until the investor reaches 66 can be years when it is relatively easy to save. In most cases, college tuitions for children have been paid. Mortgages may also be paid off. (If there are still mortgages

outstanding when the investor is 62, then it's even more important to postpone retirement). Retiring at 70 rather than 66 provides four more years of savings (and four more years of asset appreciation if markets behave).

The impact of early retirement on future income is quite substantial. And postponing retirement by a few years has a big impact on future income.

To provide estimates of how much is lost or gained if investors retire early or postpone retirement, I will consider once again a married couple who would have saved $1.1 million if the couple had retired at the full retirement age of 66. Consider first the impact of early retirement on the savings process. Recall that in Chapter 5, I assumed that an investor was able to earn 5.5 percent in real returns during the savings years. Investors who are close to retirement probably don't earn that high a return because they are likely to have reduced their stock market exposure the closer they came to retirement. (Recall the discussion of target date portfolios in Chapter 14). So let's assume a return of 4.5 percent real return from a 50/50 portfolio in the years between 62 and 66.

A couple that retires at 62, four years earlier than the "full retirement" age of 66, will fall short of the goal of a $1.1 million portfolio for two reasons. (1) The couple misses out on four years of savings. Since this hypothetical investor was saving 15 percent of a $100,000 income, the savings shortfall over four years totals $60,000 even if no return is earned on these savings. (2) More important, the couple is not allowing the portfolio to continue to grow (i.e., without withdrawals) for an extra four years. Those are important years because the portfolio is so large. If the investor already has (say) $900,000 at 62, four years of compounding at 4.5 percent/year results in an additional accumulation of about $173,000.

The result of the extra saving and compounding of returns is that the couple accumulates almost 27 percent more if retirement is at 66 rather than 62! More precisely, a couple who had managed to accumulate $869,000 by the age of 62 succeeds in growing the portfolio to $1.1 million by the time of retirement at the age of 66. It should be noted that this is what happens if the portfolio earns normal returns over the four years involved. If a bull market occurs in those four years, the couple retiring at 66 is even better off. If a bear market occurs, then they are probably thanking their lucky stars that they have four more years to save.

What is the overall impact of this decision to retire early? The answer is found in Table 18.4, where the combined effects of lower Social Security payments and investment returns are detailed. As stated earlier, retiring at 62 rather than 66 lowers Social Security payments both for the retiree and his or her spouse. And, as already discussed, the drop in income from the portfolio is dramatic because the couple has accumulated $869,000 rather

TABLE 18.4   Effect of Retirement Age on Spending by Married Couple

Retirement Age	62	66	70
Portfolio size	$869,000	$1,100,000	$1,380,000
Spending out of portfolio	$ 34,800	$ 44,000	$ 55,200
Social Security benefits	$ 28,600	$ 39,000	$ 47,300
TOTAL INCOME	$ 63,400	$ 83,000	$ 102,500
% of previous income	63.4%	83.0%	102.5%

Notes: Social Security benefits are based on $100,000 income with maximum spousal benefits. The couple is assumed to be the same age. Spending is based on 4% spending rule. Portfolio size is based on savings of 15% per year prior to retirement and 4.5% returns.

than $1.1 million by the time of retirement. The overall impact of the decision to retire early is to reduce lifetime income by about 24 percent (from $83,000 to $63,400). The couple generates only 63.4 percent of preretirement income rather than 83.0 percent.

Postponing retirement beyond the full retirement age of 66 also has a big impact. In this example, the couple has saved enough to retire at 66. So by postponing retirement until 70, the couple manages to replace more than 100 percent of previous income. Retirement income is almost 24 percent higher at 70 than at 66. Yet the case for later retirement is weak in this example because the couple was already well fixed at age 66. In reality, however, many couples fall short of their savings goals when they reach 66. So postponing retirement until 70 may give them a chance to achieve their goals.

I must reiterate that the discussion focuses on financial wellbeing. The decision on when to retire depends on a lot more than that. First, someone may not be capable of working past 62. Second, many workers are in industries where it is difficult to retain their job or find new work when they are in their 60s. Third, the sickness of one spouse may limit the ability of the other spouse to work. Fourth, the couple may value retirement highly enough that financial incentives take second place. Retirement is a lifestyle decision. This book focuses only on finances. Besides, it's difficult to fit the number of extra days on the golf course or years of relaxation in an investments table.

A RETIREMENT PLAN INCORPORATING ANNUITIES

Retirees could stretch their spending a little further by investing some of their wealth in an annuity. Let's assume that $250,000 is invested in an immediate fixed annuity at retirement with the remainder of the portfolio invested in stocks and bonds. This will give the single investor or married couple more to spend than if these funds had been invested in a portfolio of stocks and bonds with a 4 percent spending rule.

To modify the analysis of retirement income to include annuity payments, we have to distinguish between men and women because their annuity payments differ. The retirees to be studied are now assumed to base their retirement on Social Security benefits (at full retirement age), withdrawals from their portfolio, and income from annuities. Using the figures reported in Table 17.2 for a $250,000 immediate fixed annuity, total spending provided by this retirement plan is reported in Table 18.5.

Let's start with the single man. He can fund his spending out of $26,000 in Social Security earnings, $17,400 in annuity payments and $34,000 spending out of his $850,000 (i.e., $1.1 million less $250,000 spent on the annuity) portfolio of stocks and bonds. The three sources of retirement spending add up to $77,400 or 77.4 percent of his preretirement income. The single woman must spend a little less because private annuities base their payments on life expectancy. Women live longer than men on average, so annuity payments are smaller. The single woman can cover 75.9 percent of lifetime earnings.

The married couple fares better than the single man or woman. That's because this couple is assumed to qualify for the maximum 50 percent spousal benefit. On the other hand, the couple receives a lower annuity payment for the simple reason that joint life expectancies are longer than those of a single man or woman. The couple is able to replace 87.5 percent of lifetime earnings.

TABLE 18.5 Spending in Retirement for 66-Year-Old Retirees: A Retirement Plan Based on Social Security, Savings, and an Immediate Fixed Annuity

Retiree	Man	Woman	Couple
Social Security benefits	$26,000	$26,000	$39,000
Spending out of portfolio	$34,000	$34,000	$34,000
Income from annuity	$17,400	$15,900	$14,500
TOTAL	$77,400	$75,900	$87,500
% of previous income ($ 100,000)	77.4%	75.9%	87.5%

Assumptions: Retiree (man or woman) has qualified for Social Security benefits at full retirement age (66) based on $100,000 income. Couple is assumed to qualify for maximum spousal benefits. Retirement savings is $1.1 million of which $850,000 is kept in a portfolio of stocks and bonds supporting a 4% spending rule. $250,000 is invested in an immediate fixed annuity.

The spending plan outlined in Table 18.5 has one serious flaw. The annuity is not indexed to inflation. So over time, the annuity will remain fixed while Social Security payments will keep pace with inflation. Our 4 percent spending rule is also designed to keep pace with inflation, although portfolio setbacks could cause us to cut back in spending later in retirement. Most defined benefit pensions are also fixed in nominal terms. So over time, the pension payments shrink in real terms. Or, if we are measuring everything in current dollars, the pension payments fail to rise with the cost of living.

Figure 18.1 illustrates the evolution of nominal income in retirement. The figure is based on a 2.5 percent inflation rate. A married couple starts retirement with almost $87,500 in "income" consisting of Social Security payments, spending out of savings, and either an annuity or defined benefit pension as outlined in Table 18.5. That's a comfortable level of income for a couple used to earning $100,000 per year. But over time, the retirement is increasingly constrained by the failure of other sources of income, annuities and defined benefit pensions, to keep pace with inflation. Over a 20-year retirement, Social Security payments increase with inflation from $39,000 to $63,900. And 4 percent spending increases with inflation from $34,000 (4 percent of $850,000) to $55,700. But in this example, annuities and defined benefit pensions stay fixed at $14,500.

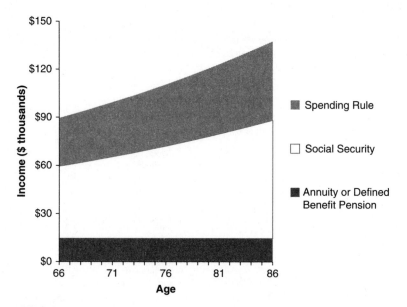

FIGURE 18.1   Evolution of Income for a Married Couple in Retirement (in nominal dollars)

What does this example show us? First, it illustrates once again that the indexing of Social Security is very important. Second, it justifies having a modest 4 percent spending rule throughout retirement. Keeping pace with inflation is essential if the retirement plan is to be successful.

The spending plan outlined in Table 18.5 also has another flaw. It's designed for a retiree who is used to spending based on an income of $100,000. The same plan will not work as well for someone used to a higher level of income. Social Security benefits are a major source of income for a retiree earning $100,000 per year prior to retirement. But as shown in Chapter 4, those benefits cap out near that level of income. Retirees who have earned $200,000 or $300,000 a year prior to retirement qualify for only slightly higher benefits than those who have earned $100,000 a year, since there is a cap on Social Security benefits and taxes (based on a $113,700 maximum income in 2013). As discussed in Chapter 4, those individuals fortunate enough to make these higher incomes will have to accumulate a much higher level of wealth by the time they retire to make up for the lack of higher Social Security benefits. Those individuals therefore will have to save a higher percentage of their income throughout their working years.

WHAT IF THE RETIREE HAS A DEFINED BENEFIT PENSION?

If the retiree has a traditional pension in addition to Social Security, then it will be possible to retire earlier with less wealth accumulated. Consider Figure 18.1 again, where the income of a married couple is traced throughout retirement. In addition to Social Security and withdrawals from savings, the couple will base spending in retirement on the income from the traditional pension. Like annuities, most defined benefit pensions are fixed in nominal terms. So over time, the traditional pension will play less of a role than at the time of retirement. But this pension will always be there for the couple (as long as the pension provider remains solvent).[8]

How might a defined benefit pension modify the retirement plan outlined in Table 18.5? Suppose that the defined benefit pension provides a couple with the same income ($14,500) as an immediate fixed annuity. Then the couple can dispense with the annuity. So the couple need not accumulate the $250,000 required to purchase the annuity. In some sense, an annuity is a substitute for a defined benefit pension. Those Americans fortunate enough to still have these pensions are relieved of some of the burden of savings that the rest of us bear. Those of us without such pensions have the option of purchasing an annuity, but we must save more than those with an old-style pension.

WHAT COULD GO WRONG WITH THIS PLAN: THE NEW NORMAL

A successful retirement plan seems almost too difficult to put together. It depends on foregoing early retirement even though there are so many (nonfinancial) advantages to retiring early. It depends on a program of saving that seems unrealistic to most families. To save 15 or 20 percent of income throughout most of the working years is a tall order. A successful retirement plan also depends on not having financial setbacks such as bouts of unemployment or unusual expenses associated with sickness or the care of parents or children. If all goes well, we can retire comfortably, but so much has to go well.

All of these plans also depend on investments behaving as well as they have in the past. As explained in Chapter 4, we have based spending rules on the real returns that markets have earned in the past 60 years or the past 90 years. What if markets perform badly in the future? What if the New Normal becomes a reality? Or what if we are hit by the kind of terrible financial crisis that we experienced recently? How would retirements do in those circumstances? This will be the subject of our last chapter.

NOTES

1. This is especially true for those retirees with high medical bills because inflation in the medical sector is considerably higher than in the economy as a whole.
2. These figures were obtained using the Social Security system website, www.ssa.gov, for a hypothetical investor who is earning $100,000 in 2012 and retiring in 2013. The figures cited have been rounded to simplify the analysis.
3. It should be mentioned that some members of Congress would prefer to curtail the Social Security benefits of the wealthy including those already retired. But Congress will remain wary about making major changes in benefits for those already retired or close to retirement because seniors vote in higher proportion than any other segment of the population.
4. English and Lee (2010) cite Social Security statistics to show that in 2008, 52.3 percent of women received their own benefits, while 34.9 percent received benefits based on their own work histories plus the spousal benefit.
5. Gustman and Steinmeier (2000) discuss these and other features of the Social Security system.

6. See Social Security Administration, "Benefit Amount for a Spouse," SSA website. Note that spouses of those retiring at 70 receive the same spousal benefits as those retiring at 66.
7. If one spouse is younger than the other or if both spouses have qualified for Social Security benefits, the calculation becomes even more complex. The Social Security Manual is over 2,200 pages long.
8. In the event of the default of a private sector pension plan, the Pension Benefit Guaranty Corporation provides benefits to retirees in the plan (although there are limits on benefits).

REFERENCES

English, Ashley, and Sunhwa Lee. 2010. "Women and Social Security: Benefit Types and Eligibility." Institute for Women's Policy Research, #D488.

Gustman, Alan L., and Thomas L. Steinmeier. 2000. "How Effective Is Redistribution under the Social Security Benefit Formula?" NBER Working Paper No. 7597 (March).

Purcell, Patrick. 2009. "Older Workers: Employment and Retirement Trends." Congressional Research Report for Congress (September 16).

Social Security Administration. 2012. "Social Security Annual Statistical Survey." Washington, DC: U.S. Government Printing Office.

Stein, Michael K. 1998. *The Prosperous Retirement: Guide to the New Reality*. Boulder, CO: Emstco Press.

Thaler, Richard H. 2011. "Getting the Most out of Social Security." *New York Times*, July 17.

CHAPTER 19

The "New Normal" and Retirement

Icannot emphasize enough how important it is for investors to start planning for retirement early in their working years. Savings are the key to a successful retirement. And savings have to start very early. Then when investors retire, they have to set out a reasonable spending plan based on the resources that are available. If investors are prudent in their investments and if they adopt a reasonable spending rule, then they can begin their retirement with a solid plan in place. But what if investment returns fall short in the future? What happens to retirement plans if we have entered a "New Normal" of lower investment returns?

Since 2000, investors have had to contend with a "lost decade" of stock returns. By the end of 2012, the S&P 500 stock index was hardly above where it had been in 2000, 12 years earlier. In Chapter 3, I tried to convince the reader that the lost decade represented a payback for the absurdly high stock returns of the 1980s and 1990s, which drove price-earnings ratios to almost unprecedented levels. The abysmal returns of the lost decade have brought valuations back to more normal levels. But perhaps Bill Gross is right in warning that slower growth in the industrial world will depress stock returns in the future. Instead of earning average real returns of 6.5 percent on U.S. stocks as in the past 60 or 90 years, perhaps the returns will be significantly lower.

As I explained in Chapter 3 on the New Normal, I worry more about future bond returns than future stock returns. With bond yields at near record lows, I worry about how retirees are going to cope with losses on their bond portfolio as yields rise to more normal levels, or, if low yields continue to prevail, how they will cope with the miserably low bond returns implied by these yields. Retirees in the past could count on average real returns on bonds of about 2.5 percent. As Chapter 2 discusses, bonds earned about that much on average over the past 60 years as well as the past 90 years.

What if bonds earn much less in the future? We cannot ignore the possibility that the New Normal will extend to bond returns as well as stock returns.

What will happen to retirement plans if a New Normal for stocks and bonds prevails? This chapter will modify these plans for lower investment returns.

RETIREMENT IF THERE IS A NEW NORMAL

Retirement plans are designed to guide the investor through several decades of retirement. Retirees do not know how long their retirement will last, but the spending rule is kept low precisely because the portfolio must sustain spending through a potentially long retirement. Any spending rule must be based on long-run expectations of investment returns, not on expectations about returns over the next few years. Of course, what matters are the future *real* (inflation-adjusted) returns, not nominal returns. If real investment returns are 20 or 40 percent lower than in the past, then spending rules must also be lower. Retirement plans will have to be scaled back.

Let's first consider how the New Normal might affect that retiree whom we have focused on throughout most of the book—the retiree who has been used to spending out of a $100,000 income. If this retiree had been successful in saving 15 percent of income during his or her working years, then the portfolio would have grown to about $1.1 million by the time of retirement. Withdrawals at a 4 percent rate combined with Social Security payments would have allowed this retiree to come close to matching preretirement income less savings of $85,000 per year. In fact, if the retiree was married and the spouse was eligible for a 50 percent spousal benefit, then preretirement income would have been almost completely matched in retirement (as shown in Table 18.3).

How badly is this plan affected by the New Normal? If returns on stocks and bonds are lower in the future, then the spending rule must be reduced to reflect these lower returns. Table 19.1 shows the effects of lowering the spending rule from 4 percent to 3.5 percent or 3.0 percent to 2.5 percent. Most readers will probably agree that lowering spending from 4 percent to 2.5 percent is drastic enough to capture the most pessimistic versions of the New Normal. Lowering the spending rate to 3.0 percent, for example, forces the couple to reduce withdrawals from the portfolio from $44,000 per year (4 percent of $1.1 million) to $33,000 per year. But in all cases, Social Security payments stay intact. As a result, total retirement income falls by $11,000 from $83,000 to $72,000 per year. So the couple has to find ways to reduce spending by about 13 percent relative to what they spent prior to retirement.

TABLE 19.1   Effects of the New Normal on Retirement for a Couple with
$100,000 Income

Sources of Spending in Retirement	Retirement Spending Rule			
	4%	3.5%	3%	2.5%
Spending out of portfolio	$44,000	$38,500	$33,000	$27,500
Social Security	$39,000	$39,000	$39,000	$39,000
TOTAL	$83,000	$77,500	$72,000	$66,500
% of previous income	83%	77.5%	72%	66.5%

Assumptions: Retirement occurs at full retirement age (66 in 2013). Retiree has accumulated $1.1 million by the time of retirement. Spouse has qualified for maximum spousal benefits.

Cutting spending by 13 percent will be painful. But let's put this cut in perspective. By retiring at 62 rather than 66, many Americans cut their retirement spending by much more than this.[1] If the New Normal prevails and the retired couple is forced to cut their spending rule by 25 percent (from 4 percent to 3 percent), Social Security still partially insulates the couple from a bad investment environment because it stays intact no matter how badly stocks and bonds are faring.

Retirees with higher incomes than our couple are affected more by the New Normal. Recall that Social Security benefits are capped because Social Security taxes are also capped. In 2013, the maximum Social Security benefit is $30,400 for an individual. So a couple that has earned $200,000 or $400,000 per year in the past will receive Social Security benefits that are not much above those in Table 19.1. Retirees used to that level of income have to rely much more on their own savings. Consider the extreme case of a couple that has retired so early that they are not yet eligible for Social Security. If the New Normal prevails, this couple may be forced to cut spending from 4 percent to 3 percent of the portfolio. So spending is curtailed by 25 percent. That makes the New Normal a more serious threat to their retirement plans.

How might retirees prepare for the New Normal? No one knows how low investment returns will be in a New Normal (and no one knows if a New Normal will actually occur). So it is difficult to know how much to lower spending rules. A prudent approach might be to start off retirement with a lower spending rule (if the retiree wants to be cautious), but make that rule *proportional* to wealth rather than fixed at the time of retirement.

Recall the discussion in Chapter 17 where I compared a fixed rule with a proportional rule. With a fixed rule, the retiree starts off spending X percent of the portfolio (e.g., 4 percent of $1 million or $40,000 per year), then adjusts the spending to keep up with inflation. With a proportional rule, the retiree starts off spending X percent of the portfolio but then keeps spending proportional to the current value of the portfolio. If poor returns lead to a fall in the value of the portfolio, then spending is cut back. For example, if the retiree starts off spending 4 percent of $1 million but the portfolio falls to $900,000, then spending is cut back to $36,000 (i.e., 4 percent of the lower amount). Many institutions follow a proportional rule, although they usually base this year's spending on an average of portfolio values over the past few years. If a retiree were to face lower returns early in retirement, the proportional rule would lead the retiree to cut back spending in proportion. That might be a practical way to adjust to a New Normal if it does turn out to be the reality in the years ahead.

If the New Normal prevails, there is no doubt that retirement spending will have to be curtailed. But there are ways for retirees to adjust to this new reality if it does prevail. In my view, retirees should worry more about another threat to retirement that is more serious. I believe that retirees *should worry much more about their own behavior than about the behavior of markets*. Many retirees have a tendency to overreact to current events. They panic when markets perform badly. The best illustration of this tendency comes from the period of the financial crisis. Investors made decisions during that crisis that will forever undermine their retirement future. Let's review that episode in detail.

DID THIS RETIREMENT PLAN SURVIVE THE FINANCIAL CRISIS?

When markets tanked in the financial crisis of 2007–2009, a lot of investors panicked. That's understandable because this crisis was extremely serious. If the Federal Reserve and Treasury had not carried out a rescue plan, some major banks may have failed and the economy probably would have suffered a far worse recession than we experienced. Give credit also to the foreign central banks that intervened aggressively to save their own banks.

In the midst of this crisis, here is what investors should have done. Investors should have stuck to their plan. This required steel nerves. The 50/50 portfolio recommended to retirees in this book fell over 30 percent. When investors see their retirement plans begin to go up in smoke, it's very difficult to stand by.

What if an investor had left the portfolio alone? Let's be specific. Assume that the investor has $1 million at the peak of the market in October 2007. The $1 million is invested in the 50/50 portfolio shown in Figure 19.1. The bond portion of the portfolio is invested in U.S. investment grade bonds (measured by the Barclays Aggregate investment grade bond Index) plus 5 percent in one-month Treasury bills (the safest short-term investment).[2] The stocks are

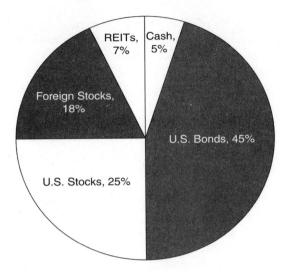

FIGURE 19.1   Portfolio for a Retired Investor

diversified among U.S. stocks (represented by the Russell 3000 all-cap index), foreign stocks (EAFE), and REITs (NAREIT index).[3] I will consider the cases of two different investors. The first is that of an investor who is not yet retired, so there are no withdrawals from the portfolio. The second is that of an investor who is drawing 4 percent from the portfolio each year.

If the investor is not yet drawing from the portfolio, the $1 million falls to $701,300 in February 2009, then recovers all the way to $1,174,600 by December 2012. So the portfolio bounces back as markets recover. Not all of the assets in the portfolio regain their full values. U.S. bonds perform well throughout most of the period, rising 36.3 percent by December 2012. Stocks, in contrast, drag down performance. The Russell 3000 all-stock index falls sharply during the financial crisis, but then rebounds enough so that by December 2012 it is up by 5.0 percent. Foreign stocks perform worse. The EAFE index has a net loss of 19.7 percent! REITs fall sharply in the early stages of the crisis, but then recover fully to post a 12.6 percent overall return. Once again, diversification is shown to pay. This time it is the bonds that save the portfolio.

Figure 19.2 shows how the value of the portfolio varies through time. If the investor is not yet drawing from the portfolio (the dotted line), the value of this portfolio rises by over 17 percent from its initial level. If we adjust portfolio values for inflation, the real value of the $1 million rises by almost 7 percent over the period since October 2007. A cynic would say that this is not much of a return. After all, the investor has had to wait over four years for this return. But remember that in 2007–2009, we experienced the worst financial crisis since the 1930s.

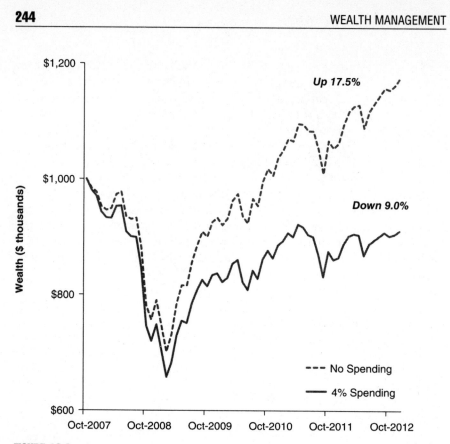

FIGURE 19.2 $1 Million Portfolio during the Financial Crisis: Effects of 4 Percent Spending Rule
Data sources: Barclays, Russell®, MSCI, and NAREIT.

What if the investor is retired? Then the 4 percent spending rule will drag down the performance of the portfolio (as shown by the solid line in Figure 19.2). Recall that the 4 percent rule sets spending at $40,000 initially, but spending has to rise over time to keep up with the cost of living. Over the period from October 2007 through December 2012, the cost of living rises by more than 10 percent. So spending eventually rises to $44,100. The retiree has to watch this portfolio fall to about $658,000 in February 2009. That is probably the point at which many retirees panicked. But if the retiree stuck to his or her plans, the portfolio rose back to $910,300 by December 2012 (or to $826,200 in inflation-adjusted terms). So the retiree definitely suffered as a result of the financial crisis. But it has not been a disaster for those retirees who stuck to their plan.

Now let's consider what happens if the retiree panics during the financial crisis. Assume that the retiree had set up a sensible retirement plan back when markets were behaving well. But when the financial world seems close to imploding, the retiree abandons the plan and shifts the entire portfolio into bonds. Asset allocation is left behind as the retiree panics. How might the portfolio have fared if the retiree panicked in February 2009 just as the stock market was about to bottom out?

Figure 19.3 shows how disastrous the retiree's behavior would be. By February 2009, the 50/50 portfolio had fallen to $658,000 as stocks collapsed. But from that low point the 50/50 portfolio rallied so much that by the end of 2012 it was only 9 percent below its peak in October 2007. If the retiree had panicked and abandoned the 50/50 allocation, however, the all-bond portfolio would have stayed roughly constant at its depressed level. By the end of 2012, the retiree would have to live off a portfolio worth $664,000 or 66 percent of its original value. Adjusted for inflation, the portfolio is down almost 40 percent.

Too many American investors panicked during this crisis. In early 2013 there are stories about investors who have finally gained enough courage to get back into the market. But Figure 19.3 tells a sad tale. Those retirees will never fully recover from their panicked decisions during the crisis. It's this type of behavior that I find more distressing than talk of a New Normal.

FIGURE 19.3   Steady Investing versus Panic during the Financial Crisis
Data sources: Barclays, Russell®, MSCI, and NAREIT.

THE MOST DIFFICULT FEATURES OF THE PLAN TO FOLLOW IN PRACTICE

I think it is very difficult to sit tight and follow an investment and spending plan when markets tank. Some financial planners suggest that retirees keep a cash reserve for such hard times. The cash reserve might be large enough to finance spending over a three to five year period. Since the spending plan calls for 4 percent spending each year, this might require that we keep in cash up to 20 percent of the portfolio (4 percent × 5 years). By "cash," I certainly don't mean that 20 percent of the portfolio is kept in a bank deposit or even a money market fund. Instead, the retiree could keep a smaller percentage (say 5 percent) in bank deposits or other very liquid assets, and the rest of the cash reserve in short-term bonds or similar investments. Some financial advisors even suggest a "ladder" of short-term investments ranging from one year to three or five years (depending on the size of the cash reserve).

How does the cash reserve help if the economy tanks (as it has done twice in the past 15 years)? Well, the cash cushion is there to fund spending for as long as five years. In the meantime, the stocks in the portfolio are left to recover. That is, the cash cushion *allows the portfolio to rebalance back to normal*. In a typical recession, stocks might fall 20 percent or 30 percent or even more. This leaves the portfolio too heavily weighted to bonds. So when stocks finally turn up, the portfolio is underweighted in stocks. Ideally, the retiree would rebalance yearly as discussed in Chapter 14. But in reality, it is hard for retirees or any other investors to rebalance. Rebalancing requires that the investor start buying stocks while they are still falling. Spending out of the cash reserve does the rebalancing for us. Because only cash and bonds are being sold to fund spending, the portfolio gradually moves toward the desired allocation of stocks and bonds. So a cash cushion makes sense for this reason as well.

A FINAL WORD OR TWO

Investing for a lifetime is hard. If an investor does everything right, then a comfortable retirement will be possible. But there are so many pitfalls along the way. Investors have to keep saving at a brisk pace. Consistent saving is essential. In the meantime they have to weigh the needs of their children against their own future needs. Education is the most expensive draw on retirement savings, but children have other needs as well. So do aging parents. If an investor is sick or unemployed for extended periods of time, the task is that much harder. And investors always have to invest wisely. The latter is not all that hard, but many investors seem to make it so.

I hope that this book will help investors get started on a reasonable plan for saving during the working years, spending in retirement, and investing wisely throughout their lifetimes. If the reader is someone who is close to retirement, the advice in the book may be a little late in coming. In that case, I hope that the chapters on retirement are helpful. And once you read the book please give it to your children. They still have time to save.

The baby boom generation may prove to all of us that the defined contribution retirement system is a failure. In that case we will have to invent a new one that doesn't depend so much on farsighted savings decisions, wise investing, and careful husbanding of wealth in retirement.

NOTES

1. Social Security payments are 25 percent less at the age of 62 relative to the full retirement age of 66. Because savings are also curtailed by retiring early, a couple retiring at 62 rather than 66 must cut its retirement spending from 83 percent of a $100,000 income to 63.4 percent of that income. See Table 18.4.
2. If the investor is in a high tax bracket, municipal bonds could replace taxable bonds. See the discussion of municipal bonds in Chapter 16.
3. Emerging market stocks might replace some of the foreign industrial country stocks (as shown in the portfolio of a younger investor; see Chapter 14).

About the Author

Richard C. Marston is the James R.F. Guy Professor of Finance at the Wharton School of the University of Pennsylvania. He holds a BA from Yale University, a BPhil from Oxford University where he was a Rhodes Scholar, and a PhD from MIT. He has been a research associate of the National Bureau of Economic Research since 1979, a visiting professor at the London Business School, ESSEC in Paris, and the Sasin Institute at Chulalongkorn University in Bangkok, as well as a visiting scholar at the Bank of Japan.

Marston is a long-standing faculty member in the Certified Investment Management Analyst (CIMA) program at Wharton, a program that has trained over 5,000 financial advisors in investment management. He has also taught in many other investment programs at the Wharton School and given investment presentations in over a dozen countries in Europe, Latin America, and Asia.

He has consulted for many of the top firms in the investment industry including Citigroup, Merrill Lynch, Morgan Stanley, Delaware Investments, and Lincoln Financial. He has spoken at numerous industry conferences and has frequently addressed client seminars sponsored by investment firms.

Since 1999, Marston has been the director of a unique program at the Wharton School for ultra-high-net-worth investors, the Private Wealth Management Program. In this program, the investors themselves come to Wharton for a week to learn how to invest their wealth. As of 2013, almost 700 ultra-high-net-worth investors have taken part in this program.

Marston is a member of the board of W. P. Carey Inc. and serves on the investment committees of several ultra-high-net-worth families.

His work has been widely cited in the press, including publications such as *Barrons*, the *Financial Times*, *Newsweek*, and the *Wall Street Journal*, and he has appeared on television programs such as the *Nightly Business Report* and *CNBC*.

Marston has written or coedited five previous books on finance. His latest book, *Portfolio Design: A Modern Approach to Asset Allocation*, was published by John Wiley & Sons in March 2011.

About the Companion Website

Investing for a Lifetime has a companion website at www.investingforalifetime.com. The website includes many free resources for the reader, including:

- Excerpts from the book
- White papers on topics related to the book
- Regular commentary on developments in the financial markets and the economy
- Annual updates of the tables and figures in the book as well as current market data

For even more free resources, go to www.richardcmarston.com.

Index